TALKING
OF SPORT

The story of
radio commentary

TALKING OF SPORT

The story of radio commentary

Dick Booth

SPORTS
BOOKS

Published in Great Britain by
SportsBooks Limited
PO Box 422
Cheltenham
GL50 2YN
Tel: 01242 256755
email: info@sportsbooks.ltd.uk
www.sportsbooks.ltd.uk

Cover design by Alan Hunns

A catalogue record for this book is available from the British Library.

ISBN 978 1899807 64 2

Printed and bound in England by
Cromwell Press

Before I joined the BBC ... I rarely listened to anything except concerts and running commentaries on sports events. These latter, which gave me a pleasure distinct from that which lies in seeing a game or race, should have provided a hint of radio's possibilities.

Louis MacNeice

CONTENTS

PART FOUR

ACKNOWLEDGEMENTS

This book would have been impossible without the help of many commentators and others working in broadcasting, given with enthusiasm and openness. I have drawn freely on their contributions in the text and I owe them many thanks:

Audrey Adams, Tony Adamson, Unni Anisdahl, Jonathan Agnew, Trevor Bailey, Nick Barnes, Peter Baxter, Harsha Bhogle, Knut Bjornsen, Geoffrey Boycott, Steve Bunce, Bob Burrows, Iain Carter, Pedro Costa, Mike Costello, Tony Cozier, Tony Delahunty, Sushil Doshi, Raj Singh Dungarpur, Angus Fraser, John Fenton, Gavin Eaves, Bill Francis, Arve Fuglum, Iain Gallaway, Alistair Hignell, John Hunt, Mike Ingham, Ron Jones, Chris Laidlaw, Mike Lewis, Des Lynam, Jimmy Magee, Lee McKenzie, Simon Mann, Victor Marks, Christopher Martin-Jenkins, Edson Mauro, Luiz Mendes, Alison Mitchell, Peter Montgomery, Adam Mountford, Reon Murtha, John Murray, Grant Nisbett, Rob Nothman, Jacqui Oatley, Micheál O'Muircheartaigh, Seán Og, Jonathan Overend, Shilpa Patel, Bob Phillips, Arne Porsum, Keith Quinn, Narrotam Puri, John Rawling, Washington Rodrigues, Pat Rowley, Andy Rushton, Dicky Rutnagur, Suresh Saraiya, Mike Selvey, Anant Setalvad, Mark Sharman, Bob Shennan, Jasdev Singh, György Szepesi, Graham Taylor, Brendan Telfer, Gordon Turnbull, Pradeep Vijaykar, Harry Walker, Murray Walker, Richie Woodhall.

Many radio listeners have shared their memories of commentary: I drew on all their contributions, if not always through direct quotation. Thanks especially to John Eaton, Anne Roberts, Clive Shippen, Ian Smith and Mick Tompson. I am grateful also to the librarians and archivists who helped me, especially at the British Library and at the BBC Written Archives Centre.

In addition to the broadcasters named in the text many other people have provided me with valuable help. In relation to Brazil they included Alex Bellos, Fernando Duarte, Paulo Cesar, Marcello Fernandes, David Macedo, Manuel Sá and Ricardo Visser. My main, and very conscientious guide, on matters to do with Brazil was Frederico Aragao. Nelly Lawrie found valuable material relating to France and Spain. Diane Millar went to great trouble to plan and host my stay in Georgia. My thanks to Nino Avaniashvili, Nino Shubladze and Nutsa Ubilava for their assistance in Tbilisi. Through Tibor Gold's help I was able to ask Robert Sikos to conduct and transcribe an interview with

György Szepesi in Hungary. The chapter on India benefited greatly from the help given by A D Bhogle, Mihir Bose, Richard Cashman, Anandji Dossa, Ramachandra Guha, Ayaz Memon, Haresh Pandya, Gurdev Singh and Vasant Raiji. On issues relating to Ireland I was helped by Tim Carey, Mike Cronin, Neal Garnham, Brian Lynch, and Paul Rouse. In New Zealand I received guidance from Patrick Day, Harvey McQueen, Harry Ricketts, Joseph Romanos and Greg Ryan. Most important, Rachel Brown was a tenacious and creative researcher who found remarkable material and helped me with many additional contacts. Arve Fuglum went out of his way to help me understand the history of commentary in Norway; Peter Dahlen did the same for Sweden.

The translation of original material could not have been achieved without the help of: Polo Arteaga, Cristina Devicchi, Tibor Gold, Nelly Lawrie, Régis Peyraque, Juliette Scott, Nidhi Singal, Peter Svaar and Ricardo Visser.

I also received help from: Steven Barnett, Grant Coleman, Eleanor Ellison, John Fenton, Brian Furniss, Richard Haynes, Mike Huggins, Anne Karpf, Frank Keating, David Lowe, Alan March, John Millar, Robin Millar, Peter Nasmyth, Mitch Pryce, Anne Roberts, Pat Rowley, Sean Street and Michael Whalley.

Audrey Adams, A D Bhogle, Chris Laidlaw, Alec Laurie and Rob Nothman read drafts of sections of the manuscript and made valuable comments. Sally Heighway transcribed innumerable tapes with care and accuracy. Kay Rowley was a tenacious researcher of photographic material.

Lesley Dee, Bryan Merton, Sally Twite and Roger Williams have provided consistent encouragement and support. In addition to his continuing enthusiasm for the project my friend Oliver Williams saw me through some of the difficult moments that beset the author: I'm sure he will be rewarded at the crease.

My partner, Sandra Nicholls, has tolerated my incessant need to talk through what I was doing and regularly helped me re-think the structure of the book. She read and commented on successive drafts meticulously, vastly improving it but always helping me to find *my* meanings. Above all, she enhanced my sense of what the book might become.

PROLOGUE

OVER TO TEDDY WAKELAM, Raymond Glendenning, John Arlott, Peter Bromley, Brian Johnston, Bryon Butler, Alan Green... studio words that over the years have meant so much to so many people. They have introduced live sport into our living rooms and made our lives brighter for it.

Live commentary on sport has been one of radio's great inventions. It has nourished the imagination of generations of listeners. The voices of the best commentators command our attention and remain with us long after we switch off.

Radio commentary first grabbed my attention as a child. My brother and I were so taken by broadcasts from big sporting events such as the Olympic Games that we marked out a track in the garden and conducted our own championships, urging each other on with mock commentary. A lap was all of eighty metres.

Talking of Sport explores the origins of commentary and how the BBC ran into all sorts of problems trying to get live sport onto the radio. There are portraits of some of those great commentators who were among the best-known voices of their time and descriptions of the different ways, some of them quite unexpected, in which people have become commentators, and how they develop their skills.

The book explores the story of radio commentary in countries where one sport has influenced many peoples' ideas of themselves as a nation. The distinctive techniques of broadcasting required by different sports are illustrated through extracts from commentaries, and the reflections of commentators. The book draws on what commentators have written about their time at the microphone, and on conversations with some seventy broadcasters from around the world who have talked to me about their work.

Speech and story-telling are at the centre of human experience. The voices in which we speak are statements of our *selves*, and of our individuality. This surely, along with the fascination of sport itself, is why radio commentary is still popular. Its story has not yet been fully told but *Talking of Sport* is a start. Perhaps it will encourage others to explore aspects in greater depth.

If you listen to sport on the radio, this story is for you.
Dick Booth
London 2008

PART ONE

HOW RADIO COMMENTARY
BECAME A PART OF LIFE

ONE

ROUND ONE

ON A HOT SUMMER'S DAY in 1921 an expectant crowd gathered outside the local newspaper office in the small town of Sanford, Florida. On the edge of the crowd hovered a ginger-haired, wiry, thirteen-year-old. It was July 2nd, just before three o'clock.

Like others in the crowd the boy was waiting eagerly for news. After a few minutes a burly man with a megaphone appeared at an upstairs window, and there was a murmur of anticipation from the crowd. They could just hear the tap of the ticker-tape machine in the room above. As the tape came out of the machine, with its messages from the stadium five hundred miles away in New Jersey, an operator wrote down the news and then passed it to the man with the megaphone. This man bellowed the latest bulletin to his audience, as if he was sitting at the ringside watching the fight.

Dempsey and Carpentier introduced to the crowd.

There was a pause of a minute or so, before the next piece of tape emerged and another bulletin was written. The crowd waited in the afternoon sun.

Gong goes for round one.

The fight had begun.

On that same day in Times Square, New York, arrangements had been put in place for another commentary on the fight.[1] Two large loudspeakers had been fitted onto the northern corner of the Times Building on 42nd Street. Through them the crowd in the street below would be able to hear the voice of a man reading from the reports as they came in from the stadium across the river. A third loudspeaker, erected on a lamp post on the safety island on Forty-Third Street, ensured that the man's voice could be heard as far north as Forty-Fourth Street, two blocks from Times Square.

There were also three bulletin boards on the building. One, used regularly for baseball scores, was up on the north side facing the same direction as the speakers. The others, on the sides of the building facing Broadway and Seventh Avenue, had been put up especially for this boxing event. The operators climbed gingerly up a ladder to a platform behind the boards, where there was a telephone. Here reports of the fight would be received on a special line from the stadium. As fast as news arrived it was to be chalked in large lettering on the boards, which would then be pushed into place along grooved runways, to be displayed to the crowds. Thus those out of range of the speakers could read accounts of the fight as they came in.

For once, it was not unreasonable to call this 'the fight of the century'. The American Jack Demspey held the most coveted title in boxing: heavyweight champion of the world. His challenger was the Frenchman Georges Carpentier, undoubtedly the best European boxer of his day. Interest in the fight threatened to spiral out of control. By three o'clock there were close to 10,000 people in Times Square and its environs, defying the summer heat and packed together like subway travellers in the rush hour. It was the largest crowd the New York police had ever had to manage in the centre of the city.

When the fight began the loud, gravelly voice of the man reading from the ticker tape soon came through the loudspeakers on the Times Building. *'Dempsey lands two rights to the body'*, he growled, and next *'Carp lands a blow on Dempsey's jaw'*.

Those within range of the speakers heard the 'commentary' first while those out of earshot craned their necks to see what was appearing on the boards. The written bulletins were only a few moments behind the loudspeakers. As news of the punches was received, two carpenters, leaning out precariously from the platform, inserted the boards on the runways and pushed them along. From high up on the building the upturned faces of the crowd seemed, as the *New York Times* said, 'like white caps on a choppy sea', swaying to and fro as moments of excitement gripped them.

The announcer told of the savage blows that the two fighters landed on each other and after each round a verdict on who was leading was announced. Slowly it became clear that Dempsey was on top. *'Carpentier down for a count of nine'* came the message. The noise in the square subsided in anticipation.

There was one new departure on that day in July 1921, momentous in its own way: arrangements had been made for the fight to be described from ringside over a phone line and then broadcast on wireless to radio receivers installed in some sixty halls and theatres around the local area. Amateur radio enthusiasts were recruited to manage the radio receivers and loudspeaker equipment in each hall, and the admission charges paid by the public were to be passed to charity.

There was no broadcasting station in New York at the time and it seems likely that the idea of using wireless was the brainchild of the manager of the Madison Square Garden stadium, Julius Hopp. The organisers of the broadcast were not allowed to transmit directly from the stadium so they installed a telephone line which ran from the ringside to a workmen's hut on railway land some two and a half miles from the arena. In the hut a radio transmitter had also been installed. The *New York Times* pronounced this as the first time in boxing history that 'wireless telephony' had been used to broadcast a fight.

A local radio enthusiast, Major J Andrew White, had been recruited to commentate at the ringside. White was editor of the popular radio paper *Wireless Age* but he had also boxed competitively as an amateur. The original idea was that as White's words came down the telephone line to the hut where the radio transmitter was housed, they would be typed by a stenographer and then read out over the air by an RCA engineer, Owen Smith. This system was used in a number of the earliest experiments with 'live' commentary.

But White himself, some thirty years later, asserted that it was his voice, talking from the ringside, which reached listeners directly. Writing in *Reader's Digest* in 1955, he described how Smith 'put a five inch diaphragm into the receiving telephone and hooked another telephone with a big diaphragm to the radio transmitter' so that the commentary could be broadcast direct. If the commentator's recollections are correct, the Demspey–Carpentier broadcast was the first truly live commentary of a major sporting event.

White rehearsed for the broadcast by 'boxing himself' in a mirror, commentating as he threw the punches at his own reflection. On the day of the fight he joined the crowds flocking across muddy fields to the new arena in New Jersey. It had been specially constructed in record time – a curious hexagonal, saucer-shaped, open-air stadium. Ninety thousand wooden seats radiated out from the centre of the arena.

By 11.30, two and a half hours before the fight was originally due to begin, White and his assistant Harry Welker were ensconced at ringside ready to start work. They were well placed in the front row, barely inches from the ropes. By 2 p.m., with the programme running late, every seat had been taken and the noise level was beginning to mount. Around White were some three hundred journalists, already tapping furiously on their typewriters, and he began to wonder if he would ever he heard.

In the event, it was the speed of the punches which caused White the greatest problem, one which was always to be a classic problem for commentators. He quickly found that he was unable to narrate every blow, and began to concentrate on the blows that really did damage. It was perhaps his good fortune, if not Carpentier's, that the fight lasted for little more than fifteen minutes. In the fourth round Dempsey delivered three blows which finished the fight: a left to the face, a fierce right into Carpentier's ribs and then another right – to the jaw.

As soon as the referee's final words – 'Carpentier down and out' – were declared the crowds in Times Square began the messy business of getting away. Everyone scrambled at once to escape, pushing for an opening in the crowd. Many men felt they had been there, at the fight, and were shaking their fists and grinning as they forced their way along the pavements. Briefly the police lost control and small fights broke out in the street.

In Sanford, the ginger-haired boy ran home to tell his parents what had happened, that Dempsey had knocked out Carpentier, and retained his title. It was to be another three years before the boy, Walt Barber, would see and hear a wireless set. But in later life, known to all as 'Red' Barber, he was to become one of the best-known radio commentators of his day, and for many years the voice of the Brooklyn Dodgers.[2]

Contemporary estimates put the number of listeners to the White broadcast at around 300,000. Accounts of the success of the broadcast came in not only from New Jersey and New York but from Vermont, Maine and Pennsylvania. The millionaire Willie K Vanderbilt listened with his guests and crew aboard his yacht on Long Island Sound, some one hundred and twenty-five miles away. A young woman in Hillside NJ, Mary Maurer, who was opposed to prize fighting, set herself against listening and refused to help her young brother tune in. But after hearing a few words, she quickly became involved, and called her grandmother to listen.

Few clues exist as to the quality of White's voice or about his approach to the task of commentary. But he went down well. Many wrote in requesting that similar arrangements be put in place for the next Baseball World Series event. Some listeners reported hearing the gong at the start of each round and a few transcribed White's account as best they could, and sent copies to him. He was grateful.

It's only through these that I know what I said. The roar of the crowd drowned out my own voice and afterward I was wondering just how much sense the description conveyed.

A little less than a year later another Carpentier fight was the subject of an experiment in radio commentary. Again Carpentier was on foreign soil, this time in London, and again he was facing a local favourite: Ted 'Kid' Lewis. Carpentier was admired in Britain as the gentleman of boxing, who always fought, said the *Daily Mail*, 'with that excellent touch of fellowship'. But Lewis was the man the crowd wanted to win.

Lewis had come a long way. He had been born Gershon Mendeloff, his father a cabinet maker in the East End. As a schoolboy he would meet the rest of the Jewish neighbourhood boys and march with them through the streets defying attack from hostile youths. He had had his first fight as a sixteen-year-old at the Judean Athletic Club; at eighteen he was European featherweight champion; then, while still in his early twenties, he had crossed the Atlantic and won the world welterweight title in Boston – the first Englishman to win a world title in the USA. In 1922 Lewis once again displayed the audacity and nerve that had made him such a favourite, challenging perhaps the greatest and most admired European boxer of his time.

At this time there was no national broadcasting station in Britain. The Post Office (the Government department then responsible) had just given permission for the Marconi company to establish experimental stations in London and Manchester. There were some 30,000 people with licences to hold radio receivers, plus others who had the equipment but had not registered with the Post Office.

A small number of radio 'stunts' were sanctioned during these early days. The *Daily Mail*, almost alone among newspapers, wanted a role in the development of radio and it knew that some attempts at live commentary on fights had been tried the previous year in America. The *Mail* persuaded the Postmaster General and the Marconi company that this was the time for a similar experiment to be tried in London.[3] The paper announced to its readers that it would broadcast a 'wireless telephonic description' of the fight between Lewis and Carpentier:

> The *Daily Mail* thus ensures that every possessor of a wireless receiving set will be able to follow round by round this great sporting event. There will be no waiting to learn

who has won or how the fight is going. Special *Daily Mail* reporters will telephone direct from the ringside every incident of the contest, and these will be broadcasted from Marconi House, Strand, WC within two minutes of the blows being struck. People hundreds of miles away from London will be able to visualise the great fight almost as clearly as those in Olympia itself.

The Marconi company anticipated how important it was to get the right voice for the occasion. From two thousand employees they identified a dozen possibles and from them a Mr W Southey was selected. The company's comments on his suitability suggest the degree to which radio was seen as a by-product of the telephone:

He has got the perfect telephone voice. To have an ideal telephone voice the operator must speak absolutely distinctly, he must not slur his words and he must practise over again and again words which might cause difficulty in pronunciation. He has to familiarise himself with foreign words which have crept into the British language, and above all he should be very human, quick-witted and shrewd.

The Mail undertook that messages would be sent out from 9.30 p.m., when the boxers were due to enter the ring, and would then be 'practically continuous until the last blow is struck and the championship retained by France or passed into British hands.'

Not far from Olympia, Florence Parbury, a well-connected society hostess, was holding a soirée in her Chelsea studio. She was keen to entertain her guests to a broadcast on her recently acquired 'wireless'. She may well have had had one of the new Burndept four-valve receivers popular at the time. She would have placed the receiver near a window and suspended a copper wire to the far end of her garden; a second wire would probably have run from the receiver up an external waterpipe. No doubt she herself put on the headphones and tuned in to the Marconi station. Her visitors included several MPs and a group of Danish visitors, including the remarkable singer Lauritz Melchior. Florence settled them comfortably on the sofa and the easy chairs around the loudspeaker horn.[4]

Elsewhere, at Harrods' department store in Knightsbridge a loudspeaker had been put up in the restaurant and here some five hundred people gathered to listen. In a garage at Leigh-on-Sea a crowd of three hundred assembled to hear the broadcast. Away from London, and spread around the country, a small number of wireless enthusiasts who had read about the broadcast in the *Daily Mail* were hoping to follow the fight as it unfolded.

The fight was timed for 9.30 p.m. on the evening of May 11th 1922. By 8 p.m. the contestants were already at Olympia in West London surrounded by their teams of assistants. Through the closed doors of his dressing room Lewis could hear the impatient, raucous cheers of 16,000 people who had come to see him fight. They were crowded into the cavernous hall, with an arched roof of glass and steel and he knew there were more fans in the streets outside – thousands of them.

Just before 9.45 the boxers made their entrances. Lewis was first, in a glittering, gold dressing gown, followed by a long line of assistants and hangers-on. Carpentier followed, in grey kimono, bowing to the crowd when he entered the ring. All were there, the Duke of York and other dignitaries, the business parties from the continent, the glamorous women in shimmering gowns, but most of all the thousands of boxing fans from across London. In the crowd too was Jack Demspey who had come from America to see the fight. Struggling against the shouting and cheering, a hoarse Master of Ceremonies made his proclamation: 'For the light heavyweight championship of' – he paused, and there was a moment's respite in the deafening noise – '*the world.*'

Lewis was a fast, aggressive fighter and he was quickly in close, punching hard. Carpentier held Lewis, they parted, and then clinched again. Carpentier struck with a left to the face and then more blows to the body. Carpentier's skin tended to mark when blows landed and, as Lewis struck him, tell-tale red blotches began to appear. Carpentier was warned for low punching. A left jab from Lewis made the Frenchman's mouth bleed. Carpentier responded with a left, and then a right uppercut. They clinched again, and not for the first time Carpentier's head seemed to smash into Lewis's face. The referee pulled them apart, one arm on each man. Journalists at ringside could hear his warning: '*Stop holding both of you, watch your heads.*' It was then that Lewis stepped back a little, dropped his arms, and turned towards the referee as if to complain.

It takes only one blow to end a fight, but that blow must be struck with full force and be unimpeded. At that moment Carpentier was in perfect balance, his left foot a few inches in front of his right, his knees slightly bent. As his body moved to its full height, Carpentier's right hand came through with great speed to land on Lewis's jaw.

Lewis – his hands still at his side as he looked at the referee – went down like a stone. The fight had lasted two and a half minutes.[5]

Next day the *Daily Mail* pronounced the broadcast a 'Listening-in success'.

Messages had been received from across London testifying to its clarity. There were calls too from towns across southern England, and even as far west as Devonport. A Mr Hodgson in Salford picked up parts of the broadcast and later reports came in from Doncaster and from Scotland and a ship off the Lizard. As one listener put it: 'Aberdeen knew the result, before Lewis properly realised it himself'.

The fight of course was a disappointment, indeed the *Daily Mail* itself called it 'a fiasco'. Carpentier's action in striking Lewis while the Londoner was listening to the referee led to him being booed from the hall. But the experts pointed out that the rules of boxing require a contestant to 'defend himself at all times'. The referee had no choice but to award the fight to Carpentier.

And the broadcast? There is no doubt that listeners were impressed by the clarity and quality of the voice transmitting the reports. But in truth, as a 'telephonic description' it too was a disaster.

The *Daily Mail* reported that one 'listener-in', whose name was not given, had kept a log of the announcer's messages. These began promptly at 9.30 and continued every few minutes until the fight began. At 9.35 the announcer reported that the preliminary fight was still in progress but at 9.46 he was finally able to give the news that Lewis had entered the ring. At 9.56 listeners were told that the referee was giving final instructions to the boxers. At 9.57 the message was: *'Seconds out of the ring. Fight started'*.

Now came the challenge, if not for live commentary as we know it today, then for the sequence of rapid and descriptive reports that would bring the unfolding fight alive to people in their homes. Perhaps so overwhelmed by the ferocity and excitement of the opening round, no telephone calls seem to have been made for at least two minutes. Then Carpentier struck. The journalists had no choice: they had to report that the fight was over. At 9.58, according to this listener's log, the result was announced and only a minute or two later was a description of the first round given.

In the restaurant at Harrods, in the garage at Leigh-on-Sea, in domestic living rooms across the country, the last message came through at 10.10. Miss Parbury and her party heard it too:

Referee was going to part the boxers from a clinch when the

9

blow was delivered. Lewis was able to walk to his corner after taking the full count. Carpentier waved his arms in his usual manner and immediately left the ring, none the worse for the encounter. This completes our programme. Goodnight. Goodnight.

So the first experiment was over. The *Daily Mail* certainly ensured that those of its readers who listened in were first with the news. However, the newspaper had expected more. It had reasonably envisaged that regular reports over several rounds would give listeners a sense that they were hearing a description of the fight as it developed, a real running commentary, but the unusual circumstances of the Olympia fight conspired against this.

In years to come boxing was to become one of the great radio sports. This happened quickly in America, and some European countries, especially France, soon followed suit. In Britain however the advent of live commentary was delayed by fierce resistance from other interests, especially the press.

In the early days of broadcasting wireless was a more commonly used term than radio. It had an all-purpose function, serving to describe a method of transmission, a broadcasting station and – well into the 1950s – it was widely used to describe the receiving set itself. In the 1990s wireless returned to the language in a new context – that of the router, not the set. Curiously, wireless has, via the new digital platforms, given radio a new lease of life.

1 Descriptions of the scene in Times Square and extracts from the 'commentary' are drawn from the *New York Times*, July 2nd and 3rd 1921. Details of the broadcast and responses to it draw on *The Wireless Age* July and August 1921, G L Archer *History of Radio* (American Historical Society 1938) and *Battle of the Century: The WJY Story*, by Thomas H White on the website *earlyradiohistory.com*.

2 Barber's own account of listening to the man with the megaphone is in his book *The Broadcasters* (Dial Press 1970).

3 Details of the arrangements made by the *Daily Mail*, extracts from the telephone 'commentary', and listeners' comments are taken from *Daily Mail* May 11th, 12th and 13th 1922.

4 Information about Florence Parbury's soirée draws in part on letters in the Marconi archive (HIS 154-156), Bodleian Library, Oxford.

5 Accounts of the fight draw on *Daily Telegraph* and *Daily Mail* May 12th 1922, from *Boxing* May 17th 1922 and from *Ted Kid Lewis – His Life and Times* by Morton Lewis (Robson Books 1990).

TWO

BRITAIN LAGS BEHIND

IN AMERICA IT WAS not boxing, important as it was, that first took radio commentary into people's lives on a regular basis. It was baseball which kick-started the process. Here was a sport played by clubs across the country, each with a devoted following. It was tailor-made for all the new radio stations growing up in the big cities.

In 1920, Westinghouse Electric had launched KDKA in Pittsburgh, widely accepted as the first commercially licensed station in the world. Among the small number of staff it recruited was an enthusiastic young engineer called Howard Arlin. Arlin did a little 'moonlighting' in the evenings as an announcer and the station liked his style so much that in 1921 they offered him a full-time post in the role. In the late summer of that year, a little after the big fight in New York, KDKA decided to try an outside broadcast from a baseball match. There was no obvious candidate for the job of commentator, so Arlin, who was known to be a baseball enthusiast, was asked if he was interested. He agreed to give it a try.

Westinghouse had little idea what they were starting. They were only vaguely aware of the huge market they were tapping into, a market made up in large part of the millions of people who had entered America in the previous decades from many different countries. Organised sport, especially baseball, offered excitement and distraction to the swelling populations of the great cities and a shared experience to those of different heritages. Reports and scores of baseball matches were a matter of wide public interest and the sport helped to sell newspapers. There was just a chance it would help to sell radios too.

So, on August 5th 1921, and at the age of only 26, Arlin found himself at Forbes Field, then the main baseball stadium in Pittsburgh, for the match between the Pittsburgh Pirates and the Philadelphia Phillies. There Arlin attempted what was almost certainly the first live 'play by play' commentary on baseball – his microphone nothing more than a converted telephone. Many years later he recalled that first broadcast:

I was just a nobody, and our broadcast – back then, at least – wasn't that big a deal. Our guys at KDKA didn't even think that baseball would last on radio. I did it sort of as a one-shot-project... Sometimes the transmitter worked and sometimes it didn't. Sometimes the crowd noise would drown us out, and sometimes it wouldn't. And, quite frankly, we didn't know what the reaction would be – whether we'd be talking into a total vacuum or whether somebody would actually hear us... No-one had the foggiest idea, the slightest of an inkling, that what we'd started would take off like it did.[1]

A few weeks later Arlin gave the first commentary on college football for KDKA but it took time to sort out the technicalities of live commentary coverage for baseball. The accounts of World Series matches in the autumn of 1921 broadcast on the Newark station WJZ were not broadcast live but phoned in from the stadium and recreated in the studio before being broadcast to listeners. Once again the 'commentator' was a serving announcer, in this case Tommy Cowan, who happened to be available. Cowan operated from the studio – actually a hut on top of the Newark Westinghouse Building – and a local journalist, Sandy Hunt, was installed in a telephone box in the stadium within view of the play. When Cowan heard 'Strike one' he quickly repeated 'Strike one'. After 'Ball one' he said 'Ball one', and so on. Fortunately the game was not a fast-moving one. Cowan later remembered:

> I sat in our studio in Newark with earphones clamped on as my colleague called the plays into the telephone. I would repeat each word before the mike but the strain was great and I did not have the slightest idea of what I was saying.[2]

True commentary on World Series baseball came a year later. The matches between the Yankees and the Giants in October 1922 were described live from the Polo Grounds in New York, this time by sportswriter Grantland Rice. Rice worked for the *New York Tribune* and was beginning to establish himself as a legendary figure in sports journalism. The broadcasts reached people three hundred miles away, and some estimated the audience as over five million.

Rice was not comfortable in his new role. After the bat hit the ball, he would wait for the shout of the crowd, hesitate a few moments, and then describe what had happened. One listener wrote: 'I would hear the crowd let out a terrific roar and it would seem ages before I knew whether it was a single or a three bagger that had been made.'[3] Rice himself acknowledged later that the station wanted him to keep talking, but that he did not know what to say.

Rice had been confronted with another classic commentary problem: he could not always tell exactly what had happened. This was to prove a particular problem in American football, where a team of associates, the forerunners of today's touchline reporters, would have to be installed to send signals to the main commentator. But newspapers were impressed with Rice's efforts. The *New York Times* contrasted the broadcast with the old system of billboards and loudspeakers:

> Radio for the first time carried the opening game of the World's Series, play by play, from the Polo Grounds yesterday to great crowds throughout the Eastern section of the country... In place of the scoreboards and megaphones of the past, amplifiers connected to radio instruments gave all details and sidelights of the game... not only could the voice of the official radio observer be heard but the voice of the umpire on the field announcing the batteries of the day mingled with the voice of a boy selling ice cream cones.

Through the early twenties radio commentary grew steadily in popularity in America, and so did the reputation of some of those who spoke at the microphone. To most listeners, letting radio into the home was like opening the door to a stranger and broadcasting stations hoped that announcers would help persuade the listener to accept that stranger as a friend. The first commentators were not just inventing a new form of narration but becoming the voice of the station, and indeed the voice of the sport. Soon the great commentators began to establish themselves, and for the first time became known by their distinctive and much-loved voices. Graham McNamee, who started with the New York station WEAF in 1923, was the first to become a household name. He established a new format by introducing himself personally, and beginning each broadcast with what became a legendary greeting:

> *Good evening ladies and gentlemen of the radio audience. This is Graham McNamee speaking.*

McNamee's rich baritone voice, recalled Red Barber later, was the one that electrified everyone. When he came on air 'The nation hugged itself happily… and waited for something vital to come right into the living room, into life itself instantly.'[4]

WHILE AMERICA FORGED AHEAD, the development of commentary in Britain was blocked by restrictions. A few months after the Marconi 'broadcast' of April 1922, the British Broadcasting Company was set up. With government backing, six firms with an interest in wireless came together to pilot a national broadcasting service. But the BBC operated under strict conditions, enforced by the Post Office. The Company was forbidden to broadcast any news other than that supplied to them by the press agencies, and then only at agreed times. As further protection to the press, live commentaries were prohibited. Newspaper owners feared that live broadcasts would reduce sales of their papers.

It fell to John Reith, the first general manager of the British Broadcasting Company, to construct a place for this new organization in the life of the nation. Reith had his own vision of what was worthy of transmission. He was not a great sports enthusiast, but he wanted the BBC to broadcast the big events of contemporary life – 'music, news and the other happenings of the great cities'. Reith understood the unique quality of radio when compared to previous means of communication – that it went directly into the heart of peoples' homes, 'not even left like milk on the doorstep'.[5]

He and his colleagues knew of the developments in sports broadcasting in America. They also knew that more and more people with wireless sets were tuning in to broadcasts from abroad, especially the famous concerts from The Hague. The BBC began to plan its own experiments with programmes from outside the studio and the first of these – although not related to sport – proved a turning point in demonstrating to British listeners the wider potential of outside broadcasts.

In January 1923, engineers from the BBC met with staff from the Post Office and the Royal Opera House in Covent Garden to discuss the possibility of mounting a dramatic experiment: a direct transmission of Mozart's *The Magic Flute*.

Many theatre owners and impresarios were opposed to live broadcasts of this kind, fearing the impact they would have on attendances. But the managers at the Opera House were keen to make the idea work. It seemed to them that it could do nothing but good for the fortunes of opera, and for their business. The Post Office was persuaded to collaborate – it was their department after all which was charged with helping the BBC make a success of its new role. Agreement was reached.

An underground cable was installed between Covent Garden and Marconi House in The Strand, so that the performance could be relayed to the studio and then transmitted over the air. Two microphones were concealed among the footlights and connected to the speech input amplifier, which was located in a room beneath the stage.

On the Monday evening the BBC's Director of Programmes gathered with his staff to monitor the transmission in a small room on the top floor of Marconi House, where a loudspeaker stood on the table. With a loud click, the speaker was thrown into a circuit and the listeners could hear with clarity the talk and rustling of programmes in the auditorium. There was a burst of clapping, a short period of silence, two sharp raps and then the orchestra 'leapt into its stride, and swelled up to a great crash of cymbals, which could be heard all down the corridor at Marconi House.'[6]

The Covent Garden broadcast was the most dramatic demonstration to date in Britain of the possibilities of wireless. *The Times* said that, on a good set, rightly tuned, 'the performance was heard as distinctly as if the listener was in the audience'. It was so successful with listeners that other operas were broadcast in the days that followed.

Most important perhaps was the reaction of Peter Eckersley, the BBC's legendary Chief Engineer. Eckersley had previously worked for Marconi at the experimental station in Essex where he had occasionally led impromptu concert parties over the air. He had been brought into the BBC as a man not just with technical know-how but with imagination. Yet it was not until the Covent Garden broadcasts that Eckersley realised fully the potential of radio:

> My attitude towards broadcasting completely changed when I first heard the BBC transmit an opera. Special microphones, developed in America for high fidelity, had been placed along the stage floodlights and connected to the 2LO transmitter. The result was staggeringly different from anything I had heard before. I sat for three solid hours while the performance lasted, rigidly clamped by headphones, completely absorbed, oblivious of discomfort. There were no interrupting announcements, no 'dead' studio feeling. I had been to the opera without going to the opera. Broadcasting, I realized, would let me join

in events without having to drag my body all over the place ... for one who had come to broadcasting through the evolution of the wireless telephone it seemed like a revelation. A real invention had been made, much more profound in its implications than the invention of the wireless telephone.[7]

So it was this experiment which convinced Eckersley, already an experienced radio man, that outside broadcasts could transport listeners to events which they had no chance of attending. And it was Eckersley who was to supervise the production of the BBC's first sporting commentaries.

Despite the restrictions faced by the BBC on news and sport, radio gained steadily in acceptance and popularity. There were those who loved the technical side of the new invention, the chance for self-assembly, and others who were simply keen to 'listen-in'. For all, there was the excitement of having a new toy. Wireless sets – like computers some seventy years later – had to be ordered, unpacked and set up. One magazine described the process:

A knock at the door, a large packing case, straw and paper everywhere and the broadcast receiver is proudly placed on the table... Naturally the family are anxious to hear the evening broadcast concert... impatient is perhaps the better word to use. ...the aerial has already been erected and an 'earth-plate' has been buried in the flower bed beneath the window. How shall we proceed to get the music from the air?[8]

Local wireless societies, and popular publications about wireless, flourished. By 1922 more than one hundred stations could be picked up in the UK during a twenty-four hour period, and the most enthusiastic listeners kept written records of what they heard. New aerials sprouted across the house tops in every suburb, and not just in middle-class homes. 'The prevalence of radio surprises me,' wrote EV Lucas in *Radio Times* in 1924. 'I am impressed coming into London by any line that intersects mean streets by the number of "the poor" who can afford wireless sets.' Mary Bartlett, who was born in 1915, remembered the excitement when the first station opened in Birmingham:

Poles and aerials sprang up in all the gardens and my father was very interested in the new technology. He made his first crystal set comprising a crystal, cat's whisker, wire coils round a cylinder, which I helped to make, and headphones. It was earthed to the metal bedstead. Mum and Dad used to listen in bed to the Savoy Orphans and often drop off to sleep.

As wireless ownership grew, the BBC sought ways of overcoming press opposition to live coverage of sport. Reith was skilful in turning his opponents' arguments on their heads and he began to argue not only that live coverage would not harm newspaper sales, but might even benefit them:

> Many know from their own experience that even presence at a rugby international has not deterred them from anxiety to live the game over again from beginning to end, through the eye and pen of a graphic reporter in an evening paper. Rather the contrary.[9]

Reith's first opportunity to press his case came in 1923, a year after his appointment. The government had asked a group of public figures, chaired by Lord Sykes, to review funding arrangements for the British Broadcasting Company. Reith was a member of the review group.

In June the committee explored the role of the BBC in news gathering and live sport.

Lord Riddell – giving evidence on behalf of newspaper proprietors – told the committee that live broadcasts, and the announcement of racing and football results, would seriously interfere with the sale of newspapers. He warned of the danger to newspapers of public houses installing radio sets. 'For example, a publican with a broadcaster would be able to supply the requirements of his customers, who would be waiting on the bar for the results.' Riddell – and Sir Frederick Jones of Reuters – argued that the impact on the sales of evening papers would be severe.

The Sykes Committee broadly accepted these arguments but the BBC did obtain one small concession. Just before Jones left the hearings Reith made a successful intervention.

> Reith: *Have you any objection to the broadcasting of a speech at a dinner, which speech may contain an element of news?*
> Jones: *I think news agencies would cover this.*
> Reith: *I mean the actual transmission of the speech.*
> Sir Henry Norman: *Mr Reith means putting the microphone in front of the speaker.*

> Jones: *It is a matter for the Broadcasting Company. I agree an occasional speech here and there is not a matter to worry about but no more.*

Reith had established a small beachhead. Provided that no commentary was given, the BBC could now broadcast some outside ceremonies and speeches. It was a start.

MEANWHILE OTHER COUNTRIES, France in particular, were beginning to follow America's example and experiment with live coverage of sport. In Paris it was a young journalist with a passionate enthusiasm for radio, Edmond Dehorter, who led the way. Dehorter had read about the experiments conducted in America and was determined to emulate them. He did not wait for the broadcasting stations to come round to the idea – he took the initiative himself, and he showed great persistence and imagination.

Dehorter saw an opportunity in May 1923 when Georges Carpentier was due to fight Marcel Nilles for the heavyweight championship of France at the Stade Buffalo in Paris. Carpentier had only recently lost his light heavyweight championship, and the boxing public were keen to see if he could revive his career. Dehorter persuaded the fight promoters to allow him to install a telephone line linking the stadium to the Radiola studio in Boulevard Haussmann in Paris. The studio manager, fearing a blunder or slip of the tongue, would not allow direct broadcasting of the words from ringside so two shorthand typists were recruited to type up Dehorter's account as it was phoned through. It took about four minutes for Dehorter's words to be prepared by the typists before the radio announcer Marcel Laporte read out the 'commentary'.

Dehorter kept his notes from this fight – which Carpentier won in the eighth round – and one extract survives:

> *The sixth round has just started, it's Nilles who attacks again;*
> *he hurls himself at Georges Carpentier who dodges and feints.*
> *He wants to tire out his adversary, his footwork is magnificent.*
> *Carpentier has just hit Nilles right in the stomach.*

But Dehorter was frustrated by his studio's manager's attitude – he wanted to do a proper live commentary and a few months later, in October 1923, he got his way. It was boxing again, a fight between Eugene Criqui and the Belgian Henri Hebrans at the Velodrome D'Hiver and almost certainly this was the first true live sporting commentary in Europe. Contrary to expectations the fight lasted the full fifteen rounds – Criqui winning on points – and the commentary was an instant success. The weekly French journal *Radio-Magazine* reported with surprise that the reception was so perfect that listeners could hear the noises of the crowd.

By now Dehorter had acquired a nickname – 'Le Parleur Inconnu' (the unknown speaker) – and something of a national reputation. In January 1924, he described live the rugby match between France and Scotland at the Stades Pershing in Colombes, probably the first broadcast of any field sport in Europe. French soldiers stationed in North Africa radioed their thanks to the station in Paris for allowing them, as they put it, 'to attend the match as if we were there'.

But there were still some obstacles in Dehorter's path. In France, as in Britain, some sections of the press were unhappy about the idea of commentary. They raised their objections later in 1924 when Dehorter tried to report the final of the Olympic Football tournament in Paris.

This turned out to be his most difficult assignment yet. Newspaper reporters were unhappy when they heard of his plans and physically prevented him from entering the stadium. But Dehorter could not be easily deterred. He had noticed that a bicycle shop nearby was using a balloon for publicity and he persuaded the owner to allow him to go up in the gondola with a microphone. High up in this observation post he commentated as best he could on the game that took place below. Uruguay beat Switzerland to take the gold medal. Dehorter recalled later:

> A devil of a wind blew, the balloon swayed so much that I was not able to see anything. In one hand I had my microphone, in the other my binoculars. And in the third... I had my balance. I spoke on my knees, and I nearly went over the top of the gondola.

Elsewhere around the world, other 'firsts' were being established. In March 1923 in Toronto, Foster Hewitt gave the first ice hockey commentary, and started a long association with the Toronto Maple Leafs. In July of that year, *The Herald* newspaper in Melbourne reported what may have been the first live broadcast of horseracing, though it was not clear if the commentary was directed to listeners in their homes or only those at the racecourse.

Intense excitement prevailed at Wirths' Park where a vivid description of the Grand National Hurdle was broadcasted while the race was actually in progress. Large crowds gathered round each of the sets ... the diction of the broadcaster was perfect.[10]

A few weeks later, in September 1923, when the Argentinian boxer Luis Firpo challenged Jack Dempsey for the world heavyweight title in New York the commentary was taken direct to Buenos Aires and broadcast over loudspeakers to people standing outside newspaper offices in the Argentinian capital. The first commentary on a rugby league match was in Sydney, Australia, in July 1924. And in the same month a rugby union match from the Newlands ground in Cape Town was broadcast. The commentator Jimmy Dunn talked over a telephone line. Dunn was not a rugby expert and listeners heard:

He's going... he's going... He's almost there. He's going to score... God! He's down... The poor chap, he's wounded. Good God! He's dead.

Another voice could then be heard in the background: 'Don't be a fool man. He's only winded.'[11]

The first live report from a cricket match was made from the Sydney Cricket Ground in November 1922 but it is unclear whether this included live commentary. It seems almost certain that there was some ball by ball commentary from the England v Australia Test Matches at Sydney and Adelaide in December 1924 and January 1925. In June 1925 came the first live sport on German radio, commentary on the Frankfurt regatta. And in December of the same year the BBC's *World Radio* reported that Union Radio in Spain 'has had great success with listeners who like to hear wireless comments on bullfights made by specialists, together with the shouts of the crowd, creating in the imagination the illusion of being in the arena.' Cross-country skiing was covered in Sweden in 1925, and in 1926 there were commentaries on rugby and hockey in New Zealand, cycling in Belgium and hurling in Ireland.

So radio commentary was spreading around the world. What form it was taking, and whether different styles were establishing themselves in different countries, is difficult to ascertain. From the snippets that survive it seems likely that most commentators followed broadly the approach later advocated by George Allison in England: 'You just repeat what you see happening ... talk as the words come into your head'.

In Britain, meanwhile, there was still no live sport on radio.

DURING THIS PERIOD, the BBC was developing some expertise in outside broadcasts by covering other kinds of live events. In 1924, the King's speech from the opening of the Empire Exhibition was transmitted direct from Wembley Stadium, a broadcast which Reith described as 'the biggest thing we have done yet'. In June 1924, a church service was broadcast from St Martin in the Fields. Later that year, in November, the BBC broadcast live the speeches after the Lord Mayor's banquet in the City of London. But still no sporting events were covered.

During the early months of 1925, Reith launched another campaign to persuade the press and the Post Office that the BBC be allowed to undertake a small number of running commentaries. He requested what was described as:

> A running story of the first half of the England versus Scotland Rugby match; a coded narrative of the Boat Race from a wireless-equipped launch, the key to the code, together with a plan of the course, having been published in early editions of newspapers on the morning of the race; a coded narrative of the FA Cup Final; and the broadcasting from Epsom on Derby Day... of the actual microphone record of the noises of the race.[12]

The choice of these three events – the Boat Race, the Cup Final and the Derby – was important, as they all excited national interest among the general public and not just keen followers of sport. The BBC was beginning to formulate an important idea: that such events were shared national occasions, and as such were the proper business of a national broadcaster. If the BBC could get its way it would help it to become a shared national institution too. But again the press objected.

The proposal was sent to a meeting with the Post Office for 'arbitration'. Reith received some support from the Postmaster General, Mitchell-Thomson, who tried to mediate by asking the press if they would at least allow commentary on the first half of a rugby match. The press, led by Lord Riddell, would not budge. They agreed only that the BBC could be at Epsom for the Derby and that the sound of the hoofs of horses and the shouts of the crowd could be transmitted.

However, in July of the same year, another committee of enquiry – under Lord Crawford – was established, this time to look strategically at the future organisation of broadcasting. Now the Post Office, realising that income from licence sales was at stake, shifted its position. In a document prepared for members of the committee, civil servants made a proposal for change:

> If events of public interest, such as the Derby, Boat Race, election results, could be broadcast immediately they are available, they would be of enormous interest to the public and probably increase the number of licence holders. It seems difficult to justify a restriction which results in the large body of listeners being deprived of a service which would be attractive to them... because of the immunity from external competition to which the press lay claim.

Reith was not a member of this committee but he submitted evidence. He made it clear that being present at big events was not enough:

> The BBC can broadcast functions and speeches at any hour of the day so long as the transmissions are limited to what the microphones can pick up, that is to say, without the interpretation of a narrator. The presence of a narrator describing what is happening... would make transmissions much more valuable.

The committee met at the House of Lords in December 1925 and Reith attended as a witness. He was asked directly if it would be possible to provide a more interesting service to the nation. His reply was unequivocal. 'Yes – most obviously – the description of an event as it is taking place.'

Equally important perhaps, the voice of the consumer was now heard. The number of licence holders was growing rapidly and some of them were organised. The Wireless League had more than 80,000 members and its secretary was called to give evidence. He stressed how inadequate the BBC's current coverage of sport was and gave voice to the views of listeners.

> Committee Member: 'What complaints have you had?'
> WL secretary: '(It is) absurd that in the case of a motor car race they should have to wait to receive the news of the race, although there are representatives of the BBC attending the race and reporting these particulars. There

have been cases in which the BBC could not state whether number four has passed ... they had to keep up a running fire of commentary – 'What a lot of fire and smoke' – and remarks of that kind.'

Member: 'Do you want the USA model where there is broadcasting of all matches and races telling (people) the results as they occur?'

WL secretary: 'Subscribers would like this'.

The Press Association was represented by the chairman of its management board, Sir James Owen. Sir James was a keen supporter of provincial newspapers, many of which were published in the early evening, and felt particularly threatened by radio. When a member of the committee pressed Owen about commentaries he made one final effort to defend the press monopoly.

> Member: 'Could not the BBC give the results of the Derby as soon as it is run?'
> Owen: 'Yes, but there is such a thing as a slippery slope. You say you think these people are entitled to have the news of the Derby?'
> Member: 'If they want it very badly?'
> Owen: 'Well, they may want it very badly. But people want many things very badly which they are not entitled to have. If you begin by giving a broadcast account of the signing of the Locarno, you come onto the Derby, the Boat Race and so forth, you gradually come to give a broadcast description of every important event.'
> Member: 'Will the public tolerate restrictions which prevent this marvellous advance of science giving them the fullest of its advantages? This is the broad question.'
> Owen: 'The broad question is, it being a luxury, whether in ten years time people will be so very keen on broadcasting as they are today.'

But Owen's position was being overtaken by events. When the Crawford committee reported in March 1926, it recommended the establishment of a body called the British Broadcasting Corporation (helpfully retaining the same initials as its predecessor): a public corporation, with monopoly broadcasting rights. More important to the story of commentary, the committee also recommended that the BBC should have greater freedom over news and be allowed to broadcast a limited number of running commentaries of sporting events.

A little later that summer the BBC finally undertook a trial broadcast from Epsom on Derby Day. It was a shambles. Some years later Raymond Glendenning – by then the BBC's leading race commentator – described what happened:

> A microphone was installed to broadcast the crowds at Tattenham Corner. Amidst a background of tipsters and bookies, Laurence Anderson, Vera Lennox and RE Jeffrey carried on a conversation as they looked around them … though the unseen mass of listeners got a terrific thrill from the concerted shout of 'they're off', their entertainment was thereafter restricted to the murmur of the crowd and something of this sort as the horses flashed round Tattenham Corner: *'Here they come – now they're getting down to it – he's drawing ahead – it's sure to be Lex – no, Harpagon'* and then a somewhat distant voice, I gather, read from his race-card: *'It looks like nine – five – one.'* Without even translating the numbers into horses, a voice from the studio then announced the end of the broadcast.'[13]

The broadcasters now had to get their act together. As soon as the new BBC came into being in November, 1926, Reith ensured that planning began for the first commentaries. A member of Reith's staff had already been to America to report on the latest developments in radio there. He would have discovered that in August one New York station had broken new ground by staging a boxing match for radio purposes. In October the BBC heard that a football match between Sweden and Denmark in Copenhagen had been broadcast, almost certainly the first live football broadcast in Europe. The sports editor of the Swedish station and one from the Danish radio department collaborated in providing commentary from the Copenhagen stadium. The report was broadcast by the Copenhagen station and sent on land line to Malmo where it was re-broadcast in Sweden.

In London the planning continued. Finally, on December 31st 1926, the *Radio Times,* in a prominent notice, told its readers that 'descriptive reports of important events from the scene of their occurrence will be broadcast.' The first was to follow within a couple of weeks. After a delay of several years, commentary was finally to arrive in Britain.

Quotations in this chapter from evidence presented to, or discussions held at, the Sykes and Crawford committees are taken from the official records held in the Post Office Archives for June 1923 and December 1925 respectively. Quotations from Edmond Dehorter are from *Histoire générale de la radio et de la télévision en France* Christian Brochand (Paris 1994.) p 439-440. The account of developments in France also draws on *Histoire de la Radio en France* R Duval (Editions Alain Moreau 1979)

1   Curt Smith *Voices of the Game* (Simon & Shuster 1992) p7-8
2   E Bliss *Now the News* (Columbia University Press 1991) p16
3   Ronald L Smith *Play by Play* (Johns Hopkins 2001) p21
4   R Barber *The Broadcasters* (Dial Press 1970) p15
5   JWC Reith *Broadcast over Britain* (Hodder and Stoughton 1924) p15-16
6   CA Lewis *Broadcasting from within* (George Newnes 1924) p7
7   PP Eckersley *The Power behind the microphone* (Cape 1941) p45-46
8   *Conquest* (a popular science magazine, November 1922)
9   *Broadcast over Britain* p141
10   *The Herald* Melbourne July 7th 1923
11   Eric Rosenthal *You have been listening* (Purnell 1974) p90
12   Asa Briggs *The Birth of Broadcasting* (OUP 1961) p240-41
13   Raymond Glendenning *Race Broadcasting* in *Flat Racing since 1900* edited E Bland (Dakers 1950) p 224-225

THREE

'DON'T SWEAR'

ONCE PERMISSION FOR COMMENTARY was granted, an urgent task arose: finding a commentator. The BBC gave that job to Lance Sieveking. He was one of that band of men who had survived the Great War, and then went to university in their mid-twenties. He left university without a degree and joined the BBC in 1925 as 'Assistant to the Director of Education', undertaking public relations, editing news bulletins and organizing the first outside broadcasts. At the end of December 1926, Sieveking was given the news: the first running commentary would be from the Twickenham stadium in west London, on the rugby international between England and Wales on January 15th. He had just over two weeks to find his man.

The BBC had prepared its listeners for this new development in the *Radio Times*. Here the journalist Hamilton Fyfe told readers more about what was happening in American radio. In 1926 he went to the USA to study broadcasting developments, and he described for the *Radio Times* how, during some football matches, 'a continuous description of the play is broadcast from the field by an eye witness':

> He spoke as if he were telephoning. He was telephoning but in the box was a microphone and his voice, when it reached the radio station in Chicago, was broadcast into hundreds of thousands of homes all over the country... Huge numbers of fans, who would like to be on the ground, follow the play at a great distance and get a very fair share of the excitement which the spectators feel... 'How many people, do you suppose, listen to your football reports?' I asked the broadcaster as we came away ... 'Millions', he said, briefly.

Sieveking had been to the USA too, to learn about radio, and while he was there he had listened to baseball commentary. He understood the potential of live sport on radio and in searching for a commentator he was not working entirely without guidance. The BBC had already begun to establish a tradition of controlling carefully what was said at the microphone and by whom. The General Manager of the BBC, John Reith, had a strong sense of what the BBC's voice, and persona, should be like:

> I believe that those who are responsible for the conduct of the Broadcasting service ... should become known, at any rate in voice and personality, if not in body, to those for whose pleasure and edification the whole of their waking hours are spent... I believe it is a matter of great importance in the development of the service that there should be a measure of ... intimacy without familiarity.[1]

Sieveking knew that he had to find someone who was familiar with the sport in question, spoke well, could make personal contact with listeners, but could be relied upon not to depart from what was agreed in advance.

He later described how he set about his task:

> In the preceding week I got into contact with everyone I could think of who seemed in the remotest degree likely to be able to give a running commentary on a rugger match. I did not know then, and I do not know now, the rules of either rugger or soccer. But with the help of commonsense I did know how to set about finding people to do things – no matter what. I assembled a party of men. They were all connected with the game in some capacity, either amateur or professional, and among them were several sporting journalists well known all over the country.[2]

One of Sieveking's party of men was Captain HB Wakelam. He too had served in the war and had since made a career with a construction company. He played club rugby and cricket, and took time off in the summer to act as a linesman at Wimbledon. He was a convivial, talkative man, 'Teddy' to his friends, short, thick set, with a Chaplinesque moustache and a broad face that made him easily identifiable.

Wakelam had enrolled in the Officers' Training Corps at his school, Marlborough. There, one of the masters in the scouting division insisted that the boys always remembered everything they saw during the day, including details such as the colour of a man's tie, as part of improving their general awareness. Wakelam played rugby, hockey and tennis at school, saw WG Grace bat and went on to Cambridge. During a May Week ball he became engaged to a girl he never saw again, as one did at May balls. He later described himself as being, at that time, a 'regular fellow.' But it had never crossed Teddy Wakelam's mind that he would work on radio, or that one day his voice would become one of the most familiar in England.

He was leading a comfortable if rather quiet life when, early in January 1927, he received a phone call from Sieveking, requesting an urgent meeting. Sieveking had been told by a friend that Wakelam was a good talker about rugby. The BBC was going to start some running commentaries, American style: would Wakelam be interested? Wakelam was keen to have a go. His view was that if an American could do it, he could.

In addition to Wakelam, several people were approached about commentary, and some were persuaded rather against their better judgement to be auditioned. They were asked to undertake a voice test in the studio and five of them, including Wakelam, went forward from the studio audition to stage two of the selection procedure, a practical test in a London park.

By mistake the would-be commentators and the engineers went to different venues. The commentators and Sieveking went to the Guy's Hospital Ground and the engineers to Greenwich Park, where they were turned away by the park-keeper. There were now only three days left before the Twickenham match and Sieveking hurriedly arranged a new venue – the Old Deer Park at Richmond. Here the candidates undertook their practice commentaries, just for Sieveking's benefit, on a school game.

With one exception, the auditions were not a success. The candidates could not keep up with the game and find words for what they saw. One, who according to Sieveking, 'knew all there was to know about both kinds of football and the personalities in it … gradually became less and less articulate and finally gave up.' Then came Wakelam's turn, as recounted years later by Sieveking:

> He sat watching the game for a long time. Then he said in a matter-of-fact tone *'I'll call one team the Yellows and the other the Whites. There's not much going on at the moment. Sort of ding-dong messing about.'* Suddenly his voice changed and he called out sharply: *'Hey, wait a minute! That was something like a pass!'* And then began that machine-gun delivery that has been so familiar to millions of listeners. A real excitement and enthusiasm seemed to possess him, he jumped up and down on his chair and a positive cataract of words streamed out of his mouth ending in

a happy roar... He was HBT Wakelam, ex-captain of the Harlequins.

With a broad grin on my face I went along to where he was sitting and tapped him on the shoulder. He stopped addressing the microphone and looked up. 'No good, eh?' he enquired, seeing my grin.

'Exactly what I'm looking for' I said. 'Will you do it?'

Wakelam was dispatched immediately to Twickenham – it was now the Wednesday immediately prior to the game – to see the commentary arrangements that the engineers were setting up for the following Saturday. Helpfully the Twickenham official who liaised with the BBC, Colonel Cropper, was an old and valued friend of Wakelam. The newly appointed commentator could hardly have felt more at home.

Sieveking had recruited an assistant, a man called Lapworth, to sit alongside Wakelam during the commentary. There is some uncertainty about Lapworth and his role. Wakelam said that he had a vast knowledge of the American film world, but little knowledge of rugby. However, at the time Lapworth was described by *The Daily Telegraph* as 'an old rugby player,' there to supply 'local colour', while Wakelam covered the technical details. Wakelam described Lapworth as his 'number 2', in many ways well-suited because he was calm and collected. Sieveking later described Lapworth as 'a general filler-in-of-pauses-when necessary.' Whatever the truth of the matter, the precedent for a second person in the commentary box had been set.

Lapworth played one other role. In the days immediately before the broadcast Sieveking had sketched an outline plan of the Twickenham pitch, divided into eight numbered squares. Listeners were invited to send in for copies to help them follow the game. During the match Lapworth, helped by Sieveking, called out the number of the square in which play was taking place so that listeners could more easily follow the path of the game. In the second half they had to increase the frequency with which they did this because John Reith rang during the interval to request them to do so.

On the morning of January 15th, *The Times* reported: 'This will be the first time that an attempt will have been made in this country to transmit by wireless a description of a game while it is actually in progress. Captain Wakelam will speak his narrative from a portable hut, from which he will be able to obtain a full view of the ground.'

The BBC engineer Robert Wood found himself coping with fairly primitive arrangements. Standing precariously at first floor level was what looked like a wooden garden hut, supported by a set of poles. The hut was approached by ladder and just beneath stood a motor van containing amplifiers and other equipment.

Sieveking, Lapworth and Wakelam climbed up and somehow squeezed into the hut, Wakelam sitting between the other two. Sieveking wrote in red on a piece of paper the instruction 'Don't Swear' and pinned it up where Wakelam could see it. He had one other idea. With the aid of the St Dunstan's charity he had recruited a blind man, interested in rugby, to sit just in front of the open window of the commentary hut so that, as Wakelam put it: 'I could talk as if explaining the game directly to him, and so perhaps lose some of my natural stage fright.' Sieveking recalled how the blind man was guided into place:

> It was a bit of a scramble to get up the improvised ladder to the hut, but the man from St Dunstan's accomplished it safely with guiding hands above and below. I seated him immediately under the tiny window through which we other three would be seeing the game. Someone sat beside him in case he moved too near the edge.

Just before play began Sieveking set the scene and read out the BBC's inevitable statement about copyright, and then, as the referee blew his whistle to start the game, Wakelam took over.

Teddy Wakelam's account of this pioneering experience is recorded in his customary fashion. He is the unwilling victim of fate but manages to pull through:

> I mounted the ladder on to the scaffold, there to become the butt of many of my more light-hearted and evil-minded friends, who took the opportunity to gather below on the ground and pass a lot of rude and scathing remarks at my expense.[3]

As so often happens, the demands of the occasion brought forth the energy and fluency that were demanded. 'I raced away like a maniac', Wakelam recalled. His own verdict was that without foreknowledge or planning he adopted a technique – which he was to try and follow throughout his career – of trying always to stay ahead of the game:

> Then and there, I think, I got into the habit of being just a fraction ahead of the actual game. By that I mean the necessity of starting to speak of a man as passing just as he is shaping to pass, a poor description and example to

illustrate my point but nevertheless a correct one, for it is actually the truth.

But not all Wakelam's listeners felt he succeeded in this regard. In Sieveking's account (written much longer after the event) he remembered in particular how nervous Wakelam seemed at the start:

> While Lapworth and I went through our prepared routine, Wakelam sat rigid. I wouldn't have guessed how strung-up he was if I hadn't noticed that, at one point, his hand trembled and he put it firmly on the shelf before him to steady it...

It is impossible to know whether Lapworth's occasional naïve questions (for example: *'Do they always play with an oval ball?'*) were genuine or whether, prompted conceivably by Sieveking, he was gently reminding Wakelam not to get too technical and remember the less informed listener. Whatever the truth, Wakelam raced on for forty minutes, took a short break at half-time, had a drink, and then raced on again, desperately trying to ensure that the blind man in front of him had a vivid and accurate picture of what was happening. 'His words came out like a torrent, and the faster he talked, the clearer it was,' Sieveking recalled.

And all around Wakelam was the noise – the noise of thousands of people clapping and stamping, for the first time sending their songs and cheers into the homes of thousands of listeners. Spectators and listeners were rewarded by an exciting match, with England winning by eleven points to nine. As soon as the game ended the telephone in the broadcasting rang van. It was Reith, with his congratulations.

Responses to the commentary varied. The sixteen press reports filed in the BBC archives are more or less evenly divided and years later Wakelam described them with characteristic honesty as 'a trifle patchy'. The *Radio Times* published an enthusiastic letter from the novelist Fred M White. He had not been sure what to expect but had sent for his ground plan from the BBC and prepared to be mildly intrigued. Instead the BBC provided 'another miracle':

> The announcer was beautifully impartial. Not one scrap of fine play did he miss... And behind all this clarity came in a minor key the other voice from the hut telling us just how the game moved from section to section of the plan so that all the time we knew even which side of the

ground the ball was on… . Above it all, that wild glorious cheering from 40,000 throats… one long thrill from start to finish.[4]

Some newspapers were also supportive. *The Observer* noted approvingly that the cheers of the crowd were as audible as the comments of the eyewitnesses. *The Spectator* noted that although the commentary was interrupted by the noise of the spectators it was very informing and realistic. 'This kind of broadcasting has come to stay.'[5]

Others were less convinced. The 'Wireless Correspondent' of the *Daily Telegraph* thought that the methods adopted would probably have to be modified. He noted that the two commentators occasionally talked at the same time:

> Originally the scheme had been for Captain Wakelam to give details of play and Mr Lapworth to supply more descriptive touches, but there was an obvious difficulty in synchronising their efforts, with the result that some of the broadcast was almost unintelligible. Another feature … was the unceasing roar of the crowd, sometimes swelling to such a pitch that the comments of the two eye-witnesses were completely drowned.[6]

But the author acknowledged that the frequent repetition of the score was a useful guide to listeners who tuned in at different times.

A listener writing to the *Manchester Guardian* also reported that for appreciable periods the roars of the crowd were the only noise heard, reflecting in part the fact that lip microphones were not yet in use.[7] The writer questioned Wakelam's style, and his ability to keep up with play:

> He was also unable to escape the excitement of the moment – a first essential of anyone who is attempting a neutral and balanced description of events taking place before him. Descriptive accounts should not be loaded with … such phrases, uttered in excited tones, as: 'That was a fine pass to Conway' … 'Anderson is playing a fine game', 'Come on; oh, come on. It's in; no, it's in! come on, let it go.'
>
> The game appears to have been much too rapid for the commentator. For example, just before the interval he was describing a neat manoeuvre in midfield when a sudden shout from the thousands of spectators drowned his voice.

The description referred to mid-field play; the shout was
for a try.

In its editorial the *Manchester Guardian* pronounced the game itself
a great triumph but thought that the broadcast of the match was less
successful. It offered some telling and prophetic thoughts on what
was required of a commentator:

> The truth is that this is a skilled job. It is not enough to be
> accustomed to the technique of the wireless though this
> is necessary, nor to be a football expert though that too is
> indispensable. A man might have both these qualities and
> be useless at the broadcasting game. He needs also to be
> able to extract the essence of the game and communicate
> it in words at the moment when his mind and eyes are
> moving on to the next stage.

These criticisms prompted a response from another listener:

> I must say the broadcast was for me an unqualified
> success. I listened in to Daventry on a crystal and heard
> every word of it. In addition to the cheering of the crowd,
> I liked the way the commentator did his job. 'England
> have it, England have it, Worton to Laird, to Corbet, to
> Locke, Locke to Gibbs, who is running down the wing like
> blazes' conveyed much more to me than any amount of
> good reporting.

Wakelam himself was anxious to know how well he had done and
was gratified by the letters and phone calls he received, not least one
from a group of bank staff in South Wales who had gathered together
to listen to the commentary and much enjoyed it. The St Dunstan's
man who stood in front of him during the game also reported favour-
ably. Best of all, Sieveking offered Wakelam ten more commentaries
at double the fee.

The issues that listeners and newspapers raised closely resemble those
which feature in discussions about commentary today: the need to
convey and even anticipate the general sweep of the game; the degree
of partiality to be shown; the balance between factual description
and comment; the distinct role of the two members of a commentary
team; what part to give to 'outside effects', especially the noise of the
crowd; the need to give the score regularly.

No recording of Wakelam's commentary is known to exist, so the snippets quoted in letters and articles are all that we have. As far as we know Wakelam had never heard any radio commentary and more or less had to invent his style from scratch. The phrases remembered by Sieveking from the trial and some of those quoted in critical letters to the press suggest that Wakelam drew partly on the language of the touchline supporter. Other extracts, however short, – *'England have it, England have it, Worton to Laird, to Corbet, to Locke, Locke to Gibbs'* – indicate that in his speech patterns Wakelam entirely matched the rhythm of the game, as the best commentary does today. He had instinctively adopted a new kind of unscripted speech, matching the ebb and flow of the play with changes in the tempo of his delivery.

Wakelam seemed to have the necessary knowledge of the game, a 'good' voice, and a command of language. These were to become unchanging features of the role. But perhaps a commentator needs more than this – a sense of why sport matters to people, and where it stands in their wider lives. Wakelam had shared the seminal experience of his class and generation – public school, the war, the good fortune to be alive. All in all he seemed to be the part.

The BBC had recognised that they needed to go outside their own ranks – but not too far outside – to get a suitable narrator for this new kind of story-telling. They had found perhaps, to use Reith's earlier words, 'intimacy ... without familiarity.' They were pleased with the result.

1	Reith *Broadcast over Britain* (Hodder & Stoughton 1924) p53.
2	Quotations from Sieveking are taken from an unpublished memoir in the BBC Written Archives Centre (WAC) (S61 *Autobiographical sketches of Lance Sieveking*).
3	Quotations from Wakelam are taken from his book *Half-Time* (Nelson 1938); his account of the first commentary is on Pages 187-195.
4	*Radio Times* January 23rd 1927
5	*The Spectator* January 21st 1927
6	*Daily Telegraph* January 17th 1927
7	*Manchester Guardian* January 17th–20th 1927

FOUR

SUCCESSES AND SETBACKS

THE BBC NEEDED SOMEONE to take charge of this new animal: the *outside broadcast*. Lance Sieveking had set up the first commentary but he had other duties. The corporation was looking not for a broadcaster or an engineer but for someone who could build and maintain relationships with outside bodies, including the sports organizations whose co-operation was so important. They gave the job to Gerald Cock.

When Cock joined the BBC in 1925 he was already 38 and had had a varied and unusual career. On leaving school, he had joined an engineering firm, travelled widely, especially in North America where he tried gold mining and ranching, and then served as an officer in the First World War. From 1920 he was managing director of a film-producing company so he brought with him to the BBC a knowledge of the world of business.

In 1927 the BBC received its Charter, giving it a more permanent status and opening the door for it to expand its range of activities. Cock was made head of a new 'Outside Broadcasts Sub-Section' and over the following eight years he led the discussions with sporting and other outside bodies, built up the first portfolio of events and kept an eye on the emerging band of commentators. Charming and debonair, it was he who took people to dinner, arranged their theatre tickets and sent them gifts. But not all his negotiations ended in success. In Britain radio commentary was slow to grow.

In that first year, 1927, Cock targeted the most popular sports and events in the sporting calendar that had some claim to be national occasions. These included the Grand National, the Oxford/Cambridge Boat Race, the Cup Final, the Derby, and Wimbledon. In that year there was commentary on athletics, boxing, cricket, football, rugby union, rugby league, racing, rowing, cricket and tennis. Other sports, including golf and motor cycling, were covered only by reports from the scene, not commentary.

These early broadcasts presented Cock with a number of difficulties: striking a deal with the sporting bodies concerned, setting up the technical arrangements, finding the right person to do the commentary. But all presented opportunities. With the big events especially, the BBC was determined not just to provide a narrative of what happened but to capture for the listener at home something of the ambience of the occasion. A second person was sometimes added to the commentary team for this purpose.

The Grand National was the first of the big events to be covered. In an attempt to convey the atmosphere of the race, Cock placed microphones around the stands and enclosures, including the paddock. Unfortunately the commentator, Meyrick Good, was positioned in the open, rather than in a soundproof box, and at the final moment his voice was drowned by the cheering of the crowd. Inter-varsity athletics followed, then the Boat Race, the Cup Final, county cricket, the Derby and Wimbledon. For all the commentaries experts from the relevant sports, rather than BBC staff, were chosen. At Epsom great stress was laid on capturing the atmosphere of the day – 'a scene without parallel in England now' said the *Radio Times*. Finally, in September, the first boxing broadcast was mounted from the Albert Hall and there was a microphone at ringside, picking up the noise of the boxers' feet and the thump of the punches. Here were the origins of a subsequent commentary motto: *give the listener a ringside seat.*

THE BOAT RACE provides a good illustration of what was involved in these early broadcasts. BBC engineers had to find a way of transmitting commentary from the Thames, the most ambitious undertaking so far attempted. And Cock had to negotiate with the race authorities, who wanted a say in who would be commentator and some kind of remuneration. The BBC was determined it would not pay for the 'right' to commentate, arguing that it had the same rights of access as the press.

Negotiations opened on January 31st when CM Pitman, whose job it was to supervise the arrangements for launches on the Thames on Boat Race day, wrote to Gerald Cock at the BBC:

> The great success and popular standing of your recent broadcast of the international football match encourages me to ask whether you would care to consider the question of making arrangements with us for the broadcasting of

an event which excites such world-wide interest as the Oxford and Cambridge Boat Race... The narrator would be some well-known Old University oarsman to be appointed by the University Boat Clubs.[1]

By now, and Pitman may have known this, Cock had already began to investigate whether a Boat Race commentary was feasible. He had written to the Post Office and the Port of London Authority seeking their co-operation. He had also asked his staff to find a launch that could carry the commentator and transmitter. A suitable vessel was found at Henley but as one of the locks between there and London was closed, the BBC had to pay to have the boat transferred by rail. Engineers installed a receiver in Barnes from where the commentary would go by land line to the main BBC transmitting point at Savoy Hill in London. A back-up receiver was installed in a private residence, halfway along the course.

Cock planned and costed out a forty-five minute programme, estimating the budget at £94, including a fifteen guinea fee for the commentator. (A guinea was £1.05p in today's money.) Cock informed Pitman that the BBC was keen to go ahead but that the name of the commentator had yet to be confirmed. At the end of February, Pitman wrote to Cock pressing for a name, so he could 'put the whole thing before the two Presidents for their final confirmation'. Cock replied by return, informing Pitman that the commentator would be Oliver Nickalls, three times an Oxford Blue, and still a highly regarded rower. Pitman was relieved: Nickalls would be 'most acceptable'.

A little later the name of the second commentator was revealed: Sir John Squire, a sportswriter. Nickalls eventually negotiated a fee of twenty guineas, and Squire one of ten.

In early March, a trial broadcast on the Thames was organised with the help of the London Rowing Club and excellent speech quality received. There was some anxiety about how the commentators would be able to judge the distance between the boats but the BBC came up with an ingenious solution: at various key points along the bank assistants would raise flags, one dark blue, one light blue, as each boat passed, so that those in the following launch could be sure who was leading, and by how many seconds.

In the week before the race, the *Radio Times* included two full pages heralding the broadcast, including a Victorian-style drawing of the course and the landmarks that might be mentioned. The Boat Race was a great spring event in London, with a considerable following. People with no Oxbridge connections of any kind sported light and dark blue favours and many thousands lined the bank of the Thames. It was the brief of the second commentator, Squire, to capture the pageantry of the occasion.

Commentary on the Boat Race was a more ambitious venture than the rugby and football commentaries, more ambitious in some ways than the Grand National. 'Are you sure you have the times right?' scribbled John Reith on a scrap of spare paper passed down to Cock. Someone remembered they might need a spare stopwatch: a messenger boy was dispatched to a shop in Ludgate Hill to borrow one. Cock produced a detailed plan for the day: a car would collect him from the BBC at 9.30, pick up Nickalls and Squire from their club in Piccadilly, and Sieveking, who was helping out, from his home in Notting Hill. The engineering team had a special place on the riverside at Putney where they could assemble.

There was one outstanding issue: money. Pitman seems to have believed he could winkle a little out of the Corporation, and the University Boat Clubs were pressing him to do so. One of their arguments was that the BBC had been allowed on the river, a privilege denied to many others. Pitman wrote to Cock a few days before the race. The alleged favouritism shown to the BBC, he said, had caused 'just a little resentment… I cannot help feeling that a voluntary subscription from the BBC to the Boat Clubs would ease the situation.'

It was nicely put. There is no written reply from Cock on the file but perhaps he phoned Pitman. After the race a cheque for £25 was sent.

Whatever reservations emerged about the Nickalls/Squire team in the following years – and there were many – the experiment was deemed a success. The race was a good one, with Oxford twice taking the lead before being pulled back and finally overtaken. The transmission went well. It was a considerable technical achievement. Reith rang his chief engineer soon after the race was over to congratulate him and his team and tell him that everybody in the BBC was proud of them. He wrote a few days later: 'There is no doubt it was a unique event in broadcasting and I believe it may also prove to have been the most outstanding feat ever brought about by any broadcasting authority.'

In the upper echelons of the Corporation it was certainly seen as the most successful event yet broadcast. Cock was well pleased. As well as the roars of the crowds along the bank, and the crescendo of cheering as Cambridge crossed the line, listeners heard for the first time the distinctive incantation that was to be the hallmark of the commentary for years to come: *in, out – in, out.*

BY THE END of 1927 more than seventy commentaries had been broadcast. This figure includes all the broadcasts on regional stations, some of which were simultaneous with each other. Of the total, almost half were on football, with rugby and cricket the next most frequent. The *Radio Times* acted as a cheerleader. 'These sporting broadcasts are, we believe, having the effect they have had in America; they are opening up all the interest of sport to thousands of people who would never have gone in person to a sports ground.' Full page features setting up each of the big events, and introducing the commentators, were commonly used. Diagrams of the pitch, divided into squares, or maps of the course were provided to help listeners follow the event. Some listeners attempted to mark the movement of the ball on the pitch and sent in their resulting drawing to the BBC. Manufacturers of radio loudspeakers and batteries began to exploit the appeal of commentaries in their advertisements.

The BBC openly embraced the big events on behalf of the nation, indeed it was quietly annexing them to its purpose. 'This Derby race belongs to all of us,' claimed *Radio Times*. Reith recognised that major sporting occasions were widely shared and enjoyed and that commentary added a new dimension to them. He wanted these special commentaries to be highlighted in the national diary, helping him position the BBC at the centre of national life. Cock's contribution to the realisation of this ambition was considerable.

But in other respects 1927 proved a false dawn. During the years that followed the BBC found it difficult to expand its coverage of live sport, and indeed the number of commentaries declined. The continuing opposition of some sporting bodies, who feared the impact of live coverage on attendances, was something that not even Cock's patient diplomacy and lobbying could always overcome. Rugby and racing were among those which presented difficulties, but it was football which presented the biggest problems.

The BBC had to deal with two national football organisations – The Football Association (FA) which ran the FA Cup competition and included the amateur side of the game, and the Football League which ran the professional game. To complicate matters further league clubs were represented within the FA. The Cup final broadcasts of 1927 and 1928 were among the most popular of the early commentaries, providing the BBC with some of its largest audiences. In 1927, when Cardiff City played in the final, Cardiff Council placed speakers in a local park and thousands gathered to hear the commentary. The Cup final was archetypal of the events which the Corporation wished to cover – a high spot in the national calendar, anticipated and talked about by many, played at a showcase new arena, Wembley Stadium. The broadcasts included the singing of *Abide with me* before the game, lending a moving aura of unity to the occasion. The BBC needed the Cup final.

The problems with the FA were to do with money. The selling of film rights had proved lucrative and by 1929 it seemed obvious to many members of the FA that they should charge the BBC for commentary. Early in March the FA phoned Gerald Cock and told him they would require payment for the broadcasts that year.

Cock offered to pay £100 to a football charity in return for permission to broadcast one semi-final and the final. When the FA turned down the proposal, the BBC counter-attacked by setting up a temporary studio in a house just outside Wembley Stadium. A team of commentators paid for admission to the final in the normal way and at ten-minute intervals they rushed to the house and recounted what they had seen. The BBC later described the experiment as 'entirely successful' but in truth it was a poor substitute for the real thing, and was badly marred when one of the commentary team attributed the first goal to the wrong team.

When the time came to think about the 1930 final, the BBC renewed its offer to make a payment to charity and the FA again refused. Cock pressed the case, not easy to sustain, that the BBC's position was analogous to the press and that broadcasters should have the same rights as newspapers. If the press paid no fee, he argued, the BBC should not be asked to pay either. This view obscured one crucial difference: that broadcasting was simultaneous to an event, while press reports were published after it.

In March 1930 the BBC published its correspondence with the FA prominently in *Radio Times* and Cock attempted to drive a wedge between the varying interests that made up the Association:

> It is a dismal prospect that when the governing body of a sport originated, built up and entirely supported by amateurs, should be captured by professionals, whose whole interest is apparently commercial ... and who are unable to see that broadcast commentaries actually increase and spread interest in the sport described.

In the end, an intervention by the Bishop of Birmingham helped to break the deadlock; he criticised the BBC but argued that many patients in hospitals would suffer as a result of the ban. This galvanised the FA to climb down – they accepted the idea of a gift to charity and the game was broadcast. It was to remain a highlight of the commentary year.

League football presented a more intractable problem. Most matches were played simultaneously at three o'clock on Saturday afternoon, many before smallish crowds at clubs struggling to survive. Such clubs could legitimately argue that the loss of a few hundred spectators, staying home to hear live coverage of a top game, could threaten their financial future.

Cock was alert to this concern. In February 1928 he wrote to station directors round the country asking them to collect figures for attendances at matches that had been broadcast, with the equivalent figure for the preceding year. Regular articles in *Radio Times* extolled the virtue of attending matches, and the many delights of live sport. One writer waxed lyrical about '... the wonder of the crowd, all lighting their cigarettes together at half-time'.

But in 1931 came the major setback. In April, the Arsenal club, from which so many commentaries had been given, withdrew its co-operation. Its manager Herbert Chapman had never been entirely reconciled to the idea of live broadcasts and George Allison, at this stage a director of the club but not present at the crucial meeting, was out-manoeuvred. Finally, in June of that year, the league clubs agreed at their AGM that broadcasting of league matches should be prohibited.

To deal with this latest rebuff, Cock produced figures in the *Radio Times* which suggested that attendances at some grounds on days when there were no commentaries were no less than on days when there were. In general the press weighed in to support the BBC, and many listeners' letters were published, some bewailing the fate of the sick and the elderly who could not get to games and had to rely on commentary for their contact with the game. George Allison warned his listeners, at his many after-dinner engagements, that if football was banned from the air, rugby would take its place.

Radio Pictorial reported a possible compromise, suggested by one reader: details of the game on which commentary was to be given would be withheld until kick-off time on Saturday afternoons. It was a prophetic proposal – this was the procedure which the BBC would follow in the post-war years.

But the Football League would not budge. They were not part of that consensus of amateur sport – rugby, rowing, tennis, athletics, for example – to which BBC men found it so much easier to relate. When a circular was sent to league clubs in 1933, almost all came out against live coverage. In the years that followed football commentaries were severely restricted – Cup finals and some internationals were the only top games to be covered. The Football League had emerged as the one major sporting body in Britain to enforce a sustained ban on radio commentary.

This was a substantial setback to the development of live sport on radio in Britain. Saturday afternoon was beginning to emerge as the focal commentary point of the week and although the BBC may never at that stage have envisaged weekly broadcasts it certainly saw football as a key part of its portfolio. It was to be many years before the issue was resolved.

COCK'S POWERS OF PERSUASION hit another barrier in 1927, in the form of the Welsh Rugby Football Union (WRFU). The economic depression had hit south Wales badly and had affected gate receipts at club games. Some members of the Welsh union were concerned that if international matches played in Wales were broadcast even more supporters would stay away from local matches.

In October 1927 Cock secured an introduction from Teddy Wakelam to Horace Lyne, the chairman of the Welsh Union, but was rebuffed. In early November, Cock decided to go to Wales in person. He spent a week in Cardiff and Swansea, having protracted discussions with a number of officials, but to no avail. Lyne wrote to Cock just before Christmas:

> We are mainly dependent on working men for our gates. … trade is so extraordinarily bad … over 100 men went to one of the public broadcasting stations where they heard an excellent description of one match for nothing.[2]

It subsequently transpired that this broadcasting point was outside a men's hairdressers in a shopping arcade in Cardiff.

Cock did not give up. In November of that year he finally managed to secure a face-to-face meeting with the WRFU. Before he left London, Cock persuaded his superiors in the BBC that, if he could secure agreement to commentaries, a donation of one hundred guineas should be made to the Union's fund for new ground developments.

There was one additional caveat: the BBC would not appear in the public list of subscribers.

This time Cock's preparations bore fruit. In December 1928, the WRFU agreed that an international match could be broadcast the following February. Lyne now felt able to seek advice from Cock on which receiver the BBC would recommend for his home – Cock sensibly passed the enquiry to the engineering department. In 1933 a further donation of one hundred guineas was made to the WRFU 'to be distributed to clubs most needing financial support'. Contributions of this kind, Cock argued to his colleagues, 'may quite easily save the awkward position by which we might have to pay for broadcasting facilities'. It was a fine distinction.

RACING, NOT LEAST THE GRAND NATIONAL, caused persistent problems over the years. In 1930 a payment of £50 for 'out of pocket expenses' was made to Tophams Limited, who owned the Aintree course. Cock developed good relations with Edward Topham but he knew that the issue of payment would rear its head each year. In 1933 Topham died and the board of the company now run by Mirabel Topham, Edward's daughter-in-law, decided to raise their price.

In a memorandum to colleagues, Cock summarised the dilemma in which the BBC found itself.[3] In deference to Reith's view, he restated that the Corporation must stand by its stated principle that it did not pay for the right to broadcast. He acknowledged that the BBC was to some extent being exploited by Tophams because the commentaries had further raised the profile of the event, to such an extent that it was now almost impossible for the BBC to leave it out of their schedules. But he also pointed out that national events were critical to the BBC: 'their programme value is enormous and they must be a great factor in selling licences.'

In summary the BBC would 'not get facilities unless we agree to pay in some form'. The alternative was to try and describe the race from outside the course (following the Cup final precedent) and incur inevitable public criticism. Cock proposed £200 a year for the next five years, describing this as 'rental for the three necessary positions'. He added ominously: 'The talkie people pay £1000'.

Reith was not happy about the payments being made: 'I am apprehensive on the score of precedent and I do not know that Cock's feeling that paying for rent rather than for broadcasting does safeguard us'. Eventually the payment was made, on a confidential basis, and with the proviso that it was understood that 'no payment is being made for the right to broadcast'.

Apart from the Grand National there were also difficulties with the Jockey Club and with individual racecourse managements about radio coverage. At Newmarket, the Cesarewitch and the 2000 Guineas were not broadcast until 1937 and 1938 respectively and there were no broadcasts from Ascot until 1937.

In 1927 the BBC broadcast live commentary on almost fifty days, including eight successive Saturdays in the spring of 1927. But after that the momentum slackened considerably. In 1933 there were live commentaries on only thirty days in the year, and the total number of commentaries, including regional broadcasts, had fallen by over half from its 1927 total. However, the summer of 1934 did see a significant experiment. On one Saturday afternoon the BBC mounted *'An afternoon of broadcast sport'* with visits to five venues. This was a forerunner of what was to become a centrepiece of radio on Saturdays, the continuous afternoon coverage of several sports, culminating – from 1948 onwards – in *Sports Report.*

Cock, of course, was busy, not only with sport but with a range of other outside broadcasts including public events, plays and concerts. Furthermore, there was a view in some quarters of the BBC that live commentary should be restricted to the major sporting events. An article on *'Commentaries'* (clearly written from inside the BBC) in *The Times* special supplement on radio in 1934 stated that the ideal broadcast commentary 'should be of outstanding interest to a national and not merely sectional audience'. The 1934 BBC Handbook referred sympathetically to those 'for whom sport holds no attraction'. It added:

> The interest of this sector of the community cannot be overlooked and sporting commentaries are limited to events of national importance such as the Derby, the Boat Race, international football matches etc.

There was no mention of the fact that the BBC had sought, and been refused, coverage of other events.

1   This account draws on BBC WAC R 30/135 OB Sound Boat Race 1927
2   See BBC WAC R 30/3 572/1 Welsh Rugby Union 1927-39
3   See BBC WAC R 30/19 Grand National 1933-35

FIVE

NEW PEOPLE, NEW WAYS

WHAT KIND OF PERSON – with what kind of voice – makes a good commentator? What constitutes a good commentary? These were the two key questions about radio commentary with which the BBC struggled throughout the pre-war years.

John Snagge said of the first football commentary he did with Rex Palmer in 1927: Neither of us knew much about the game or the players in it. We made a howling mess of it at first.

Nearly sixty years later, he recalled: 'We didn't know what a good commentator was … a lot of it was very bad.[1]

The initial instinct of Gerald Cock and others was to find someone who knew a lot about a sport and who could 'talk well'. In an article in the BBC Handbook of 1928 he listed the main requirements: technical knowledge of the sport, 'a good voice', fluency, and the ability to select things which were most relevant to a clear narrative. At this stage little attention was being given to other important factors – for instance how a commentary should be structured, what the balance should be between technical information about the event and background material, and what the role of the second commentator should be.

Nor was there a systematic programme of training or induction for commentators. Occasionally individuals would be taken aside if someone spotted a fault.

Wakelam, generally a great favourite with listeners, got an ominous letter after one of his early commentaries from Sieveking, who was still assisting with outside broadcasts: 'I would like to have a chat – when would you manage to look in for five minutes?' He went on to tell Wakelam:

> You have been tending recently to throw your voice all
> over the keyboard and to talk very much more quickly,
> so that it becomes on the last occasion very nearly

incomprehensible. To a certain extent this excitement contained in your voice is good, but the listener can get a very large proportion of the excitement from the sounds of the crowd. Therefore, it is not only advisable, but absolutely necessary that you should keep your voice much more even and speak slower.[2]

A few years later, in 1933, the BBC set down in its annual handbook what it saw as a good microphone voice. It should be 'primarily one which is easily audible and one which is sufficiently flexible and expressive to reveal the personality of the speaker. ... undoubtedly the ideal microphone voice is one which adds beauty of tone to audibility and expressiveness'.

And writing for a major supplement in *The Times* in August of 1934, someone from the BBC, Cock again perhaps, added a little more: the voice should be in a 'neutral or at least not inappropriate accent', and the commentator should sound cheerful and be humorous 'without being facetious'.

So the personality of the speaker now entered the equation: a commentator needed to be someone a listener would be pleased to meet. Some voices were more acceptable than others but it was not clear what 'beauty of tone' and 'neutral accent' meant.

––––––––––––

AT THIS TIME THE BBC was also struggling with finding effective ways of auditioning potential commentators. 'The discovery of talent is by no means easy,' a BBC writer complained in the same *Times* supplement of 1934. 'Trials during actual events are seldom possible. Impromptu descriptions of imaginary happenings before a microphone, in the cold atmosphere of a studio, must generally suffice as a basis of selection.'

In 1936 the young Michael Standing, later a director of Outside Broadcasts, conceived the idea of erecting a mock commentary point on the roof of Broadcasting House in Portland Place. This at least had the merit of giving candidates the scenes in Upper Regent Street and Oxford Circus to describe. The first tests were held there in January 1937, involving nine people in all, of whom three were listed as 'possible'. The assessor (presumably Standing) did not seem to be working to any explicit criteria. These notes on the rejected candidates are typical:

Rather high pitched and strident voice. Unattractive inflexions. Commentary fair but her voice rules her out.

Average cultured but quite undistinguished voice.
Poor voice. Slight cockney accent. Poor commentary.
One of the 'possibles' had a 'north country accent; quite good continuity and description; rather thin voice'.[3]

But almost no new commentators emerged from these tests. In practice the BBC spent the years from 1927 to 1937 believing that the best commentators could be found in the world of sport. The success of Teddy Wakelam and George Allison seemed to confirm that this was the way forward, especially as Wakelam was able to turn his hand to both tennis and cricket. Neither had 'posh' voices but they spoke within the parameters of what is often called 'standard English' and used the 'received pronunciation' favoured by and associated with the BBC. By chance the BBC had stumbled across two unusual people, and other sports did not throw up good commentators so readily. A number of cricketers were tried without success and it took some time before the BBC found someone who could develop the right style for the game. There were also problems with boxing, horseracing and rowing.

For some time the BBC used Lionel Seccombe as their first choice boxing commentator. He was very much the type they favoured at that stage: a boxing blue at Oxford, he seemed to know the sport and 'spoke well'. But Seccombe had what John Snagge later called 'bad luck with his verdicts'.[4] Boxing is almost unique among sports in that there is no public score or race position to indicate to the spectator who is in front. Seccombe covered a fight between Len Harvey and the Canadian Larry Gains from the back of the Royal Albert Hall in 1934 and 'gave' the fight to Gains, when almost everyone else, including the referee, awarded it to Harvey. Harvey and his manager were so annoyed that the boxer subsequently announced that he would not do another fight if Seccombe was commentating.

Horseracing presented a particular challenge. In setting up the first Grand National commentary in 1927, Gerald Cock told his colleagues that they must get an experienced racing person for the job:

These specialists are so good it is said of them that they can read the whole race 'in a black fog'. I once heard one myself at Aintree and the precision of his spotting the order of running, the falls, the distances between horses, and other incidents, was astounding, and was proved perfectly correct afterwards.[5]

47

But the chosen person, Meyrick Good, was soon discarded, and a number of others struggled with the race in the years that followed. A transcription of the 1928 Grand National commentary published by the BBC indicates that, even when only three horses from the original forty-two starters were left standing, the commentary team struggled to identify the eventual winner. In the 1932 running of the same race there is much whispering off mike to try and help the commentator identify horses.

One of the two men the BBC used for ten years or more was Captain RC Lyle, the racing correspondent of *The Times* (the other was Geoffrey Gilbey). Lyle was a former cavalry officer, and deeply immersed in the sport. He covered many of the classic races for the BBC between 1928 and 1939. But, as he admitted in an interview in 1932, Lyle was also colour-blind:

> I hope it won't lose me my job to tell you this. But honestly I could not tell you whether your tie is green, or brown or blue. Of course I know yellow when I see it. But brown and green and certain shades of blue, and even red, are all the same to me. I was ploughed for being colour blind in the Navy and but for that I might now be an admiral.[6]

Lyle tried to memorize owners' colours in terms of shades of light and dark, but in following the races for radio he relied largely on knowing the faces of the jockeys. His views on broadcasting technique were fairly simple, and would be sharply contested by some commentators today:

> The broadcaster must get excited. It is only fair to his invisible audience, who cannot see anything, for him to do so. The first rule about broadcasting is never to stop for a single instant. If you do, you are done. You must keep on.

On the morning of the race in 1932, Lyle told readers of *The Times* that *Orwell* was justifiably the favourite for the Derby. That year he was in a much improved commentary position on top of the royal box. He had beside him a 'race reader', William Hobbiss, whose job it was to pick out individual horses and riders. The commentary they managed between them was a continual struggle. The account is punctuated by pauses – about twenty in all, some of them quite painful in length, and all rather underlining Lyle's 'first rule of broadcasting'. There was a sharp disagreement early on with Hobbiss, and two apologies from Lyle that he could not see what was happening.

Cockpen's gone to the front ... Cockpen in front, on the far side, the middle of the far side ... Now it's either Summer Planet or the other one of Gulliver's ... (another voice, off mike: 'It's Bacchus in front')... Bachuss is not in front... Cockpen is there... Orwell's quite well away... Summer Planet is there, Cockpen is there ... Orwell is not in the front, he's quite well placed... Still Summer Planet I make it. (Something indistinct said sotto voce off mike). What? They're going behind the cars, still Summer Planet. Orwell is all right... Not left or anything like that, they're going to the top of the hill now... It's almost impossible, I'm sorry, to tell you the colours exactly...

At the climax, Lyle is quick to spot that the favourite had run out of steam but he then prematurely awards the race to *Dastor*, only just catching the winner's late run in time:

Here's the favourite on the outside, here he comes. ... here's Orwell on the far side ... (cheering mounts). The favourite's beat, whip on the favourite. Miracle's coming ... Dastor's won it ... the favourite's beat. Here's April Fifth coming, April the Fifth has won it, April the Fifth has won it, April the Fifth has won it...

In his column in *The Times* next day Lyle complained that a thick haze over the course had made it difficult to distinguish colours. This was not an isolated case. BBC staff were regularly frustrated by Lyle's inability to place the horses in a race in relation to the distance left, as well as in relation to each other.[7]

The Boat Race commentary also caused problems. By the autumn of 1930, Cock had decided he had to get rid of Nickalls and Squire. He admitted in a letter to the Boat Race organisers in 1930 that commentary 'for the last year or two has been rotten and we know it. Nickalls gets so hysterical and sounds as if he were almost crying,' he recorded.[8]

Nickalls blamed the debacle on Squire and his alleged interruptions – 'it became worse every year and this year it reached such a point that it entirely disintegrated me.' As a further humiliation, the recording of the commentary made with the BBC's permission by HMV was played back to would-be commentators at Broadcasting House as an example of how not to commentate.

At first Cock toyed with the idea of getting another rowing blue from outside the BBC to take over the commentary but eventually the job was given to John Snagge, a staff member with rowing experience. Significantly, when Pitman asked who Snagge was, Cock pleaded with him to give the idea a chance but added: 'We would not do anything which should be disapproved of by you.'

IT WAS NOT UNTIL the mid-1930s that the BBC began to think again about how to find good commentators. At the same time a more adventurous and expanding programme of commentaries began. A key factor was the arrival of the man who replaced Cock (who was appointed as the BBC's first Director of Television) as head of Outside Broadcasts in 1935: Seymour Joly de Lotbinière, known in the BBC as 'Lobby'. Within three years de Lotbinière reversed the BBC's policy on the selection of commentators, developed a theory of how good commentary worked and greatly expanded the range and number of sports covered. Live commentary was about to enter its golden age.

Son of a senior army officer, de Lotbinière went to Eton, had a distinguished academic record at Cambridge and was called to the Bar. But the work of a Chancery barrister failed to challenge him and in 1932 he left the legal world and joined the BBC as a talks producer. He was responsible for all radio outside broadcasts – not just sport – from 1935 to 1940, and again from 1945 to 1952. No single person had more influence on the style of radio commentary on the BBC.

De Lotbinière quickly raised the profile of outside broadcasts and particularly live commentary on sport. He understood the fundamental difference between the two: that the first was usually scripted, predictable and controlled, the other unscripted and with a strong element of spontaneity. But he also knew that both required careful preparation. He was meticulous in monitoring the performance of commentators and overhauled BBC policy towards their recruitment. But, most important, he developed a theory about how good commentary worked.

In 1935 the overall coverage of sport was thin. The BBC had secured the great annual occasions but there was no routine coverage of sport on a weekly basis. It was not unusual for Saturday afternoon programmes on the main network to consist of organ recitals and gramophone records. But within a year or two of de Lotbinière's arrival the outside broadcast department began to commit more resources to areas such as cricket, boxing and rugby and also to experiment with sports which had previously not been included.

By 1938 de Lotbinière had greatly widened the spread of sports covered: there were thirty-seven in all, compared to ten or twelve a few years previously. Of these some received only one or at the most two visits: badminton, bobsleighing, diving, fencing, racquets, rowing, shinty, skittles, show jumping, shooting, squash and wrestling. But other sports outside the top group were given regular coverage: billiards (five commentaries), cycling (five), darts (five), ice hockey (eleven), swimming (five), speedway (eight), snooker (eight), table tennis (five) and water polo (six). 'Joly is nothing if not adventurous,' commented *Radio Pictorial* in 1938, when it picked up that the BBC was going to cover bobsleighing.

De Lotbinière seemed determined to go to every part of the social spectrum. Racquets, a game largely restricted to a small number of public schools, was tried in 1936 and Aidan Crawley given the task of commentary:

> *A man is just going to serve. That was a fault. Well served …
> its very difficult to describe it's so fast. Well hit, sir, well hit.
> … terrific pace they're playing. It's Winchester three Rugby ten.
> Lord Abbeydale has just served.*
> *'This is a game that requires great hand and eye ability, so
> inheritance is a factor, so there are a lot of public school par-
> ticipants. A certain amount of mothers and sisters are here. I
> wish more people could see this game. I'm sorry … it's a very
> exciting game. Well hit sir. I'm trying to hear the score, you'll
> hear it in a moment.*

In the same year Charles de Beaumont, president of the Amateur Fencing Association, was asked to describe an international women's foil event. He did a little better:

> *Now they're sparring again. Miss Lachmann is pressing her
> now, she's coming out, coming out again. She came out, and
> she was parried, she parried the riposte from Miss Adams. Miss
> Lachmann continued and landed, and that is given against
> Miss Adams, that is two against Miss Adams and three against
> Miss Lachmann.*
> *There's an attack from Miss Lachmann, it was parried but the
> riposte was short and nothing happened. Now Miss Adams is
> pressing, she's pressing, she made an attack which was parried,
> she went on, took the blade in carte … very, very well, and ar-
> rived on target. Of course there was no riposte on that as she*

was holding the blade, and therefore that was against Miss Lachmann.

De Lotbinière also gave darts and snooker regular coverage but neither sport lent itself easily to radio. Darts was enjoying a boom period, with some twenty thousand entries for the national championships in 1938. In his commentaries on darts, Charles Garner often confessed that he could not see exactly what was happening. And de Lotbinière concluded that the problem with snooker was that it was a 'long drawn-out affair and it is therefore not easy to strike the psychological moment when a match is in the balance.'[9]

No sport could say it had not been given a chance, but greyhound racing proved the most contentious and it took several years for de Lotbinière to get it into the schedules. Reith, supported by religious pressure groups, had always set his face against any connections between broadcasting and gambling. In 1933 he had reacted with alarm to news that a talk about greyhound racing was to be broadcast:

> I think it is one of the most degrading sights in England. The element of sport is reduced to a minimum, is in fact almost non-existent. It is a betting ramp, and betting is a worse evil in this country now than drink.[10]

Public interest in the sport, he added, 'is by no means necessarily a recommendation'. The greyhound racing industry pressed the Corporation to give results of races as they did with horseracing and, after some discussion, the BBC finally agreed to announce the results of the eight main races during the season.

The industry saw a further opening when Reith left the BBC in the June of 1938. They invited his successor, Frederick Ogilvie, to the Catford Stadium but he declined. De Lotbinière however had an acute sense of how the BBC needed to position itself in the burgeoning world of professional sport. He knew that by covering greyhound racing at the White City stadium he could improve his chances of winning a contract to cover boxing there. He went to see George Lansbury – the Labour MP who led the opposition – and persuaded him of the inconsistency of covering horse but not dog racing. The Greyhound Derby, he argued with colleagues, could win more listeners than any other evening outside broadcast apart from boxing. 'If we could do 3 or 4 of the big greyhound races each year,' he wrote, ' I feel certain that we would find it would make it easier in negotiating for some of the big fights'.

It seems likely that de Lotbinière went to a track so see a meeting for himself and he now began to argue that the sport deserved coverage in its own right:

> Greyhound Racing provides a very interesting puzzle, with more to it, I sometimes think, than *The Times* crossword, which evokes so much laborious attention from the better educated.

In the end it was the war which made the difference. In January 1940, the BBC Control Board agreed occasional commentaries 'partly in recognition of the special needs of the Forces, now that the Corporation is giving them a programme ...' So, in March 1940, the Greyhound Derby was broadcast for the first time.

TO GET CONSISTENCY OF STANDARDS across the BBC, de Lotbinière needed to bring the scattered team of outside broadcast assistants and commentators together. After careful preparation, he managed to ensure that almost all were released for a short residential conference in London. This was to be the first of a series of annual events at which he promulgated and discussed policy and set standards. The agenda for the first gathering, in February 1937, included 'commentators' qualifications and tests.' Among those attending were Raymond Glendenning, Wynford Vaughan-Thomas, John Snagge, Michael Standing and Thomas Woodroffe.

At these meetings de Lotbinière played recordings of past commentaries and invited discussion of them. It was at the 1938 conference that racing commentaries were scrutinised and the death knell for Lyle's role as a racing commentator sounded. In 1939 there was discussion about the need for a small portable transmitting set so as to enable commentaries to be made from different parts of a golf course. And de Lotbinière circulated guidance notes for would-be commentators which remained in use for many years.

Reith had established the habit of ringing broadcasters from his home after they had completed an event and giving them almost immediate feedback, and de Lotbinière would sometimes do the same. But he sought more systematic methods of monitoring and improving quality. He held regular Monday morning meetings to discuss the previous week's broadcasts and to report on whether they met his expectations.

De Lotbinière also called individual commentators into his office.

Max Robertson recalled that when he first joined the BBC in 1939 as a young broadcaster he found the experience of going to see his new boss an ordeal. De Lotbinière's office was at the end of a balcony in an annexe of Broadcasting House and to enter it you first had to pass through an open-plan area where a number of experienced announcers including John Snagge and Wynford Vaughan-Thomas had their desks.

> Going through their ranks as they sat looking you over with amusement or disdain was quelling enough but when you came into Lobby's den you quailed even more before his mild manner.[11]

Harold Walker, who began football and swimming commentaries with the BBC in 1938, was a great admirer of de Lotbinière but he remembered his anxiety on being summoned to receive feedback. De Lotbinière used a small ball on a board to illuminate what he was saying about a football broadcast:

> Lobby was a very strict disciplinarian, and he listened to everything meticulously. He'd call me up to his offices on a Saturday morning, and you'd be thinking: I wonder what the old man's got to say to me now. He would put on a piece of your commentary and with his finger he'd follow the ball on the board. 'I want you to listen, Harry', he'd say. 'You see, Harry, I'm lost, here. I'm lost. Let's play that again.' After an hour's drubbing you felt a bit drained. I can see him now walking up and down jingling the coins in his pockets taking the rise out of my last commentary. 'You've lost me, Harry, You've lost me.'[12]

―――――――――

BETWEEN 1935 AND 1938 de Lotbinière began to change his mind about where to look for good commentators. When he took on the post of head of outside broadcasts in 1935, he at first accepted the necessity of asking sporting specialists to undertake commentary, particularly as he was committed to widening the range of sports covered. For speedway he turned to Frank Buckland, who had ridden for England; for snooker to Willie Smith, finalist in a world championship; and for bobsleighing he recruited the skating judge and owner of Richmond ice rink, Hubert Martineau.

At the two-day meeting on outside broadcasts in 1938, he told regional staff directly that BBC racing commentaries were not good enough. He played them recordings of both Lyle and Gilbey and it was agreed that at the forthcoming Cheltenham meeting Thomas Woodroffe – a staff member, not a racing expert – should do the commentary. In an internal memorandum written that year de Lotbinière noted:

> I believe that at the moment we are doing better horseracing commentaries than we have done for the past ten years, only because we have given up trying to find horseracing experts for the job.[13]

There were probably several reasons why de Lotbinière changed his mind about where to find good commentators. His experience in managing the great state occasions of the time – the funeral of George V and the coronation of George VI – was almost certainly one factor. On these occasions experienced broadcasters, including Howard Marshall and John Snagge, had found the appropriate notes of solemnity and celebration, and the broadcasts had provided a compelling narrative for some listeners. Marshall and Snagge were also beginning to demonstrate how much microphone experience counted in covering sport. And in other countries, notably America and Germany, de Lotbinière noted, sports commentators were drawn largely from the ranks of professional broadcasters.

In 1938 de Lotbinière argued in a memorandum that the BBC should not look for sporting experts to undertake commentary, but for people with a general aptitude for broadcasting. He acknowledged that some 'expert listeners' to each sport might suffer but he argued that more general listeners would gain. He made his point forcibly in an article in the BBC Handbook in 1939 which contained a cruel dig at those experts who had made a mess of their attempts at commentary:

> In arranging, for example, a circus broadcast, it has been found more satisfactory to employ a regular commentator who can learn about circuses than to search amongst the clowns for someone with the requisite natural abilities and then teach them commentary technique.

By the end of 1938 he was committed to training BBC staff commentators for all-round work, so as not to be dependent on the outside specialist. Writing in the BBC Handbook in 1939 he announced cautiously that the technique of commentary had improved in the previous year, but that 'further study' was still needed.

Lobby also had to deal with the large numbers of people writing into the BBC to say that they thought they would make good commentators. He was finding it difficult to reply to all their letters, let alone arrange auditions. And he was irritated by the failure of some unsuccessful candidates to accept the BBC's verdict on their performance with good grace. He began to give up on general auditioning of members of the public because he found so few of them had any talent at all.

He wrote an uncompromising piece for *Radio Times*: *Would you like to be a commentator?*:

> I believe that commentary work is as difficult as anything in broadcasting ... during the previous ten years some hundreds of commentators have had the chance of actual broadcasts and several hundreds more have been tested and rejected. Yet at the end of it there are only perhaps half-a-dozen persons who would now be accepted generally as successful commentators.

The last point was bad news for some of the fourteen existing commentators whose pictures appeared alongside the article.

De Lotbinière advised those sitting at home who thought they could do the job to give themselves an audition before they wrote in to the BBC. They should set themselves a target time during which they would 'commentate' and keep to it; they should speak aloud and have someone listen; and their listener must judge them against the best on the radio.

During this period, de Lotbinière was also exploring whether he should use women commentators for women's sports. He employed Marjorie Pollard for cricket, Thelma Carpenter for snooker, and Mrs Garner for darts, all for women-only events. In 1936 *Radio Pictorial* reported that he was looking for a women's commentator to cover women's fencing, and hockey. There was a conviction in some quarters of the BBC that women were being excluded from announcing and commentary jobs. For example one BBC producer, Hilda Matheson wrote as early as 1933:

> Do the British feel that no women could read the football or cricket results with the peculiar conviction which a male voice alone would convey to them?[14]

For his part de Lotbinière told colleagues in 1937:

> BBC policy was to use women commentators occasionally

if any with the requisite qualifications could be found, not in order to present the so-called women's point of view on dress or fashion, but on their merits as commentators; the difficulty was that women answering to the necessary qualifications appeared to be excessively rare.[15]

However, within a few weeks, in the notes he drafted for would-be commentators and which were sent out to those who wrote in seeking an audition, he struck a rather different note:

It must be remembered that for technical reasons a woman's voice will only rarely be at such a pitch that sustained listening can long remain a pleasure.[16]

WHILE HE EXPERIMENTED with different sports and, to a lesser degree, with different commentators, de Lotbinière was also musing on something even more fundamental: what is a good commentary?

He had sounded a prescient note in his *Radio Times* article of 1937:

The art of the 'sound' commentator is scarcely ten years old, and it still has a long way to go. But there may not be much time left for its normal development, as television will soon be making a different demand on the commentator and, I believe, a lighter one. In the meantime, if only for the sake of 'sound' listeners, commentaries must improve.

By the beginning of that year – in an internal memorandum – de Lotbinière was beginning to articulate some important ideas about the structure of a broadcast, the sequencing of information and the use of additional material. He warned of the need to keep people abreast of the score – though his suggestion that in football it be given 'every five minutes' now seems unrealistic.

But the most significant idea, again owing something to experience of the wider field of outside broadcasts, was for the commentator to bring in the broad context of the event. This should include scene setting, perhaps prepared on paper, though never read out verbatim, and reserve material. De Lotbinière could see that there were things that sports commentaries had in common with public events and state occasions: both needed a proper narrative structure, and material whereby the commentator could depict the whole scene for the listener; including the distinctive sounds of the occasion.

When, later that year, he produced his famous 'Notes for would-be commentators' these ideas were incorporated. Fluency and 'microphone personality' were included as desirable characteristics. But the stress was now more on weaving scene-setting information and the description of events into a continuous narrative, and the need to give shape to that narrative. It was not enough for commentators just to describe what they saw. They must convey its significance, add human interest and suspense, and give their story a felt beginning and ending. Some of these things perhaps came to Wakelam and Allison by instinct but they needed to be written down and practised if other people were to acquire them.

The war, and his transfer temporarily to another post, delayed de Lotbinière in finally setting out in detail what he had learned. In 1942 – a year in which very few people were thinking about the subject – he produced a twenty-page typescript on *Outside Broadcasts*.[17] The shift of emphasis from the early days of BBC commentary is striking. Then, the focus was on the commentators, their knowledge and their voice. Now the focus was on commentary, as a certain kind of broadcasting, requiring a certain kind of narrative technique. The requirements were framed by a consideration of the listener's experience.

The first of two prime considerations was that 'the listener must be persuaded that he really is in a "ringside seat". It followed there could be no faking of what was seen or said, because listeners could detect quickly what was not 'true'. Descriptions of the event should be delivered swiftly and effectively. There should be full use of 'effects', for instance crowd reaction and background noise, and these should have precedence over the spoken commentary.

Having got the listeners in their 'seats', the second priority was to 'hold their attention'. Commentators must be well informed on whatever event they were covering and tell their story 'attractively' and with competence. The core of the attractive style to de Lotbinière was effective story-telling: a striking start, maintaining speed and showing assurance, blending all the material together, creating suspense, retinterest, and finding a neat finish.

A third section of de Lotbinière's paper dealt with the need to match the commentary to different types of event and different sports. He gave as examples athletics, billiards, boxing, cricket, football and rugby (he grouped these two together), racing, tennis and rowing. He also had something to say about the second commentator. The task, he said, was to be concise, and not to intrude. De Lotbinière had already pronounced in an earlier document that in general dialogue between commentators was not appropriate. It was in this one respect that his approach was eventually to be not only abandoned but systematically reversed.

1	J Snagge and M Beesley *Those Vintage Years of Broadcasting* (Pitman 1972) and interview with Ivan Victor August 27th 1986, held in British Library.
2	BBC WAC Rcont. 1, HBT Wakelam Talks 1927-36
3	BBC WAC R 30/428/1 Commentators 1936-39
4	*Radio Pictorial* December 9th 1938 p38
5	BBC WAC R30/16 Aintree
6	Charles Graves *As it happens* in *The Strand* magazine, June 1932
7	BBC WAC R30/428/2 OB Commentators File 2 1940-47
8	Quotations in this story from BBC WAC R 30/138 Boat Race 1930-32
9	BBC WAC R30/3,144/5
10	Quotations from the debate about Greyhound Racing taken from BBC WAC R30/1,078/1 (Greyhound Racing 1934-1953)
11	Max Robertson *Stop Talking and give the Score* (Kingswood Press 1987) p45
12	Harold Walker in conversation with the author
13	BBC WAC R/30/428/1 Commentators 1936-39 (8.9.38)
14	Hilda Matheson *Broadcasting* (Butterworth 1933) p 56
15	BBC WAC R30/428/1 Commentators 1936-39
16	BBC WAC R/30/428/1
17	BBC WAC R30/428/2 Some notes on commentary

SIX

THE GOLDEN AGE

DE LOTBINIÈRE'S WORK BORE FRUIT. In 1933, John Snagge's account of the university Boat Race consisted of little more than a series of announcements about the race strung together. Stuck for what to say, he falls back regularly on reciting the strike rate of the rowers, continuing with this when the race is effectively over. He is not helped by altercations with his back-up commentator who urges him: 'Give the time, John.' Snagge digs his heels in: 'I think we'll wait.' More seriously, Snagge is slow to recognise that the Cambridge boat is pulling ahead – they have a lead of a length before he recognises that it is decisive. At the end of the race, there are prolonged consultations before the confirmed time, almost half-a-minute different to the provisional one given, is announced.

By contrast, Snagge's commentary in 1939 is enriched by descriptive detail, and a greater feel for the colour and atmosphere of the occasion. The context is set first by Snagge with accounts of the weather (*'perfectly wicked last week'*) and the scene at Putney – the trams passing up and down and the policemen standing on the bridge. He invites listeners to share the emotions of the rowers as they prepare:

> *This is the worst moment. As they paddle down from the boat-houses … it seems like about five miles. It seems heavy and it seems long. And your sweater never seems to fit and you always think your shorts are coming off … or something like that.*

The expert summariser, JM Duckworth, describes the role of the coxes:

> *We have these strange little men who do a lot of shouting… and seem to control the destinies of a whole race … little Massey is perched like a sparrow on the house top, looking over the heads of his men … with the muggy, dirty Thames and with a fog over the course, usual landmarks are completely obliterated.*

As an experiment de Lotbinière himself was reporting from an aeroplane above the Thames. He is handicapped by foggy conditions but adds to the picture:

All along the bank ... it looks from here as if someone's drawn
a black line with a thick bit of charcoal along each bank and
those I suppose are people.

Snagge gives an assured and rounded account of the race. This change in commentary style helped to make the race an annual radio ritual, even among those with no direct links to the universities involved. For one young listener, Michael Firth, it was the first memory of commentary:

> It was just before the war and I was about six years old. We lived in Balham and my grandmother and two aunts lived next door. When the Boat Race came round there were light and dark blue rosettes on sale everywhere and people were milling around to choose the colour of their favourite. We all went to Grandma's house and sat down together to hear John Snagge's commentary. That year I picked dark blue and although Oxford lost I've supported them ever since.

One or two commentators led the way in these changes and probably influenced de Lotbinière's thinking. Howard Marshall's gradual development of cricket commentary during the 1930s – of which more in Chapter 20 – is the best example. And the arrival of television was also a factor. Cricket was first shown live in 1938 and people soon began to ask whether, since TV could show the pictures, there was anything left for radio to do.

It was de Lotbinière who thought hardest about this. He understood the unique quality of radio and its potential for a different kind of commentary. He grasped the importance of good story-telling and he knew that radio could nourish the imagination of listeners in a way that television could not. It was a tribute to his success that some of radio's best story-tellers acknowledged that good commentary provided them with a model to emulate. Edward J Mason, who wrote many episodes of both *Dick Barton – Special Agent* and *The Archers,* said that a sixty-minute omnibus edition should be 'packed with as much incident and action as the broadcast of the Cup Final or Grand National.'[1]

LIKE COCK BEFORE HIM, de Lotbinière also proved a skilful negotiator with sporting bodies and one who, in the post-war years especially, helped the BBC come to terms with their growing influence. Before the war he had one particularly tricky situation to resolve. In

1938 the five-year agreement with Tophams regarding the Grand National commentary came to an end. Mirabel Topham, now managing the company, requested a fee of £500 per year. When the BBC turned this down she informed de Lotbinière that the Board would 'delete the broadcast for a year or two.'[2]

This was a difficult moment for de Lotbinière. He had extended sporting coverage and could not now afford to lose one of the jewels in the crown. Sparring took place between the two organisations and a certain amount of courting of Mrs Topham by de Lotbinière. Their backgrounds were rather different. His parents lived in India and he had spent his youth at boarding schools in England and his school holidays with aristocratic relatives. After Eton, it was Cambridge and then the Inns of Court. She had grown up in a London hotel, managed by her father, and had a short stage career as an actress. She married into the Topham family and eventually became the owner of the Aintree racecourse (which she finally sold in 1973). Mirabel Topham, someone said, 'enjoyed the scent of battle', but she also had a winning and warming side. She was undoubtedly a tough negotiator but she knew when to strike a deal.

It was agreed that Victor Smythe, the BBC man in Manchester, should prepare 'Plan B', a strategy for describing the race from outside the course. After considerable research, and not a little haggling with local residents, he came up with a plan costing thirty-six guineas. The BBC would rent a private house overlooking the starting gate. A platform would be erected on property belonging to two householders near the start and at the Canal Turn the commentator would be placed on a veranda of the premises of a small general store. Smythe thought Mrs Topham might possibly be able to sabotage the third position but not the first two. Unsurprisingly, the London Midland and Scottish railway company had rejected his proposals for stationing a commentator on their railway embankment.

While the Manchester end of the BBC was doing this, and the corporation's lawyers were reflecting on the legal position, de Lotbinière travelled up to Lancashire and met Mrs Topham in her home. It must have been an interesting encounter. Lobby's notes to colleagues indicate that he found her an engaging woman, and someone with whom he could do business. Mrs Topham knew that radio coverage brought her race free publicity. He made it clear the BBC could not go to £500, and she pointed out that the 1933 figure of £200 was no longer enough. A sum of £350 was agreed. As part of the deal the BBC agreed to give publicity to the race on other radio programmes including *In Town Tonight*.

Tommy Woodroffe and Richard North undertook the commentary, receiving help from two young men who were just at the start of their commentary careers: Michael O'Hehir and Raymond Glendenning.

The commentary figures for 1938, the last full year before the war, illustrate how dramatically de Lotbinière extended the coverage. There were one or more commentaries on one hundred and ninety days, more than double the figure when he took over in 1935. Cricket had now been established as a favourite and, including broadcasts of county games on regional stations, around sixty commentaries were scheduled covering twenty-six different matches. Boxing came next with thirty-five broadcasts, followed by rugby union (twenty-one) and football (twenty).

By the time war broke out, radio commentary was playing an important part in the leisure time of many people. A survey of several hundred households and individuals in Bristol confirmed that radio had extended their interest to new sports.[3] People who had never seen the events live said they always listened to the Boat Race, ice hockey matches, Wimbledon, motor racing and the Derby, plus eye-witness reports on golf. Many women listeners said they listened to football commentaries, especially the Cup final. Boxing was very popular.

> In a group of ten middle-aged and elderly women, six said they habitually listened to boxing, while a group of fourteen young mothers all listened, and some even took the wireless up to bed with them, when there was a relay from America.[4]

Cricket had a big following. The leader of a boys' club reported that when he and a group passed a field in which play was taking place, the boys 'criticized the play most intelligently in phrases actually used by wireless commentators'.

DURING THE SECOND WORLD WAR, radio in Britain acquired a new significance. The voices of newsreaders and of reporters at the front line brought the drama of the conflict into people's lives on a daily basis. Some of those who had commentated on sporting events now described victories and defeats of a different kind. A news bulletin read by John Snagge might be followed by reports from Howard Marshall in North Africa, Stewart MacPherson on the Normandy beaches or Raymond Glendenning on a London rooftop. The war confirmed the process whereby radio became an everyday, shared experience and the best-known voices were offered as sources of reassurance and unity.

At first, sport had to take a back seat. Commentary was banned by the BBC Board as soon as war was declared on September 3rd 1939. The Corporation was reluctant to provide much live coverage partly from a desire to avoid the impression that 'we are not buckling down to the job.'[5] However, the ban was partially lifted on September 24th and in October some football and boxing was covered, plus a darts match between firemen and wardens from a pub in Islington. In November, de Lotbinière decreed that outside broadcasts might slowly be increased because they 'give the public a reassuring impression of normality'. There was a growing feeling that sport was good for morale. Within a few months the Football League agreed that matches could be broadcast on the services channel – *For the Forces* – which the BBC had introduced to meet the needs of service personnel around the world.

In August 1940, Michael Standing – standing in for de Lotbinière, who had been put in charge of the BBC's West region – pressed the case for a resumption of wider coverage. 'We want to show the world that we can still play football, whether Hitler likes it or not', he argued to colleagues. That winter he prepared a schedule of commentaries for the following summer, about twenty broadcasts in all, most on the Forces network.

During 1942 and 1943 there were some thirty commentaries during the summer months, and occasional football internationals in the winter. Some of what was offered had a service slant or else a home front angle – a darts match between the Navy and Army for example, and the Central London Busmen's boxing championships. Instructions were given to commentators not to mention weather conditions, whether the King was present and other security details. This meant that when Sidney Wooderson made his attack on the world 1,000 yards record the *Radio Times* announced that the broadcast would be 'from a northern athletic ground'.

By 1943, a Saturday afternoon programme of commentaries was beginning to appear more regularly but with a limited range of sports. Young boxers like Freddie Mills and Bruce Woodcock were receiving attention and Raymond Glendenning covered international football and rugby matches. As the end of the war approached there was an explicit attempt to capture a 'back to normal' atmosphere. 'Saturday Sport' in June 1945 featured swimming, athletics, cricket, football and water polo, and there was boxing in the evening. Finally, in August 1945, for the first time since 1939, sport featured on the front cover of the *Radio Times*. By then the Forces Programme had been replaced by the Light Programme, the lead network for sport.

De Lotbinière's expertise in the field of outside broadcasting had been put to good use in the later stages of the war when he became head of the war reporting unit. The style of the live front-line dispatches on the war owed much to the expertise developed in producing outside broadcasts in the 1930s. Equally the imperatives of war broadcasting impacted on the style of broadcasters. John Arlott, who began his long career as a cricket commentator in 1946, recalled:

> The men sending back the stories of battle ... were not concerned with the politeness of the mannered broadcast, but with action, violence and death. They were the people who changed broadcasting, who gave it urgency, on-the-moment drama and yet also the common touch... Essentially ... a new way had been cut to the listener's consciousness. So, for those who were to broadcast in time of peace, a new formula had been created. Essentially this was so in the case of outside broadcasts, of ceremonial and great State occasions, but most of all, of sport.[6]

IN THE SUMMER OF 1945 de Lotbinière returned to his old job. Brian Johnston, who delivered his first cricket commentary in 1946 and seventeen years later became the BBC's cricket correspondent, recalled that when he joined the outside broadcasts department just after the war, Lobby's Monday morning meetings had been resumed:

> There, sitting humbly with notebooks in hand were well-known commentators like Raymond Glendenning, Rex Alston, Wynford Vaughan-Thomas and Stewart MacPherson. They listened quietly while Lobby criticized, praised, or completely pulled to bits the programmes which they had broadcast during the previous week... How Lobby managed it I don't know but he tried to listen to all the output of OBs and record his findings in a little black book. He was a perfectionist, but completely fair, never too fulsome with his praise but never too unkind either: 'Not bad' or 'On the whole a brave effort', meant that you had done pretty well. But if he began to beat his clenched right hand into the palm of his left and said, 'Brian, I was a bit puzzled', you could be sure that you were about to be

criticized. But no one resented this because the criticism was always constructive.[7]

De Lotbinière slowly rebuilt the commentary schedules, concentrating now on the most popular sports rather than experimenting across the board. In particular he sought to exploit the popularity that football matches had had with service personnel by persuading the Football League to agree to regular commentaries on the main network. This took some years to achieve.

In the years between 1945 and 1960 radio listening was at its peak. A cluster of popular comedy shows, panel games and serials – including *Take it From Here, Twenty Questions* and *Dick Barton* – drew huge audiences. Most homes had one radio, and many families listened together; research in 1947 suggested that in eight out of ten homes the radio was on during the evening meal.[8] Television was slow to take off, not least because the director general of the BBC from 1944–52, William Haley, was more committed to radio. The number of radio-only licences reached its highest point in 1950 with 11.8 million and was still nearly 10 million in 1955.[9]

It was in this context that radio commentary drew some of its biggest audiences. Football league attendance was at a peak, there was a cluster of new and promising young British boxers and, in 1948, the Olympic Games – and also the Australia cricket team – came to England. Interest in the heavyweight title fight between Bruce Woodcock and Joe Baksi in 1947 was so great that the Chancellor of the Exchequer's budget broadcast was delayed until the fight was over. Tony Challis was a teenager in the village of Foxton, just outside Cambridge:

> My brother was due home from service in Malaya that day, and we were all keyed up to meet him. Unfortunately his train was expected just when the fight was due to come on. We could see the smoke from the train as it left the neighbouring station and my mum and dad kept calling for me to get my coat on to go down to meet him. But I just had to stay in and listen.[10]

The 1948 Olympic Games proved the biggest outside broadcasting operation yet mounted by the BBC, and probably by any broadcasting station in the world. Facilities were installed at thirty points around London, with thirty-two commentary positions at Wembley Stadium alone. This was essentially a radio event: television at this stage had a range of only fifty miles and only 48,000 licences had been taken out.

The BBC did not schedule an unbroken slot of time at the Games. The *Radio Times* announced that between 3 p.m. and 6.45 p.m. scheduled programmes 'may be broken into' for particular events. The timings of high-profile finals were given but in reality the practice of going over to Wembley at set times proved problematic because much of the track and field programme did not run to time. For the main sport, athletics, radio commentaries were handled by a team of three: Harold Abrahams, Rex Alston and Max Robertson. Robertson's speed of delivery came into its own during the shorter events where he showed that he could describe a race at great speed without losing his fluency.

In this post-war period, de Lotbinière tried to nudge the BBC towards the modern world of commercial contracts with sporting bodies. By 1949 he was referring to the payments made to them as 'facility fees', a halfway house between the 'donation' made to the University Boat Clubs in 1927 and today's formal payment for 'rights'. Standard payments had been agreed for many sports but there were particular exceptions, the figures (still in guineas) forming a useful indicator of the importance that the BBC attached to particular events:

Grand National 350, Derby 300, Professional Boxing 300 (maximum), Boat Race 125, Test Matches (cricket) 40 per day.[11]

'These figures represent', wrote de Lotbinière, 'something near what the events are worth to us. (They) may be classed as 'musts' for us.' He went on to mention two other national 'musts' for which the BBC still paid no more than a standard fee: the Cup final, and the England v Scotland football international. Some other events were placed in a second tier, as 'shoulds': these were Wimbledon, other horseracing classics, and FA Cup semi-finals. Among the third tier ('mights') were speedway, ice hockey, cycling, and motor-rallying. His advice, written at the time of a battle with boxing promoters over the forthcoming fight between Bruce Woodcock and Lee Savold, was that these figures were the upper limit and should not be exceeded, even if it meant losing the Woodcock fight.

De Lotbinière was convinced that the BBC had got sport rather cheaply before the war. He always thought the Wimbledon authorities were generous and he assumed it was 'the deliberate policy of an amateur sport towards a public body'. De Lotbinière knew those days had come to an end, and when, in the post-war years, both government and BBC management were trying to limit BBC expenditure on fees, he wrote a memorandum to colleagues putting a different view: 'It does not pay us to strike a bargain that is very much in our favour ... cheapness is not always the best policy'. In this, as in his thinking about the nature of commentary, de Lotbinière had a good grasp of the future.

BY THE EARLY 1950s a pattern had been established of in-depth radio coverage, but over a smaller range of sports than before the war. This pattern was to continue in broad terms for the next fifty years but the place of particular sports on radio, and the overall amount of live commentary, was to be affected by the growth of television and diversification in the media generally.

Statistics of the number of commentaries and the number of sports covered tell an important part of the early story. It is interesting to compare three years: 1927, the first year of commentary; 1938, the high point of the pre-war years; and 1953 which was something of a golden year in sport and might reasonably be seen as representative of the post-war peak in radio.

In 1927 only nine sports were covered. By 1938, at a time when de Lotbinière was still experimenting, that figure had risen to thirty-seven. In 1953, by which time the BBC had a better understanding of which sports were most conducive to live coverage, the number had fallen back to fifteen.

The statistics for the number of days on which commentary was broadcast tell a similar story. In 1927 there was commentary on just forty-five days. In 1938, when the BBC was broadcasting live sport throughout the year, the figure had risen to an unprecedented one hundred and ninety days. The 1953 figure was one hundred and forty days.

This analysis also brings to light some figures about the sports receiving the most coverage. In 1927 over two-thirds of the small number of live sports broadcasts were on football. In 1938 cricket (sixty commentaries) was the most frequent, followed by boxing (thirty-five) and rugby union (twenty-one). Football, with only twenty commentaries, was still suffering from the Football League ban. In 1953 cricket (ninety-one broadcasts) was still the most frequent but football (seventy-five) was now second, and horseracing (fifty-eight) third.

The figures for numbers of commentaries relate to broadcasts scheduled in the *Radio Times*, with no deductions made for matches or events finishing early, and include broadcasts by regional stations. 'Eye-witness' reports after completion of events (for example cricket and golf) are not included.[12]

By 1953 a distinction between Home Service and Light Programme coverage had also emerged. Boxing and football for instance were very much Light Programme sports; rowing and tennis tended to be on the Home Service. There was still no regular Saturday afternoon programme of sports coverage (and nothing at all on Sundays), but on particular Saturdays – when the number of commentaries was deemed to justify it – a programme called *"Going Places"* was mounted and the listener was taken round a series of sporting events.

In 1948 there had been one other important development. A Saturday afternoon sports programme began, rounding up the day's sporting news. *Sports Report* quickly established itself as a favourite. The first programme was introduced by Raymond Glendenning and one of the football match reports was by John Arlott. The stirring signature tune (uninterrupted by any voice-over) was followed by a full reading of the football results. The drama of that moment, now largely lost, derived from the fact that the scores were not preceded by any headlines. *Sports Report* was sporting journalism of a new order and very 'un-BBC'. The programme was managed by the news department of the BBC rather than Outside Broadcasts. Its producer, Angus Mackay, set about changing the tone of sporting coverage, drawing on the work of journalists as much as broadcasters. There were breathless match reports from all the top games, topical interviews, and provocative comment pieces by top writers, some of whom had clearly grown up outside the home counties. It is significant perhaps that by now some people were beginning to complain of the 'astonishing tonal variety' on radio and to call for 'standards' to be restored.[13]

Sports Report was firmly a Light Programme broadcast. The 'Light' was becoming the natural home for much popular sport, foreshadowing the role of its successor networks Radio 2 and 5 Live. But there remained the problem of finding network time for a particular feature of the English summer: the five-day-long Test matches. De Lotbinière gave up his responsibilities for outside broadcasts on radio in 1952, a few years before this issue was resolved.

LATER IN HIS CAREER de Lotbinière, by then Controller of Programme Services in BBC Television, reflected on what he had achieved and offered one note of regret:

> In my sound broadcasting days I think I did do something to develop, if only by much analysis and discussion, the commentator's technique. In the process I may have concentrated mostly on the Oxford and Cambridge

accents and backgrounds, so that a Howard Marshall might have been preferred to a John Arlott. Incidentally I think a Wolstenholme was a fair compromise since he sounds neither posh nor common.[14]

Certainly some of those that de Lotbinière appointed as commentators shared an educational background and a BBC 'Home Counties' voice. But there were other commentators who offered a degree of diversity. Their varied voices and microphone personalities enriched the experience of listeners who for so long had been treated by the BBC as if they were sitting in a particularly formal school assembly.

Some commentators became closely associated with one, or perhaps two, particular sports, and in so doing contributed to the popularity of those sports not only on radio but in society generally. Those judged to have a sufficient air of authority were occasionally used on state occasions such as the Coronation. A few, anticipating a modern trend, diversified into other forms of broadcasting including panel games and quiz shows, becoming compères of the nation's light entertainment. But, as the four studies which follow suggest, each presented different facets of commentary technique and spoke in a different voice.

1   *BBC Quarterly* 1952
2   Quotations from discussions with Mirabel Topham from BBC WAC
        (R30/17-21 OB Sound Aintree)
3   *Broadcasting in everyday life* (BBC 1939) p38-39
4   Ibid p40
5   This and other extracts from wartime minutes BBC WAC (R30/3/144/1)
6   ed Bryon Butler *Sports Report – 40 Years of the best* (Queen Anne Press
        1987) p21
7   Brian Johnston *Chatterboxes* (WH Allen 1983) p35
8   David Kynaston *Austerity Britain* 1945-51 (Bloomsbury 2007) p212
9   After that date more and more people switched to the new combined
        TV and radio licence so that by 1960 there were 4.5 million with
        sound-only licences and 10.4 million with the 'sound and vision'
        version. The radio-only licence was abolished in 1971.
10   Letter to the author from Tony Challis
11   BBC WAC OB Sports 1947-49 (R 30/3/144/4)
12   Tennis and cricket pose problems for these calculations as it was the
        custom to go over for commentary several times during one day,
        as and when play demanded it. In calculating these figures broadcasts
        from a Test match or from Wimbledon on one particular day are
        counted as one commentary. Broadcasts on two different cricket
        matches on two regions are counted as two commentaries. The same
        principle is followed in relation to other sports.
13   SK Ratcliffe *The influence of Broadcasting on Public Speech* (*BBC
        Quarterly* January 1949)
14   BBC WAC R34 /1009 (Current Affairs Committee)

SEVEN

DIFFERENT VOICES

CHARMING, VULNERABLE, GENEROUS, HAUGHTY – Harold Abrahams bestrode athletics in Britain. Loved by some, detested by others, he presided over the sport, literally or figuratively, for half a century. And no sport was entrusted to anyone for so long by the BBC as athletics was to Harold Abrahams. Of that early group of experts to whom the BBC turned when it was seeking commentators, Abrahams – 100 metres gold medallist at the 1924 Olympics – was the first with a major reputation in his sport. He appeared on radio in 1924, gave the first commentary on the sport in 1927, and continued to broadcast until 1974.

Abrahams was not a skilled commentator on races and fared better in the second half of his career as an expert summariser alongside Rex Alston. But he was the major influence on the nature and extent of BBC radio coverage of athletics. Prior to many of his commentaries, the *Radio Times* carried articles by him highlighting the main contestants of interest, and records that might be under threat. This did much to create interest in the broadcasts and raise the profile of the sport. In the early days he pressed the claims of particular fixtures on the BBC with the result that events involving Oxford and Cambridge received an attention disproportionate to their role in the sport. But Abrahams had a memorable broadcasting voice and his transparent enthusiasm for athletics did much to arouse interest in the sport among the listening public.

Harold Abrahams' father, Isaac Klonimus, was a Lithuanian Jew who emigrated to England in the 1870s and changed his name to Abrahams. Harold, born in 1899, was the youngest in a family of six, including four brothers, all of whom had successful careers in public life and two of whom were knighted. He went to Repton school and Cambridge, where he was an outstanding athlete, took part in debates and drama productions, but got a poor law degree. Soon after his victory at the Paris Olympics, a foot injury forced him to retire from active sport and he quickly became a central figure in athletics administration and journalism. He worked initially as a barrister and then as a civil servant, becoming secretary of the National Parks Commission after the war.

Abrahams brought a considerable presence and a distinct sense of authority to the microphone. These derived not so much from his career as an athlete but from the fact that he knew a great deal about what was going on in the sport, and understood the importance of keeping track of performances around the world. In addition, he held senior positions in the sport's hierarchy and was one of the most prolific sporting journalists of his day. Few commentators since have combined experience as a performer, an administrator, a statistician and a writer. But his sometimes authoritarian manner led to life-long enmities with a small number of coaches and athletes.

Abrahams undertook some voice training at Cambridge, probably to assist him in his intended career as a lawyer. His radio voice was very public school ('often' was pronounced 'orphan') and sometimes had a rather magisterial, superior tone. But it was also vibrant and reassuring. In his many radio talks, and his comments on races, he spoke with eloquence and style. He fitted in well when recruited to join the team of commentators on state occasions, such as the 1937 Coronation.

There was always an individuality and authenticity about Abrahams' sporting broadcasts, deriving in part from a boyish excitement about athletics which he never lost. However, recordings of his pre-war commentaries – before he had Rex Alston beside him to undertake many of the actual descriptions of races – suggest his limitations, especially his proneness to make crucial errors of detail in the excitement of races. He also displayed partisanship towards athletes, mostly from Oxbridge, whom he knew and admired. The best-known example is his commentary on Jack Lovelock's win in the 1500 metres at the Berlin Olympics in 1936.

Abrahams acknowledged that as a result of his personal friendship with Lovelock he got more pleasure from this New Zealander's achievement than that of any British athlete. 'I had known him very intimately indeed since his Oxford days', he recalled years later.[1]

As Lovelock came nearer to victory Abrahams' excitement takes over, and the listener is left confused by a series of mistakes:

> *And Lovelock's just running perfectly now. Come on Jack ...*
> *New leading, Cunningham second, Lovelock third... three-*
> *quarters of a mile, no that's not ... a quarter of a mile to go...*
> *New setting the pace hard, as Cunningham follows on his heels,*
> *Lovelock third ... New leads by about two ... no, Lovelock's got*

up to second position, Cunningham third... three hundred me-
tres to go, Lovelock leads, three hundred metres to go, Lovelock
... Cunningham's got up to second position ... Lovelock's about
four yards ahead, Cunningham's leading. no, no... Lovelock
leads by three yards, Baccalli third, come on. ... Edwards com-
ing up for fourth position... Lovelock leads by about four yards,
Cunningham fighting hard, Baccalli coming up to his shoulder,
Lovelock leads ... Lovelock... Lovelock... Cunningham second,
Baccalli third ... Come on Jack... one hundred yards to go...
come on Jack, by God he's done it, Jack, come on ... Lovelock
wins. ... five yards, six yards, he wins ... he's won.

Abrahams often had this difficulty of maintaining his technique as a broadcaster once he became excited about the outcome of a race. During the mile race at the Oxford and Cambridge v Princeton meeting in 1934 he made mistakes about the position of runners in the race and the time at the bell. In the final of the 800 metres at the 1936 Olympics he had considerable difficulty identifying competitors.

Abrahams was aware of his faults and keen to improve them. In 1936, almost ten years after his first commentaries, he was arranging with the BBC to practise his technique at Crufts Dog Show and a six-day cycle race. He wrote to de Lotbinière seeking any opportunity to practise. Aware of a tendency by Abrahams to dramatise the prospects of a race, at the expense of the event itself, de Lotbinière sent him some advice about managing 'excitement':

> It is essential to make the race more exciting than the build up. I do not mean by this that a race which is not exciting should be made to appear so, but that the listener's attention should be held even more thoroughly during the race than during the preliminaries.[2]

Abrahams always strikes a deferential note in his replies:

> I am obstinately convinced that with a good deal of thought I can in time remedy the obvious deficiencies. (And, a year or so later) ... I am so glad that on the whole there is some improvement in my broadcasts.

Abrahams did not escape the careful scrutiny of de Lotbinière. More than once over the years Lobby was concerned at his failure to inform listeners about the nationality of runners:

> I must admit to having been a bit shaken by the athletics

broadcast on Saturday. Fortunately we had the Test Match to play around with so I don't think any serious damage was done. I only heard one of your races in which I'm afraid you confined yourself to names and avoided national cross references so that I lost most of my interest in its progress. I am sorry to resurrect this 'King Charles's Head' but I am paid to do these distasteful jobs.

Among Abrahams' post-war commentaries those which made most impact were of races involving Sydney Wooderson, including the Blackheath Harrier's great run at the European Championships at Oslo in 1946. In races like this Abrahams was skilful in bringing his statistical knowledge to bear. Before a mile race, for instance, he would read out existing records and suggest the interim times to listen out for. As his co-commentator Rex Alston brought the runners round, Abrahams would supply the lap times and indicate where the leaders stood in relation to any particular schedule. For the listener it could be an exciting combination.

There has been much discussion – and the issue was a central one to the film *Chariots of Fire* – as to how being Jewish, and the experience of anti-semitism, impacted on Harold Abrahams' life. It certainly created for him one difficult decision as a commentator. In a radio interview in 1968 he was asked about his reactions in 1936 when the BBC asked him to cover the Olympics in Berlin:

> I wasn't happy – being Jewish – about going at all, but it was an enormous temptation being asked by the BBC – the first time they'd ever broadcast the Olympics. I went – I'm not sure it was right … it's rather … you know … I was advised by Lord Vansittart that it was a good thing to do … to let the Germans see that over here Jewish people were treated just like anyone else… but I'm not terribly happy about having been there.[3]

Unlike John Snagge and Howard Marshall – both of whom conveyed emotion in a controlled and subtle manner – Harold Abrahams sometimes allowed his feelings a free rein at the microphone. This was both his charm and his undoing. But his love of the sport, his pleasure in the achievement of athletes, and his ability to put performances into context, helped transport the listener from the living room to the side of the track. He did more than anyone to make athletics a radio sport in Britain. Abrahams died in 1978, four years after his last broadcast. He was 78.

RAYMOND GLENDENNING WAS DESCRIBED by one of his successors as 'The father of sports commentary.'[4] Brian Moore – football correspondent for BBC radio before moving to ITV – said once that the greatest day of his commentary life was the day (the only day) when he shared a commentary box with him.[5] Raymond Glendenning had a descriptive technique which worked well for racing, football and boxing and he adopted an air of authority which made him one of the best-known figures in the world of commentary for some twenty years. Unlike some of his contemporaries, Glendenning had no particular sporting achievements to his name. But he was assiduous in his preparation and his speed and clarity meant he was particularly well equipped for fast-moving sports.

Glendenning was a large, convivial man, and his smart, swept back black hair, horn-rimmed glasses and handlebar moustache made him a familiar public figure. He was born in Newport in 1907, went to a local state school and graduated at London University before qualifying as an accountant. A highly satisfactory if conventional career for the son of a company director seemed to lie ahead of him. But while still a student he had begun to undertake some part-time acting work for the BBC repertory company in Wales and the lure of creative work in a new medium attracted him. In 1932 he left his accountant's job and joined the BBC staff in Cardiff as an announcer.

His duties gave him considerable experience in planning, producing and compèring programmes, including *Children's Hour*. He learned quickly how to make a radio programme work – how to grab, and hold, the attention of listeners. Three years later he moved to Belfast as an outside-broadcasts assistant. It was here, in 1936, that he first tried commentary, acting as 'Number Two' at a point-to-point race in the far north of Ulster, and stepping into the breach when the main commentator dried up. In 1939 the director of the BBC regional station in Northern Ireland wrote to de Lotbinière pressing Glendenning's claims for work on the national network and enclosing a copy of a recording of his commentary on the Irish Grand National. Lobby acknowledged the package but asked: 'Will he do so well on an English course with thirty horses?'[6]

The war provided Glendenning with his opportunity. Other commentators were drafted to different duties of various kinds and he was moved to London to help out. He was one of the few regular voices heard doing sports commentary and he also undertook a number of outside broadcasts relating to the war.

This period enabled Glendenning to establish his versatility. In 1940 the BBC advertised for experts to attend a special audition for potential commentators on greyhound racing and between forty and fifty people from all walks of life turned up. In the event the BBC decided none could master the technique of commentary in time and Glendenning was asked to take it on. He spent the next ten days immersing himself in the sport, with visits to kennels and tracks, and doing trial commentaries. On the day of the broadcast – the Spring Cup from Wembley – he had thirty seconds to describe a race between six dogs. In that time he fitted in the order of the six dogs out of the traps, the first three at all the bends, the whole lot down the back straight, and the order of the six dogs as they crossed the finishing line. 'Hi, governor, slow down a bit and give them dogs a chance to catch up' was the apocryphal remark of one bystander.

Table tennis provided another test. In 1941 Glendenning was sent to a colliery in County Durham where Richard Bergmann and Victor Barna were playing an exhibition game. These were perhaps the two best players in the world, and both had left their homelands (Austria and Hungary respectively) because of the rise of Nazism. This was a classic wartime broadcast intended to highlight the efforts being made to bring top sports stars to those involved in the war effort. Glendenning did not attempt to cover every single shot but captures the main ebb and flow of play, inserts the score, and the game position, regularly and helps the reader to picture the scene. It is one of the few commentaries on table tennis that survive:

> *Bergmann serves again, a very short one indeed. Barna hooks to the backhand, Bergmann comes racing up, you probably heard his feet on the hollow boards of the stage there as he bounded forward, chopped it back onto the table, only for Barna to come in with a vicious forehand drive that took the point.*
> *Barna takes the service and he's now four points behind, 13-17 in this second game having won the first. He's driving backhand again, beautiful backhand drive that is, and Bergmann retrieving it from five yards away and actually nearly fell off the stage trying to retrieve that one but he couldn't quite put it there.*

By 1942 Glendenning was assistant director of Outside Broadcasts. Shortly after the war he left the BBC staff to go freelance, but for another twenty years he was the BBC's most versatile and prolific commentator.

Glendenning's style favoured sports with movement, action and changes of tempo. He was skilful at changing gears, and this enabled him to adjust quickly to alterations in the pace of a game or race. He had an assured radio presence. His colleague, Wynford Vaughan-Thomas, spoke of 'his absolute confidence in himself before the microphone.' It is a measure of how the range of voices on radio has changed that Glendenning, who sounds relatively 'posh' to modern ears, once argued in *Radio Times* that 'a plain, unaffected voice usually serves best.' He meant, perhaps, that he had no aspiration for poetry. He had a businesslike and breezy style – just right for the post-war world.

When listeners joined Glendenning they were quickly and warmly seated at the scene. 'He had the precious gift,' Bryon Butler, BBC football correspondent for twenty-three years from 1968, wrote, 'of being able to make listeners feel they were sitting next to him'.[7] The delivery was disciplined, the details of the occasion immaculately paraded. Glendenning once explained how preparation informed good commentary:

> The success of a commentary depends far more on the work that is put in beforehand than on the actual performance at the microphone. By this I don't mean that any commentary should be written out. Obviously that is impossible at a sporting event, but even on, say, a ceremonial occasion it would lack the vital touch, however expertly delivered. No, the commentator, having studied the possibilities of the event in question – say a horse race – will be far better fitted to deal with it if the appropriate associative material springs to mind naturally and easily on account of his previous research.[8]

De Lotbinière – whose influence Glendenning always acknowledged – would have been proud of this.

Glendenning established his position as a football commentator during the war, a position he later came to share with Alan Clarke. The great post-war cup finals, often described by Glendenning and Clarke, confirmed the place of football commentary in radio sport. In 1948 Bolton led Manchester United 2-1 with twenty minutes remaining but United scored three times to bring Matt Busby his first trophy as manager. Over one-third of the adult population listened to the commentary. For this broadcast Glendenning (and Clarke) received a special letter of commendation from de Lotbinière: 'You and Alan achieved an outstanding appreciation index – seventy-four per cent – for a sporting broadcast'.[9]

The success helped Glendenning in negotiations over his next BBC contract. He signed a three-year deal guaranteeing him a minimum of six hundred guineas a year in fees. In return he undertook to be available to cover football, racing, boxing, motor cycling, tennis, billiards, snooker 'and other international sporting events'. Top events were earmarked with specific fees: twenty guineas for instance for the Cup final, the England v Scotland football international, the Grand National, five flat racing classics and championship boxing. The guarantee would in 2008 be worth some £50,000 a year. Equally important, Glendenning was left free to take on other work.

He covered a number of the great post-war fights involving British boxers – Freddie Mills, Bruce Woodcock, Don Cockell, Randolph Turpin and others. Beside him as 'inter-round summariser' was Barrington Dalby. Dalby had a brief boxing career in the flyweight division and then acquired a referee's licence. His partnership, first with Stewart MacPherson and then with Glendenning – and the commentator's end of round catchphrase 'Come in, Barry' – was the centrepiece of BBC boxing coverage.

Glendenning gave many hundreds of horseracing commentaries during a thirty-year period. He did not have the intimate knowledge of the racing industry many of the modern commentators have. And he had occasional failures, about which he was not afraid to reminisce, not least the running of the Cambridgeshire in 1951 in which he succeeded in completing the commentary without mentioning the winner. The horse, inevitably, was called *Fleeting Moment*. But he was a skilled racing commentator who could raise the tempo and excitement as the finish of a race approached, without over-doing the volume. *The Times* commented: 'The listener felt that however fast the horses went, Glendenning would get there first.'[10]

In racing, Glendenning was helped by two factors. First, by the assistance of an expert assistant at his side who would pass him crucial information – the 'race reader.' Tom E Webster and Claude Harrison were among those who fulfilled this role. Secondly, he owed much to his careful homework. He had a particular method of memorising the colours worn by jockeys in any race:

A week before any race I paint the colours to be worn by the jockeys on a little set of playing cards and deal them out to myself at odd moments until I am completely familiar with them. Later, on the racecourse, when any particular colour appears in sight my memory attaches a name to it. Actually the homework doesn't end there, because all those cards have to be filed under the owners' names after the race and kept for future reference.[11]

When he renewed his contract with the BBC in 1954 the guaranteed earnings he was offered had risen to £3,500. A fee of sixty guineas was now ear marked for the Derby and for world title fights, fifty guineas for the cup final and European title fights and thirty-five guineas for the Grand National. That annual guarantee would be worth close to £200,000 today and indicated that the BBC rated him among the most prized in their team.

Glendenning was helped, of course, by working largely in an era when there was little live television coverage. Some contemporary commentators take the view that he was able to take more liberties than they can today. But Glendenning knew what business he was in, and that he needed to retain his listeners' attention. 'Listen, old boy,' he once told Harry Carpenter, 'it's my job to stop them turning the knob to off.'[12]

This ability to button-hole the listener would have helped Glendenning to hold his own in the modern world. He briefly chaired the radio panel game *The Name's the Same* but he retired from the BBC in 1963 and went into business. He died of a heart attack in 1974.

IN 1937 A BRASH YOUNG CANADIAN named Stewart MacPherson unexpectedly prized open the door of the BBC commentary box. He brought with him a different kind of voice and a different style of commentary, well-matched to his favoured sports. 'I hired this colonial savage … and suddenly the entire bloody country was hanging on his every word,' said Michael Standing.[13] MacPherson became the first-choice commentator for ice hockey and boxing, and a popular entertainer who helped the BBC launch a number of famous radio programmes.

MacPherson was born in Winnipeg in 1908. His father, a factory manager, died when he was young and he left school early in an effort to supplement the family income. From an early age he had the ambition to work in journalism or radio and, in 1936, when Canadian ice hockey players began to take their skills to England he conceived of the idea that, since he knew a bit about the game, this might provide an opening for him. He caught the train across Canada, grabbed a place on a cheap boat to Tilbury and took lodgings in St Pancras with less than £3 in his pocket. Before long he was writing programmes for ice hockey matches at Wembley and refereeing the odd game.

When he first auditioned for the BBC in 1936, he was marked down for the very qualities that were to make him famous:

> Fluent; very Canadian; very dramatic; perfect knowledge of the game, but having no humour. Like Bob Bowman his rather over-powering American voice, all on one note, bores into one's head, with the persistence of a pneumatic drill. Efficient, but very newspaperish.[14]

MacPherson went back a little later, this time successfully. He made a big impression, recalling a match and narrating all the details. One interviewee asked how that particular game had finished: MacPherson revealed that he had invented it all himself.

Between 1937 and 1939, and then again for four years after the war, MacPherson covered not only ice hockey and boxing, but also speedway, cycling, swimming and other sports. His microphone presence came from a combination of two things. First, the transatlantic drawl marked him out sharply from Snagge, Marshall, Allison and others. Second, he adopted a more colourful vocabulary and a much racier imagery. 'I was always complimented,' he once wrote, 'on saying a lot of things the English commentators didn't have the nerve to say.'[15] Rex Alston later said that MacPherson 'had a sense of radio the way some dramatists and actors have a sense of theatre.'[16]

Only MacPherson – at that stage – would dare break off from the main commentary to describe a fight in the crowd: *'The man in the raincoat throws a left hook. They grapple ... hard right from the man in the blue suit.'*[17]

MacPherson's place as an outside broadcaster was confirmed by his war reports. Although he had returned to Canada on the outbreak of war, in 1941 the BBC offered him the opportunity to travel with British forces and report direct from battle. His live dispatches incorporated into John Snagge's nightly war reports after the news – at one point for thirty-nine nights in a row – were among the most vivid of the European campaign.

One night in July 1944 he stood in a darkened wood on the banks of the Marne watching the RAF bombardment of Caen:

Now we can hear that heavy, monotonous roar of the bombers ... just listen to them ... God knows, it's little wonder the Hun hasn't been able to put up anything ... just listen to this, the whole earth trembled and shook, my little portable recorder fairly leapt up in the air... it's perfect night-bombing weather, the bombs almost seem to make the stars move, you can almost reach up and touch them.

MacPherson also continued with some boxing commentaries during the war. He was at Glasgow in June 1943 when Jackie Patterson knocked out Peter Kane in the first round to win the World Flyweight Championship:

Patterson has won the world title in two punches. Jackie Patterson brought up a vicious right hand punch, a bolt from the blue. That punch came out of his hip pocket, ...that punch really hurt, it almost hurt Dalby and me here ... it cracked up like a sabre and down went Kane. He got up after a count of six, and Patterson rushed in, viciously pounded him with a left to the jaw, following him up with another right hand punch which had absolute dynamite in it.

MacPherson knew that the popularity of his reports and commentaries had raised his selling power. In 1945 he was offered his pre-war job back by the BBC at his old salary of £675 a year and in characteristically blunt language rejected it. De Lotbinière did not want to lose him and came up with an arrangement: the Canadian would be paid fifty guineas (about £500 in today's terms) for every national sporting event he did, and could keep a desk in the BBC. MacPherson negotiated one further concession: he need not go to every one of Lobby's Monday meetings. Later in life MacPherson claimed that in his first year under this new arrangement he earned £6,700 – the equivalent of over half a million pounds. Wynford Vaughan-Thomas and others soon followed him to freelance status.

One listener remembered the impact of MacPherson's boxing commentaries after the war:

The Americans had the world champions and Britain had the hopeful challengers and plucky losers – Don Cockell, Bruce Woodcock, and others. So it seemed appropriate that boxing, a vulgar but undeniably exciting sport, should be brought into British homes by a commentator with a North American accent. It was the sort of accent that we'd come to associate with Hollywood films and popular music and all the other innovations that, for good or ill, were helping to relieve the dullness of post-war life. A North American accent could make anything more exciting than it would otherwise be. So it was Stewart MacPherson's tough metallic words that we hung on while the blows were being exchanged...[18]

MacPherson exemplified one of de Lotbinière's prime requirements: he gave the listener a ringside seat. He had a gift for capturing the atmosphere of a stadium, and the sweaty brutality of the fight, almost wincing as the blows landed. When Freddie Mills met the Canadian Lloyd Marshall in the summer of 1947 the fight erupted into a fierce exchange of blows:

> *The crowd are all up on their feet, forgetting the humidity and the sweltering heat. They're mauling each other in the centre of the ring. ... those vicious short right hooks ... oh ... if he'd hit with that one the building would have come down ... they don't go very far the coloured boxer's blows but – Oh – Oh – they hurt almost down here at the ringside, they sink right in every time.*

Finally Mills goes down and is counted out.

> *It was a terrific left-hand punch, and it was on the target all the way.*

MacPherson acknowledged later that – to avoid repetition – he made a list of adjectives he might need and crossed each one off as he used it. This was a great disappointment to some of his admirers who thought that everything he said was entirely spontaneous. But recordings of MacPherson's boxing commentaries still have impact today, with their instinctive expressions of hurt that take the listener almost to where the punch lands.

In the immediate post-war period MacPherson became even better known as a quiz master on *Ignorance is Bliss* (for which future golf commentator John Fenton did the sound effects) and *Twenty Questions*, and he was also the first compère of *Down Your Way*. In 1948, *Daily Mail* readers voted him the best-known voice in Britain, ahead of Churchill. That year MacPherson was assigned to cover a number of sports – including swimming – at the Olympic Games in London, but he did not let this interfere with his social life. Harold Walker recalled that MacPherson often relied on him to do the preparation for the next day's events. 'He always had a date somewhere in the evening – Stew was happy to look at my commentary notes the next morning.'[19]

To general surprise Stewart MacPherson left the BBC at the peak of his fame in 1949 to return to North America. Ed Morrow knew that MacPherson's family wished to return and he enticed him back with a job at the Columbia Broadcasting Service. MacPherson spent the rest of his career broadcasting in the USA and Canada. He came back to Europe in 1985 to participate in a broadcast commemorating the fortieth anniversary of the Normandy landings. He died in Winnipeg in 1995 at the age of 86.

––––––––––––––

IN THEIR SEARCH – between 1927 and 1938 – for sporting experts who could become radio commentators the BBC had one other success. The sport was motor cycling, and the expert Graham Walker.

Motor cycling, and motor racing, became an important part of the commentary schedules in the early 1930s. There was something essentially modern about both sports which was appropriate to the new medium of radio. Motor cycling did not have the image problems it later gained, and acquiring the latest model gave an aura of some status to the owner. The organising bodies concerned created fewer difficulties over live coverage, so these sports helped fill the gaps when, for different reasons, football and cricket commentaries were restricted. Events such as the Tourist Trophy (TT) races on the Isle of Man, and the Ulster Grand Prix, became part of the commentary calendar.

Graham Walker was born in 1896. His father was a company secretary with the Union Castle shipping line and he was the youngest of six children. His early love of motor cycles began as a schoolboy in London when he watched the riders assembling at the start of the London to Edinburgh trial. That summer, at the age of fourteen, he bought his first second-hand bike. 'For a while,' he recalled years later, 'I was primarily interested in transporting flappers on the bracket.'[20]

But he soon began competitive racing, and enrolled as a dispatch rider during the First World War.

In the 1920s and 1930s, the great British motorcycle manufacturers, part of the lifeblood of what was then an engineering nation, fought for dominance with each other. Victory in major competitions, and all the publicity that brought, was a key means of establishing a position in the market. Graham Walker worked for a succession of these firms – Norton, Sunbeam and Rudge-Whitworth – as a works rider and then competitions director. He first rode the Senior Tourist Trophy race on the Isle of Man in 1920 for Norton. 'Oh boy,' he recalled, 'was I proud. Oh boy, was I frightened!'

Walker had a distinguished career in the sport, winning many trophies in Britain and on the continent including the lightweight TT race in 1931. His family, including son Murray, would often accompany him to Northern Ireland or the Isle of Man for the big events. It was the TT races especially, Graham Walker always argued, which helped the British motorcycle industry to survive during this period by providing conditions in which bikes could be tested and monitored.

Graham Walker began his broadcasting career in 1933, when Gerald Cock was still in charge of outside broadcasts. The BBC knew he was one of the top riders of his day, that he was immersed in the sport and well-informed about the form of the riders and the performance of the machines they rode. They quickly found that he was also someone with a natural and distinctive microphone presence. Despite initial protests from some in the motorcycle industry who feared that Walker might favour his own company's bikes, Cock gave the necessary reassurances and added:

> Mr Walker was chosen as his voice and manner were considered suitable for the microphone and because it was desired that someone who had actually taken part in the event should describe it.[21]

The protests were isolated because Graham Walker was greatly respected in the industry, a natural communicator, with a friendly and conversational voice. The affection with which he was regarded by many of his peers was captured in the *Sunbeam Club News* of September 1934:

> Father Graham's broadcast of the Ulster was excellent; we switched the wireless set on whilst digging up the garden and found it good – the broadcast not the digging. He is due to do one of the Manx next month, so get the old set de-coked and the valves ground in.

What made Graham Walker's commentaries work so well was that they were rooted in the sport itself – the surging power of the bikes, the anxious moments of anticipation, the twists and turns, and the powerful acceleration on the long straight stretches of the Isle of Man.

The world's best motorcyclists raced for nearly seventy years on this small island, thirty miles by ten, on public roads closed to traffic and providing a perfect test of motorcycling skill. During the TT races the BBC would devote two hours or more each day to the commentaries.

The format of the TT broadcasts was imposed by the format of the races. At any given point on the course there were sometimes long pauses so it was important to have a team of commentators, spaced around the course, and to plan carefully how they worked together. Murray Walker described in his autobiography some of the difficulties for the commentary team:

> The TT broadcasts were enormously demanding because the competitors started one at a time at intervals and were not seeded. The races were time trials, so you could have the leading riders separated by seconds on corrected time but minutes apart on the road... Before each race the five-man commentary team would meet to forecast the lap times of the next day's top riders and would then, with their own timekeepers, have to work out each rider's estimated arrival time at their commentary point on each of the seven laps.[22]

Small changes in the performance of riders inevitably affected the plan. 'You had to know when to expect people. If a rider was a few seconds early or late,' recalled Murray, 'the timekeeper at each point had to update the schedule.'

The care with which this planning was carried out and the skill with which the calculations were used produced extraordinary broadcasts. The commentators seemed able to describe things which were not within vision. Robert Hudson, who worked for the BBC in the north of England, remembered how father and son worked together:

> Graham would say with absolute conviction: 'Jones is approaching a long right-hand bend, down the hill, he changes into third gear and now he should be within your sight, Murray, at Ramsey'. He was. It was uncanny.[23]

Graham Walker loved the sound of a high-performance bike, and he loved to let the listener hear it. Murray Walker explained:

> Motorcycling is a noisy experience and this is part of the attraction and the enjoyment. Different engines make different noises and it was manna from heaven for

motorcycle enthusiasts to listen to them. My father and I
helped to made gramophone records of some of the great
races so that people could re-live them at home.[24]

In Graham Walker's commentary on the 1936 Ulster Grand Prix
the affection for the riders and their bikes, the technical knowledge,
and the narrative skill and imagery provide compelling listening:

> *I opened the trap at the back of my box as I know how enthu-*
> *siasts like to hear the roar of a good healthy engine as they*
> *change up from second to third ... you get a very fine idea of*
> *how the modern engine can rev.*
> *Here comes Ginger Wood. Oh, a beautiful bit of work going*
> *into the corner using every inch of the road ... Ginger's got his*
> *jaw sticking out and his face absolutely set rigid. There'll be the*
> *scrap of the day down the long straight ... the man that gets*
> *round Claddy first will be the man who will win.*
> *Listen, listen – do you hear the roar of his engine? Now here*
> *comes, here comes, the hero of the day, Freddie Frith ... listen,*
> *listen did you hear the roar of his bike? Freddie Frith has gone*
> *round for all the world like a train on rails ... every time the*
> *same neat approach ... right over to the right-hand side, then*
> *a momentary twitch of the machine as he banks it over to the*
> *left, then between the left-hand and right-hand exit he uses*
> *the tail of his body ... stands up in the footrests to swing the*
> *machine over with a little kind of flick, then settles down rather*
> *like a tortoise retiring, moves backward on to the pad, tucks*
> *his head well down and disappears out of site ... He appears*
> *absolutely effortless but the fact that he's lapping at ninety-two*
> *mph suggests that he knows exactly what he's doing.*

Walker's enthusiasm for competitive sport, and his natural honesty with listeners, were demonstrated a year or two later when he
was asked by the BBC to cover cycling championships in London.
He knew that many of his listeners, like himself, knew little about
the sport. He described the track, explained the techniques, how the
marks were given, and the build of the cyclists – '*Cousins is a short
stocky little man with tremendous thighs.*' And, as so often, there was
that gentle chuckle in his voice:

> *The modus operandi as far as I can tell, and I'm no expert*
> *on the sprint game, seems to be to play on each other's nerves*
> *as much as possible during the first lap. The riders even get*

to the point where they're balancing stock still watching each other. The art is for the man with the biggest thrust in his legs who can put the last ounce to try and get as low as possible and then jump his opponent. Once he's got his revs up, sort of like motor racing there (he laughs), *he can get into his stride and the man at the back naturally endeavours to slipstream or take the wheel, as they refer to it here, reducing the breeze as much as possible in the hope that he can pull out before the finishing line.*

Almost single-handedly – though helped from 1949 onwards by his son Murray – Graham Walker made motorcycling a radio sport and in the process attracted many new listeners. Of all the commentators who began in the 1930s on BBC radio, Walker was the most natural talker, using the friendly registers of normal speech at the microphone. His commentaries exemplified much that de Lotbinière advocated, especially in the skilful use of effects, and the ability to hold the listener's attention by effective story-telling. He supplemented this by many radio talks, edited *Motor Cycling* for many years and was instrumental in ensuring that a museum of motor cycling was established. 'The name Graham was sufficient to identify him whenever motor-cyclists gathered', it was once said.[25] He died in 1962 at the early age of sixty-six.

1	BBC Radio September 1968 (Harold Abrahams Archive, University of Birmingham)
2	BBC WAC (OB Commentators: H Abrahams 1936-47)
3	J Dunn Show July 12th 1974 (Harold Abrahams Archive, University of Birmingham). Lord Vansittart was a senior civil servant in the diplomatic service, known for his anti-appeasement views.
4	*Back to Square One* BBC Radio 4 January 27th 2007
5	ed Bryon Butler *Sports Report – 40 Years of the best* (Queen Anne Press 1987)
6	BBC WAC Rcont.1 R Glendenning OB Commentator 1937-54
7	ed Audrey Adams *Fifty Years of Sports Report* (Collins Willow 1997) p22
8	These two quotations from Glendenning are from *Radio Times* December 4th 1953
9	See note 6
10	*The Times* February 2th 1974
11	*Raymond Glendenning's Book of Sport for Boys* (London 1953) p52
12	*Back to Square One* – see note 4

13   *Winnipeg Free Press* April 18th 1995
14   BBC WAC R30/428/1 Commentators 1936-39
15   Audio extract on *www.broadcasting-history.ca*
16   Rex Alston *Taking the Air* (Stanley Paul 1951)
17   I am grateful to Wilfred Morgan for this recollection.
18   Recollections by Paul Clark
19   Interview with the author
20   Graham Walker's first article as editor of *Motor Cycling*, March 2nd 1938
21   BBC WAC Rcont. 1, G.Walker OB Commentator 1a 1933-39
22   Murray Walker *Unless I'm very much mistaken* (Collins Willow 2002) p118
23   Robert Hudson *Inside Outside Broadcasts* (R W Publications 1993) p137
24   Interview with the author
25   Obituary note, *The Times* September 14th 1962

PART TWO

THE MAKING OF THE COMMENTATOR

EIGHT

ROUTES INTO COMMENTARY

THE FIRST RADIO VOICE to become a national favourite was that of a sports commentator. Graham McNamee had heard about a thing called radio, but never listened to it, when he dropped into one of the new broadcasting stations in New York by chance during his lunch hour. It was 1923. Within weeks he was commentating on a world championship boxing event. Two years later his coverage of the baseball World Series brought him a postbag of 50,000 letters.

McNamee was born in 1888 and grew up in the north-western USA. His mother was a fine singer and encouraged him to learn the piano but when he was eighteen he branched out. 'I turned from the piano to singing and fairly ate that up', he recalled later.[1] In 1921 he took the plunge, left his day job, moved to New York and embarked on a career as a professional singer.

In early 1923 McNamee was called for jury duty. It was during a break in proceedings that he wandered down Lower Broadway and passed the premises of WEAF, just established as a radio station. Other singers had told McNamee that they had begun to get work on radio and an instinct prompted him to enter the building. A member of staff showed him round, they chatted, McNamee asked a few questions and before he left he had been offered an audition. Within days he joined the station as an evening announcer on thirty dollars a week.

American stations had by now begun to see the potential that big sporting events, including boxing, offered in winning audiences and sponsors. A world middleweight bout between Harry Greb and Johnny Wilson had been scheduled for the Polo Grounds in New York for March 1923 and WEAF won the rights to cover it. There were no commentators at the stations at this stage, only announcers. Of these McNamee seemed to be the most fluent, and he also had a voice that was easy to listen to. By chance he had done a little boxing in his youth. He was given the job.

McNamee had never attempted commentary before but he narrated the whole fifteen-round fight, and the inter-round comments, on his own:

It was my first important assignment and I was horribly nervous. In fact, none of the fighters could have been more shaky than I. Though the bouts were not to take place until evening, I went to the Polo Grounds at four o'clock and just fussed around watching the workmen fix the ropes and canvas for the ring, and men from our plant running the wires for our microphones. I don't think I actually saw what they were doing; I was really thinking of the sixty thousand fans that would line those stands, while I was up there by the ring talking to a million more. And every once in a while I would look up at the sky, praying for rain.

McNamee found, as so many do, that once the action started he began to relax. He picked out the main blows, described the men feinting and ducking and the expressions on their faces, especially when they were hit. But, most important, in between rounds he told his listeners about the scene around him. It was partly this ability to capture 'colour' that made McNamee famous. His account of that first commentary, written only a couple of years later, provides a clue to how vivid the picture was that he painted:

Before the fight I had written, rather self-consciously, a good many sheets on the crowd, for I knew what it would be like. Now I tore them all up and got down to brass tacks – the real thing. And there was a lot of color in that crowd around me – the sea of spectators, some in coats, others in short sleeves, the black varied with white, strangely like the many tiers of keys of a gigantic organ. All these things I tried to describe; the ring, too, with its fierce lights under their inverted cones beating down on the contestants, who lay back on the stools, resting their arms on the ropes, their chests heaving, their pink and white bodies glistening with sweat or flecked with blood as the handlers sponged them off...

Shortly after that broadcast McNamee was asked to help Grantland Rice with the baseball World Series, acting as the 'colour' commentator alongside the man who called the play. Following that broadcast he received 1,700 letters. McNamee continued with his career as a singer, sometimes commentating on a football game in the afternoon and giving a recital in the evening. His national popularity as a sports broadcaster was confirmed in 1925 when he appeared on the cover of *Time* magazine.

ALL THIS WAS IN RADIO'S earliest days. But for many years afterwards there was no career route into radio work and certainly not into commentary. So how did commentators become commentators?

For some the origins can be traced back to a childhood dream fuelled by a fascination with radio and a love of sport. While friends nurtured the idea of being airline pilots or pop stars they dreamed of being at the microphone, describing the excitement of a game to those who were not there. For others the opportunity arose through a chance encounter, a contact with a friend, a sudden gap in the schedules – 'being in the right place at the right time.' And then there were those who were in another profession that required good communication skills – teaching perhaps or journalism – and for whom commentary proved a natural step. Others came into commentary from another branch of broadcasting, as in his own way McNamee himself did.

As a ten-year-old, Tony Adamson, later to cover golf and tennis for the BBC, would sit at his bedroom window broadcasting to the world outside. He designed an imitation microphone and, helped by the *Radio Times*, which he thought at the time was 'the most important publication in the world', he would speak to his imaginary listeners. He not only gave sporting commentaries but branched out into other programmes, like the *Morning Service*, for which his mother provided an imitation cassock. Then, his production stint over, he would hand back to the studio.

So it was too for Jimmy Magee, who has covered sport on RTÉ for almost fifty years:

> I would have been ten or eleven years old, and I commentated to myself walking round the garden or the fields, imagined matches and did them for real. It was narrowcasting rather than broadcasting, but I talked away to myself with structure. Every Saturday night I did a programme. I presented it, I did the music myself, at that age. Then I did all the reports on matches. And my father, lord of mercy, said 'Gee, this man's talking to himself ... we'll soon have to get someone to collect him and take him away, our son.'[2]

Bill McLaren, who covered rugby on radio for BBC for ten years before moving to television, was another who played at being the commentator as child. He has told how he would mark out a running track on the road where he lived with brick and chalk markings and his friends would run races, while he sat on the garden wall doing commentaries.[3]

During cricket matches in the garden at home, Christopher Martin-Jenkins gave constant running commentaries and they became something of a family joke. 'When uncles or aunts asked what I was going to be in life the answer was unequivocal – a cricket commentator.' Much later, following advice from Brian Johnston, Martin-Jenkins took himself off to occasional matches with a tape recorder and delivered 'private, whispered commentaries' which he later played back to himself.[4]

Keith Quinn, one of New Zealand's best-known commentators for forty years, recalled that as a young boy his father had an operation to remove his voice box. 'I collected the rugby scores and took them down to his hospital bed. It was like my first broadcast – he was the radio audience listening'.[5] In the early 1950s Keith and his brothers held Olympic Games in the back garden of their house in Wellington, New Zealand. There were five boys and Keith called all the races:

> Then when Winston McCarthy broadcast the fourth rugby test against England in 1956 it was my tenth birthday. We all listened and the whole of New Zealand celebrated the win. My mother says I went out in the backyard and played the game again by myself – commentating at the same time.[6]

Other commentators can date their involvement back to the moment when they posted a letter, or made a phone call, and said: 'I think I can do this'.

In 1938 Michael O'Hehir was seventeen, still at school in Dublin and studying for his leaving certificate.[7] He heard that Radio Éireann was in difficulty, that it could not find the commentators it wanted, so much so that some top games were not broadcast. O'Hehir had a keen interest in Gaelic football and in the Gaelic Athletic Association (the GAA) which oversaw Gaelic Games in Ireland. He sent a letter to the director of broadcasting and asked for a test. That was the easy bit. But he got no reply – so he rang the station, succeeded in being put through to the director and told him: 'I can do it – let me have a go'. A few days later he was called to an audition.

The trial commentary was to be on a (Gaelic) football match at

Croke Park between Louth and Wexford. O'Hehir dressed up smartly in his school uniform and arrived at the stadium to find four other triallists present. Each of the five did a short piece of commentary during the first half of the game. At half-time a message was passed through to the group that the last to audition – this was O'Hehir – was to do the whole of the second half. The schoolboy heard no more for two weeks, but then he was called in for a meeting. The director thought he ought to give the score more often, but in general the audition had gone well. Would he do the Leinster football final – live? Within two years Michael O'Hehir was the best-known commentator in Ireland, and he was soon to become a great favourite with racing fans in Britain.

Several current BBC radio sports reporters and commentators started knocking on the doors of their local radio station while still at school. Alison Mitchell began with a two-week work-experience placement at Radio Northampton when she was fifteen.

> A few weeks after that I got a call offering me a one night a week job, at £3 an hour, as one of the broadcasting assistants, from five o'clock to 10.30 p.m. So I went straight from school into Northampton, pulling the records from the shelves for the next day's show, answering the phone in the production studio and so on.[8]

Mitchell continued her involvement with Radio Northampton while she was an undergraduate and then went on to take a post-graduate course in broadcast journalism, and get a full-time job in local radio, before moving to Radio 5 Live. She commentated for BBC on the 20:20 World Cricket Cup in 2007.

OTHER COMMENTATORS HAD NO youthful ambitions of this kind, but they did not come into the world of commentary entirely by accident. At one particular moment a friend or relative, someone perhaps who recognised their potential as communicators, dangled before them the idea that it might be something they could do well.

Kote Makharadze was born in what is now the nation of Georgia in 1926 at a time when that country was part of the Soviet Union. As a boy he trained to be a ballet dancer for seven years at the Tbilisi Choreographic Studio but his main love was acting. His success on the stage was such that he became the first actor to be named an Honorary Citizen of Tbilisi.

Makharadze was also a successful basketball player as a young man and captain of the Georgian youth team. By chance, the main football commentator in Georgia in the 1950s, Erosi Manjgaladze, was also an actor, and a friend and admirer of Makharadze. In 1958 a basketball match between Tbilisi and a visiting American team was arranged. This was a major event in any part of the Soviet Union at the time and excited great public interest. Georgian radio cast around for someone to cover the match and Manjgaladze suggested Makharadze:

> Never even in my thoughts had I imagined I would some day do such a thing. We were friends, and never, even jokingly, had we discussed this or entertained doing it. Basketball is a game three times faster than football. Besides, there was no television broadcast, and on the radio to a listener who sees nothing you must explain everything. I plucked up all my courage, made up my mind and did the sportscast. That is how it all began.[9]

Makharadze quickly graduated to covering football. In 1960 he began commentaries in other parts of the USSR and became probably the best-known football commentator in the Soviet Union.

In the case of Peter Montgomery, the setting and the sport were very different, but again a chance suggestion made a lasting impact. Montgomery grew up in the South Island of New Zealand in the 1940s and acquired a love of radio and of sport. He followed the rugby commentaries of Whang McKenzie and Iain Gallaway and also horseracing and baseball broadcasts on shortwave stations from the USA.

> Radio made a big impression on me as youngster. I loved the theatre of the mind. And it stayed with me. But I had no idea an opportunity would open for me to turn my fascination into my career.[10]

In 1970 Montgomery was busy working in the marketing division of a motor company in Auckland. For several years he and some friends from university days had sailed together. Peter had also kept in touch with an old school friend, Bill McCarthy, who worked in sports broadcasting. McCarthy needed someone to cover the world championship sailing regatta in Auckland and remembered Montgomery talking to him about his love of radio. He approached him and asked if he would try a couple of broadcasts.

Montgomery hesitated. Radio commentary had always been part of his life but he had never thought of doing it himself and, besides, his career in marketing was going well. But he decided he would try it out. There followed over thirty years of broadcasting, some of it from ocean races around the world, and including the great races for the America's Cup.

Harsha Bhogle, among the best-known cricket commentators of his generation in India, acknowledged that it was his father who steered him quite firmly towards commentary, in a way perhaps that would not happen today. At the age of nineteen Bhogle was a keen cricketer though not an outstanding one. He had also been in his school debating team and won an award for being the best speaker:

> My father said: 'Why not try and combine your knowledge?'
> By chance there was an under-19 Test Match in the city
> and he said: 'Why not tell All India Radio that they need
> an under-nineteen commentator? Go and meet AIR now,
> today, and tell them they must have an under-nineteen
> commentator for an under-nineteen Test'.
> In those days you didn't dispute what your father said.
> So I took the bus and went there, having no idea what
> I was going to tell them. Because my father had been
> in Hyderabad for so many years and knew people, they
> treated me kindly and allowed me to audition. I did two
> two-minute reports for them on local matches. And then
> I went to one of my own games with a tape recorder.
> I was batting six or seven and while the openers were
> batting I did half an hour of commentary and gave it
> to All India Radio and the head said: 'I think you have
> more promise than others – you can try the next Ranji
> Trophy game'.[11]

TEACHING AND JOURNALISM are the professions that have supplied broadcasting with most commentators. In Britain, rugby commentators Bill McLaren, Ian Robertson, Nigel Starmer-Smith and Alastair Hignell were all teachers when they first took up rugby commentary. Football commentators Maurice Edelston and Peter Jones were both teachers.

Journalism has produced Edmond Dehorter in France, 'Bobby' Talyarkhan in India, Nicolau Tuma in Brazil, PJ Carberry in Ireland,

George Allison in England – all were among the first commentators in their respective countries and all had some previous reporting experience.

Allison was recruited by the BBC in the same month as Teddy Wakelam – January 1927. His involvement with football had begun when working as a journalist in the north-east and continued when he moved to London, reporting on most of Arsenal's home games at Plumstead. When the club moved to Highbury, he continued his association and then started writing the match-day programme. The BBC rang Allison and told him that although they were not sure if football lent itself to commentary they wanted someone who knew about the game to try it out. Allison, not realizing he was one of several to be auditioned, was initially flattered to be chosen:

> The feeling and elation were short-lived. I was shown to a spacious waiting room where I found a crowd of my Fleet Street colleagues – all keyed up and rarin' to introduce sporting commentaries to Great Britain. When the BBC phoned me it had not entered my mind that I was one of the ordinary pebbles that go to make up a beach. With a 'Hello, everybody', I was once more on this planet without showing any visible sign of having left it. Anyway, all of us saw the humorous part of being marshalled for an audition somewhat on the lines of one of Mr. Cochran's famous choruses.[12]

The journalists were taken to Highbury where the Arsenal 2nd XI were playing a midweek game. Each in turn was asked to commentate for a few minutes. The BBC was in a hurry to find their man and before he left the ground that evening Allison was asked if he would commentate live on an FA Cup tie at the Crystal Palace ground the following weekend. In the years that followed both Allison's careers blossomed. He became the BBC's main commentator for football while also moving through the ranks at Arsenal until he became manager. Remarkably, for some time he combined both roles.

Others who have entered the world of radio commentary from journalism include Gerald Williams, Bryon Butler, Don Mosey and John Rawling.

Rawling, who for many years covered athletics and boxing for BBC radio, testifies to the part that an early training in journalism can play in giving broadcasters a command of language:

I worked for a local newspaper and then I worked for an agency serving the East Midlands, and that gave me a fairly sharp journalistic background. Not only was I covering sports but I also did crown courts. If you're covering a court case you have to be accurate – it's a terrific grounding, the discipline within the writing, and discipline within the use of speech is absolutely key.[13]

The importance of having a background in journalism grew when radio news departments began to play a greater role in sports coverage and some commentators were asked to take on the role of being reporters. The discipline of telling the story in a newsworthy way began to take precedence over the basic skills of description. However, John Rawling acknowledged that live commentary, as opposed to writing material to speak on radio, makes very specific demands:

I remember when I first started live commentary how difficult I found it, because the commentator's art is totally different to writing a voice piece. You're used to relying on the written word and suddenly that's gone. You make the great transition from reading a voice piece to then presenting a programme where you have to think on your feet, and then take a step beyond that when you have to commentate.

The advent of local radio, which began with the opening of Radio Leicester in 1967, had an important impact on the development of commentary. The first stations (Leicester was soon followed by Sheffield and Nottingham) were keen to establish themselves as genuinely local voices in their city or region and live coverage of local clubs was a key way of doing this. A side effect was that those working for local newspapers, who for so long had had a monopoly of coverage, found a new and vocal brand of journalist occupying the press box.

As the stations multiplied they provided new openings for those wishing to become commentators – several of those working on BBC 5 Live today undertook work experience at their local stations while still at school. A wider range of voices and accents came to be heard and, as some local radio broadcasters moved into the main BBC, the voice of the BBC nationally began to change. Today 5 Live does much of its recruiting from local stations.

IN SOME SPORTS, commentators are employed to narrate races to spectators on the public address (PA) system. In the case of horse racing and greyhound racing this commentary is sometimes carried to betting shops.

Simon Taylor was a PA commentator in motor racing before auditioning for the BBC and becoming one of their main radio commentators. Peter Bromley began his career when he auditioned in 1954 with the British Amplifying and Recording Company, which supplied PA systems to most racecourses. After giving a test commentary on tape he was given a job with the company, and worked on their panel of commentators for five years before being appointed as the BBC racing correspondent in 1959. Bromley was to become one of the outstanding commentators of the modern era.[14]

John Hunt, the BBC's main racing commentator in 2008, followed a not dissimilar path:

> It was a bit of a fluke. I was working in the police service in London but I was always very passionate about horseracing. My wife saw a tiny advert in the local paper placed by the bookmakers Ladbrokes for a trainee broadcaster. It was her thought that I would like a go at it. I'd never done anything of that kind but one thing that was clear in my mind from my other work was that I could identify certain things and that I could do that quite quickly. She thought I would absolutely love the opportunity to get into the world of racing.
> I went on to have a couple of really good years there. We developed a service purely for the betting shops, commentating off a monitor, but live. Strangely my trade was learned doing greyhound racing. I must have done 20,000 races for betting shops evening after evening. Then in I went to Satellite Information Services for two years. They wanted some new blood, and they were moving towards single commentary for betting shops and racecourses. So I began the process of country wide travel. Previously you would stand side by side with the betting shop guy on the course and in the betting shop you could hear the on-course commentator in the background.[15]

Lee McKenzie also worked both for BBC radio and for *Racetrack*, the company that provides commentaries at the racetracks. He recalled that after an audition with the BBC he was provided with an opportunity to work alongside experienced commentators:

> The BBC wrote a few days later and said I was 'promising' and offered me a day at Newmarket with Peter Bromley. I was to do the first half of each race. I really learned from Peter Bromley's ability to extract drama from a race, his unique turn of phrase, his way of using his voice, letting it go up and down. If it was a really exciting finish it was incredibly loud – like a thunderstorm. Anyway on the Monday after the Newmarket meeting they said I had made a promising start but that I needed to do some work on my voice. They offered me half a dozen days the following year.
>
> In August 1982 I did my first full commentary from Newmarket. It was an eight-runner race. I died a thousand deaths but somehow I managed to get through it. Then I did more days with Peter Bromley and in 1983 I did my first Grand National. Here I was working in the same team as Michael O'Hehir, a legend. In those days the BBC radio commentary was also broadcast over the PA and the crowd would cheer when O'Hehir came on. He welcomed me and took a piece of paper out of his pocket, wrote his phone number on it and told me to contact him if I ever needed help.[16]

O'Hehir had not forgotten what it was like to start out as a young broadcaster.

1   Graham McNamee quotations from *'You're on the air'* (Harper 1926)
2   Interview with the author
3   Bill McClaren *Talking of Rugby* (Stanley Paul 1991) p 9
4   Christopher Martin-Jenkins *Ball by Ball* (Grafton Books 1990) p 5
5   *Wairarapa Times Age* August 2007
6   Interview with the author
7   Michael O'Hehir *My Life and Times* (Blackwater Press 1996) p 1-2
8   Interview with the author
9   Interview with Marina Vashakmadze, *www.magtigsm.com/magazine*
10   Interview with the author
11   Interview with the author
12   George Allison *Allison Calling* (Staples Press, 1948) p 37-38
13   Interview with the author
14   There is more about Peter Bromley in Chapter 10
15   Interview with the author
16   Interview with the author

NINE

GETTING GOING

WHATEVER THE ROUTE INTO COMMENTARY, whether it be planned or accidental, there is always one unavoidable moment, the moment when for the first time the commentator is alone with the microphone and the listeners. There are a million people, perhaps millions, eavesdropping and there can be no pre-recordings, no second chances, no opportunity to say: 'Stop, let's take that again'. The first commentary beckons and the question looms: can I really do this?

The early pioneers – McNamee, Dehorter, Wakelam and others – must have had some sense they were making history. But it is no less demanding perhaps for everyone else, since everyone's first commentary is just that: the first commentary. Murray Walker has recalled how he obtained some experience by 'doing the PA job at a hill climb' and then, in 1949, went for an audition with the BBC. That same year he was called in for the TT races. He rode his bike round the course until he was sure he knew it and then took up position:

> There was no commentary box … I just stood in the middle of the escape road clutching my clipboard, festooned with wires, harness and headphones and with microphone at the ready, eager to give it plenty.[1]

Micheál Ó Muircheartaigh was an eighteen-year-old student in Dublin in 1949 when he successfully auditioned with Radio Éireann to broadcast some matches in Irish. Within a few days he was asked to commentate on the Railway Cup football final on St Patrick's Day at Croke Park. He was given no opportunity for preparation, except that on the Saturday before his commentary he was able to sit beside Michael O'Hehir and observe him at work. Come St Patrick's Day and Ó Muircheartaigh arrived at Croke Park to cover the match between Munster and Leinster:

> As I had not been given an admission pass I presented myself at a stile adjacent to the Corner Stand and informed the man in charge that I was broadcasting the second game. He looked bemused but admitted me nevertheless.

I felt lost and found cover in a room at the back of the Hogan Stand. The hurling game was on but I didn't know where I might go to see Christy Ring and all the others in action, so I just remained anchored where I was.

There was a telephone in the room, and at some stage close to the end of the hurling game a man came in and dialled a number. The caller asked in a worried tone: 'Who is doing this football game? Nobody has shown up yet.' It was time to identify myself and as soon as the hurling game was ended I was ushered into the box.[2]

To his relief, the young student found he knew enough about the players, their jobs and their in-laws to fill his account with personal detail:

Of course I was nervous about the whole operation, but my being only eighteen years of age must have been some help. I felt no sense of responsibility or anything of that nature. I remember feeling part of all the drama from throw-in onwards, and it was a joy to be watching the best players in the land before a crowd of 40,000 plus. I thought it was a fine game, and the teams finished on level terms at 2-7 a side. I enjoyed myself immensely, and to crown it all I received a cheque for six pounds through the post a few days later – an enormous amount of money for a student at the time.

This was the start of a career lasting more than fifty years.

Formerly a keen amateur boxer, Mike Costello found his first live commentary – at the World Athletics championships in 1995 at Gothenberg – as frightening as entering the ring:

I remember being scared to the point I hadn't been since I gave up boxing. I realised that the kind of mechanisms and habits that I'd learned when I was boxing – to keep control, to keep belief, all those sorts of things – were very important in not letting the magnitude of the job overwhelm you. Once the presenter has said 'We hand you over to Mike Costello' you are absolutely naked, it is you telling the world what is going on. It's very, very intimidating at first. There's an amazing buzz to be got once you are on air and it's very similar to my experience as boxer. As soon as the bell goes the nerves disappear.[3]

It was a heat of the 400 metres for men, run mid-morning but involving one Michael Johnson:

> I commentated as if the whole world was crashing around and it was the single most important event that had taken place in track and field athletics. Commentators in other boxes were looking at me as if to say – 'What is going on?' I finished, and then I got the message from London: 'That was fine, Mike, but you've given it so much – where are you going to go when you get to the final?' It was a case of going in much too hard, much too quickly. If you want to draw a boxing analogy, it was a case of giving absolutely everything in the first round and holding nothing back for the remainder of the contest.

Jacqui Oatley, who began her career at BBC Radio Leeds, recalled her first football commentary. It was arranged at short notice and one of the players sat down before the game and talked her through the teams:

> Some event had been cancelled and the editor said: 'How about you do some commentary?' I was a bit embarrassed because I thought people might laugh at me, because there weren't any women commentators then. It was a Unibond Premier Division game between Wakefield and Emley, and Worksop Town. I'd been up on the early shift at three in the morning and I was absolutely exhausted. I wasn't particularly nervous but I'd rather have had time to do some preparation. There was little information on the internet and it was the first game of the season so preparation was difficult. But the captain of one of the sides, a fireman who had just arrived from a shift at work, came and sat with me just before kick-off and we went through it.[4]

IT TAKES TIME TO LEARN the skills of commentary. Some of those who join the BBC's national network 5 Live have done graduate or postgraduates courses relating to broadcasting and come with experience in local radio. Those working for local stations can attend courses run by the BBC at national level. To tutor the course the BBC turned to Ron Jones, a BBC commentator for nearly twenty years, and before that a teacher:

The takers are largely people who have spent some time in local radio and some of them are very, very good. One of the side effects is that Network BBC has the opportunity to find out what sort of talent is out there.

They come to London and we do it over two days. The first morning session we talk about the essential skills – voice, style, preparation, alertness, sharpness, who you're talking to, action and comment, how to set the scene, how to build up suspense, how you point out the likely star performers, use of effects, use of the summarisers, all those sorts of things.[5]

Ron Jones uses extracts from the BBC sound archives to illustrate good practice and in addition course members bring in recordings of their own work which are discussed. In the evening they do a mock commentary on a match at Loftus Road, Queen's Park Rangers' ground, to provide more raw material to be discussed the following day.

Performance reviews also play a part in developing the skills of commentators. The days when a head of Outside Broadcasting could listen to most commentaries and then give feedback on a weekly basis are a distant memory. The BBC now follows the pattern of most organisations in providing a system of annual appraisals for its full-time staff, when commentators can receive feedback and discuss career possibilities. The appraiser will have had the opportunity to listen to some commentaries and to speak to some producers who have worked with the appraisee. Mike Lewis, former editor of BBC Radio Sport, notes that these meetings are important to those commentators who are anxious about where they stand in relation to their colleagues:

Commentary is a branch of show business. It's a performance. If you're a performer you may be quite insecure. Some are not keen to see others go past them.[6]

It was once the case that all BBC staff who worked at the microphone were sent on a general voice course. In the early years of the 21st century the provision for commentators became more bespoke. Rob Nothman, himself an experienced commentator, was asked to provide a mentoring system for individuals. He was given the names of commentators who say during their appraisal that they would like more feedback:

First I ring the commentator and ask for examples of work they think is particularly good or work they feel didn't quite come off. I listen to these extracts in the archives and make notes and then I meet with them for two or three hours and play one or two bits through. More often than not, the commentator will spot minor faults such as being behind the action or not giving the score enough. The process is one of self-evaluation – taking the time to listen back. It's nice to hear improvements in subsequent commentaries. For example, one commentator, whom I felt was struggling to keep the listeners' attention during a dull game when there was little meaningful action to describe, went away and worked hard on painting more pictures. The next time he was commentating on a Champions League qualifying tie in Europe, he really made an effort to describe the stadium and town where the match was taking place. It provided much-needed colour.[7]

Nothman undertook this mentoring with many of the newer members of the football commentary team and with people coming through into rugby and cricket commentary:

All of them crave feedback. A lot of broadcasters have certain insecurities. They often ask 'Am I doing a good job?' They need to be reassured. Also there is a measure of competition between commentators over who gets certain matches.

Attitudes among commentators to listening to recordings of their own commentaries seem to vary. Some did this a lot, some hardly at all. Rob Nothman acknowledged that some commentators were wary of listening back for fear that they might be perceived to be vain and obsessed with the 'grandeur' of their work:

The bit of advice I always give to a broadcaster who wants to listen back is: 'Don't listen back to it immediately. Leave it probably for the best part of a month or two months, probably until you've done lots of other commentaries, and then you will find that you're listening to it as a listener, as opposed to someone who knows immediately what they're about to say. You can remember commentating on that match the previous weekend and you know that

Bloggins is just about to hit the post and things are going to get exciting, so you're not listening as the listener does. Whereas if you give it enough time, and you've done enough matches in the interim, then you'll have no idea what you're going to say, your critical ear is tuned in and you're listening as a listener does.'

Training is provided for new expert summarisers, many of whom had not had the experience in local radio some commentators have had. Former England football manager Graham Taylor, picked as a summariser for Premier League and international football games, said:

After a year or so nobody had said anything to me. I assumed this meant I was doing the right thing but I wanted a bit of feedback. One of the producers arranged for Rob Nothman to bring some clips to my house and we went through them discussing how I worked with different commentators. It was well worth it.[8]

The BBC also helped to provide training to one group of volunteer commentators. *Soccer Sight* is an initiative by The Royal National Institute of Blind People (RNIB) to improve access to football venues and provide playing opportunities for blind and partially sighted people. Volunteer commentators, trained by the BBC and the RNIB, use special transmitting and receiving equipment to provide audio description to blind and partially-sighted spectators at the ground. This enables the spectators to sit in their preferred seats and receive a commentary which in addition to providing a description of the game provides more emphasis on the whole environment of the ground, regular explanation of crowd noises, and all the visual detail that goes to make up a match experience.

Hazel Dudley, a Liverpool supporter, recalled how *Soccer Sight* commentary brought the game alive:

I need a commentator to tell me the funny things which are going on – things that you mightn't expect, even things you would. How should I know that Alex Ferguson chews gum and another manager stands with their arms folded, while another dances about within their technical area? How would I know what banners are being flown, or that Harry Kewell's hair is ridiculous? Why shouldn't

I want to know that in one particular game when one of our players was meant to be wearing goggles to protect an injured eye, he threw them off and the players on the bench were trying them on and having a laugh? All this and describing the game![9]

Would-be commentators went on a training course run by the RNIB and the BBC in which some of the problems which blind and partially-sighted people encounter at football grounds were explained and which included a practice session. The RNIB also prepared additional back-up materials for those providing audio-description to spectators at a game, setting out the ways the commentator can meet the needs of someone who can 'hear' the game but not see it. The *Soccer Sight* approach has been extended to other sports, including cricket and rugby.

Established commentators have also turned to sportsmen and women for help. This may be necessary when – successful in one field – they find themselves thrown to the lions with a sport they knew nothing about. Keith Quinn was asked one day to take on boxing, a sport about which he knew little:

> John Rex Hughes was a New Zealand amateur champion, and a hard-bitten Auckland detective. So I rang him and I said: 'John, I'm going to do this commentary on radio – can I come and see you?' I went to his office and asked him how it worked. And right there in his office he showed me how boxing worked, what a southpaw is, the difference between a clinch and a hold, and I took notes and I had it at my elbow when I went into the commentator's box.[10]

Opportunities like these can be important career opportunities or lead to memorable moments. Unni Anisdahl in Norway, having gone to work as a secretary on leaving school, was drawn into commentary when she started writing articles about handball, the game in which she represented Norway. Her commentaries proved so popular that she was asked to cover alpine skiing, presenting a new challenge:

> I had no problem with handball as I knew the game, the rules, the psychology... My main asset was that I knew what the players were thinking. I knew from their body language. I could 'read' them. But I had never skied in my life. So I went to talk to the skiers and asked them all

about it, what was right, what was wrong and they were very patient and told me. Also I requested, and got, an expert summariser, a former top skier.[11]

Anisdahl then began to cover football as well as handball and skiing and attracted a considerable following in Norway.

Alan Green, better known for his football commentaries on 5 Live (of which more later), has described how he was roped in to cover rowing during the 1996 Olympic Games in Atlanta. He read about the subject, watched videos and then went to see Steve Redgrave and Matthew Pinsent, Britain's hopes in the coxless pairs event. After some initial difficulties, all went well with the commentary and Green found himself helping describe a gold medal. 'The beauty of sports commentary', he said, 'is that people like me are in a position to feel that, somehow, we share in the success of others'.[12]

1	Murray Walker *Unless I'm very much mistaken* (Collins Willow 2002)
2	Micheál Ó Muircheartaigh *From Dún Síon to Croke Park* (Penguin Ireland 2004) p 44-45
3–10	Interview with the author
11	Email to the author
12	Alan Green *The Green Line* (Headline 2000)

TEN

GOLDEN RULES

I prepare a team sheet which is literally one sheet of A4 which is divided down the middle and I have the teams either side. The most important thing about your team sheet of course is that it must be easily readable at a glance; you can't afford to be looking down trying to read things when the game is going on in front of you.

I will spend quite a lot of Friday getting my Arsenal/ Liverpool notes together, the teams, how many goals they're scored, how many appearances the players have made, whether they're coming back from injury. I put all that down in as concise a way as I can. Each sheet shows each player listed in the position they'll be in when I'm reading my team sheet...

I'll put down in a little corner how many goals van Persie has scored this season. If someone comes back in after injury I would note what the injury was, and so on. And then at the top of the sheet I would have what positions they are in the league at the moment, all the little details, how many games it is – someone may be on a winning streak – how many times they've met in recent seasons, whether there are any significant results. So all this means when you actually sit down at five to three you have in front of you a sheet which is really there as a reference point. I will probably only glance at it maybe ten or eleven times throughout the whole game and it will be simply to check on goals scored.[1]

THIS IS RON JONES, a man with a lifetime's knowledge of the game and of commentary, the day before an Arsenal/Liverpool game. Another BBC football commentator, John Murray, said that a Premier League game will involve five to six hours of preparation. Edson Mauro, a veteran Brazilian radio commentator, stressed that the voice too has to be prepared:

The day before each transmission I try not to drink alcohol or any cold drink. I consider that preparing myself for a transmission is a very strict process. When I have to transmit an evening game I try to sleep for at least eight hours. When I wake up I spend one hour in complete silence. According to my voice doctor, in that way you are automatically preserving all the voice's potentiality and power.[2]

Commentators need to be steeped in a sport, to love it and to know its rules and its history to be really at home in the commentary box, and to help them hold their listeners' attention. And they need to be able to call on a wide range of material whenever they need it. A major event demands extra preparation. Before a big fight in the USA John Rawling would fly to America a few days in advance:

I would have taken with me every available bit of stuff that was written about the fight, I would have read all the newspapers, plundered the internet for records, anecdotes, anything which had been useful. During the week you're rubbing shoulders with trainers, sparring partners, people around the fights, hopefully the fighters themselves, journalists from all over the world. You're set up in a big press room, probably in Las Vegas, and you're swapping information, eating out together, talking about it, and people who are not steeped in it probably would find it profoundly boring, because you're banging on about what might or might not happen and why.[3]

Rugby, the game which provided the first running commentary on the BBC, requires similar preparation to football, perhaps even more so as thirty players can get very muddy, and hard to identify, by the end of a game. Bill McLaren was renowned for the depth of his preparation before rugby internationals. He made a point of going to see each team in training, even when he was combining teaching with weekend commentary work for the BBC. On one occasion he arranged to be released from school in Scotland on a Wednesday and left home at four in the morning so he could catch a flight from Newcastle to London and then go on to Bridgend to see the Welsh team in practice. He got back at 11 p.m. and was in front of his class at 9 a.m. the next morning.

The main rugby commentators on BBC radio in 2008 included two ex-internationals, Alastair Hignell and Ian Robertson. Hignell stressed that although the natural drama of the game lends itself to commentary, there remains the underlying importance of getting the names right:

> There are moments of sheer physical grunt and grind and the more balletic, poetic movements at the back. The combination makes for an enthralling spectacle. But the most important thing for the commentator is getting the names right and the rhythm right. Your confidence derives from getting the names right. You're on top of the game if you recognize people and identify them and build up the whole thing by mentioning names.[4]

But international rugby teams stopped welcoming outsiders at their practice, and this prevented commentators from following McLaren's methods of preparation. Hignell regretted this:

> The thing about training is that you learn how people run, so you can spot their body movements. There are people that lift their knees up or scuttle, or spread their arms about – but you can't go to training and see them nowadays... During the week when the teams are announced you put names to numbers. Because I'm disabled I have to use my laptop, I can't write, so I put names against numbers. I have a team sheet on my laptop with all the basic facts – caps, tries, points – for each player – so during the course of the week I would fill that in and come back to it several times.

In horseracing correct identification of the runners is critical. Those listeners who have placed a bet want to know the fortunes of their horse and, especially in the early stages, the commentator must try and indicate the position of all the runners. This may mean committing to memory up to twenty-five sets of colours, or even more. Raymond Glendenning's painted cards, described in Chapter 7, are one method of solving this problem. Peter Bromley followed a similar system. 'His cards were a work of art', remembered Bob Burrows. Bill McLaren also used the Raymond Glendenning method for remembering the names of rugby players. He had a pack of playing cards numbered one to fifteen and each evening prior to a match he would turn them over and ask himself the player's name.

John Hunt stressed that preparation is something that goes on all the time:

> I'm seeing these horses five days a week every week, not just seeing them but having a working relationship almost every day of the week so although there are a lot of them, I feel I know them quite well anyway ... It's an ongoing thing, preparation, through the week ... I don't have a time in the week when I say, right, preparation time, I just pick up and soak things up as it goes on. But certainly in terms of doing a commentary itself I wouldn't have looked at it until that morning. I'd look at the details over breakfast. In the case, say, of the Cesarewitch in 2006 with thirty-four runners I'd have thought I know twenty, twenty-two of these anyway, they won't cause me any problems. The closer the race gets you bring yourself to a peak almost in terms of short term memory, because I can guarantee that the fourteen I didn't know that morning would be the same fourteen that I would struggle to recognize at tea time that day.[5]

Many commentators would get to know scores and even hundreds of players by sight over a number of years. Obviously it would be the teams the commentator has not watched before, who may pose the greatest difficulty. Mike Ingham, appointed BBC football correspondent in 1991:

> The truly challenging games are cup ties involving non-league teams or unfamiliar overseas opposition. If possible I will try and watch a training session or a video of the club. Relying on photographs can be unhelpful as players never seem to look the same in the flesh on the pitch. To distinguish a player I might try and liken him to someone else and make a note – for example the number sixteen who is tall with curls reminds me say of Chris Martin. I do try and remember squad numbers – though many on striped shirts from a distance can be almost impossible to read.[6]

Jacqui Oatley had a similar problem before the Women's European football championships. She knew few of the players from outside the UK so she approached journalists from the other countries involved and also got hold of a video of Sweden playing Denmark:

I contacted all the press officers, and did image searches on the internet. This was slightly extravagant but I got mental pictures of all the players. I copied and pasted images from the internet. Going to a Finnish training session also helped. I got the physio to tell me who the players were. I wrote down what each player looked like, ponytail, etc. I tried to get individual stories about them – one a nanny, one a cleaner etc. And then I kept testing myself. I knew that listeners didn't know what the players looked like, so I needed to give more description than usual. A game like this is a different type of commentary, probably even more descriptive.[7]

Preparation of this kind is the bedrock of commentary. Moments of hesitation when a fielder or a striker cannot be instantly identified are avoided. It is a pleasure for the listener too if the commentator has taken trouble to consult colleagues from other countries, or the players themselves, and get name pronunciation right. Similarly listeners expect commentators to have done the basic research about the countries taking part in international competitions. Keith Quinn remembered veteran BBC cricket commentator Henry Blofeld welcoming one group of competitors from Samoa coming into the stadium at the Commonwealth Games in New Zealand with the words: '*Oh look – more Maoris.*'

'BEGIN WITH THE SCORE', said de Lotbinière in his policy paper about outside broadcasts in 1942. In 1937 he had suggested that the score be given by the football commentator 'every fifteen minutes.' He must have soon realised this was a mistake – in 1939 he suggested 'at least every five minutes'. Even this would be frustrating today for the listener who switches on for the latest news because in many sports this is the first fundamental of commentary.

Thousands of new listeners join a broadcast every second – to check on the score or see whether a wicket has fallen – and a delay of two or three minutes can seem like an eternity. A BBC aide-memoire on commentary of 1978, designed to guide producers across all sports, and written at a time when there were no female commentators, asked:

'Does he repeat the score regularly but not monotonously, varying the ways in which he does it?' The skilful commentator can weave in an update without repeating the same phrase – 'Villa still looking for the equaliser here at Anfield', 'everything still going with serve', 'Wales still eight points adrift'. Other basic arithmetic, which puts the score in context, is also important – minutes elapsed, time added on, overs remaining, holes left to play.

Providing information of this kind is the commentator's primary task. In some sports it assumes crucial importance. Knut Bjørnsen, drawing on more than thirty years' experience as a radio and TV commentator in Norway, stresses the particular challenges of speedskating:

> It is a very mathematically orientated sport. Two athletes compete against each other on the ice, but also against athletes who have already finished their race, and other athletes still to come. The commentator has to compare lap times, intermediate times and also stipulated times. So you actually create a news situation while waiting for the next intermediate time. And you alone can break that news – approximately each thirty-third second![8]

Listeners began to expect some indication of the score to be given with great frequency. Ron Jones recounts how mortified he was when, at an early stage of his career, his boss, Cliff Morgan, picked him up on this issue after a midweek game at West Ham when his commentary seemed to have gone well. He had been congratulated by his co-commentator, Peter Jones (who did not give praise lightly), and by colleagues in the office the following morning:

> And then in the afternoon, Cliff Morgan, who had done it all in broadcasting terms, and was an icon, a fellow Welshman as well, patted me on the back, and said: 'I listened to the commentary last night. Excellent, top class, best you've ever done. My wife and I had been in the supermarket, we got in the car and listened and my wife said: "Who is this guy, isn't he good?" I said: "Yes, new fellow, come up from Wales." And I really was glowing, you know, and he said: 'You were so sharp, the words were good, and the excitement and the effects were good: well done'.
> He started to walk away, and I thought I've really cracked it now, and then he suddenly turned and he came back.

And he said: 'There's one thing – I'd have liked to have known what the score was. You know, you must give the score. I'd been in the supermarket, I'd got into my car, switched the radio on, and for two, maybe two and half, maybe three minutes I listened to the commentary and I didn't know what the score was.'

It became the norm for BBC football commentators to make a point of giving the score regularly. In each half of a match it was not unusual for it to be announced, or referred to indirectly, between fifteen and twenty times. Just occasionally, dramatic events on or off the field might cause commentators to forget but they would usually have the producer quickly prompting them through their headphones.

Cricket is a sport where the score is central to commentary. 'Keeping the score' has always been a way of following the game and when commentary grew in the post-war years the BBC began to realise that some listeners were indeed maintaining their own record of the game. Rex Alston and John Arlott set out in *Radio Times* the plans at the start of the 1948 season:

> Our ideal listener is the man who knows cricket and can listen all the time. We shall try and show him the game growing and developing in detail so that he could if he wished keep the score.

A year later, writing in *Radio Times* again – and still ignoring the female audience – Alston identified two kinds of listeners to cricket commentary: 'Mr Stay-at-Home' who listened to the wireless all day; and 'Mr Everyman', who listened only for certain periods and 'is irritated if he doesn't, within a minute of switching on, know the score'.

In his memoirs, Alston reprimanded Arlott for neglecting to give the score in his early days as a broadcaster. Fortunately, added Alston, 'stern mental self-discipline gradually brought him into line'.[9]

But cricket, of course, is not just a game where the score is important, it is a game of statistics. The scorer, first attached to cricket commentary in the 1930s, has evolved into a statistician for the *Test Match Special* commentary team and Bill Frindall has fulfilled these roles since 1966. His scoring methods have ensured that patterns of play that might otherwise be hidden to the listener are revealed – the performance of one batsman against one bowler, for instance.

As his experience on *TMS* grew, Frindall was allowed to become more adventurous in his comments, and even to speak when not spoken to. One commentator at least found his interventions intrusive at times.[10] As the years went by they seemed to have become less common and more subdued, while no less important in informing the listener. When baited, Frindall was still allowed to reply in kind, sometimes in a deliberate tone of irritation: *'I've given you the figures – all you have to do is read them out'*, he will say. But his prime value was as the voice of authority on facts – a Delphic figure in the corner whose *sotto voce* asides feed the commentators with crucial details. In June 2007 when Matthew Hoggard equalled Alec Bedser's total of test wickets there was discussion in the commentary box about their relative standing. Frindall rapidly supplied a summary of the two bowlers' averages, strike rates and economy rates, and an indication of the kinds of teams they had played against. It was a crucial contribution.

Statistics also play a crucial role in athletics. Bob Phillips was an expert summariser and statistician covering athletics on BBC radio for nearly twenty years. The task is a demanding one because of the range of events to be covered, and the level of detail required. For him preparation was a year-round affair:

> I maintained profiles of thousands of athletes so that there was always something ready to hand to say about anybody. It might seem odd, but the more obscure the athlete the more important it was to know something about him. If the commentator is able to say of an athlete of whom almost nobody has heard – reading from a race card prepared for him by the expert summariser – 'And in lane five we have Joseva Levula, of Fiji, who is the South Pacific Games champion' this gives greater credibility to the whole presentation … For any particular meeting … it is vital to know who has won medals in previous years and for which countries. All this data would be carried by me in files and handbooks in a large holdall and the night before an event I would check on any facts and figures which I anticipated could be of interest. The secret is not to necessarily have the facts in your head but to know where to find a piece of information in a matter of twenty or thirty seconds or so.[11]

The first radio car! Twickenham in 1927 – a far cry from today.

(top) Teddy Wakelam with buttonhole, and his no. 2 commentator, a young John Snagge.
(bottom) Twickenham 1927: the primitive arrangement for the BBC's first commentary.

Graham McNamee with the legendary American baseball star Babe Ruth. (Corbis)

HOW DID YOU HEAR THE BOAT RACE?

COULDN'T have heard it better, did you say? The announcer's voice sounded as clear and loud as if you were sitting next to him on the launch? And you only paid 54/- for your loud speaker?

Then you must have been one of the many thousands who listened in with the Lissenola, the full-toned, sweet-voiced loud speaker which has delighted enthusiasts in every town and village of England.

Yes. The Lissenola is an instrument

to be proud of. No loud speaker, no matter if it costs £20, is more natural in its utterance, more pure in its tone, or more powerful in its volume. You can prove this for yourself at home for 7 days, and then, if within that time you do not definitely prefer the Lissenola to any other loud speaker which you may have tested it against, irrespective of price, return the Lissenola and your money will be refunded in full.

The Golden-toned **LISSENOLA** 54/-

LISSEN LTD., 300-320, Friars Lane, Ri...

FULL-SIZED. — FULL-TONED — FULL

HOW THE COMMENTATOR SEES IT
Broadcasting a Football Match

*(top) Radio Times 1 April 1927
Manufacturers cash in.
(bottom) Explaining things to the
listener.*

Football in Brazil and cricket in India. (top) Brazil's Ary Barroso perches on a roof. (below) AFS (Bobby) Talyarkhan, wearing dark glasses.

(top) Henry Longhurst — "filling in the gaps.".
(bottom) Graham Walker in the Radio Times.

Seymour Joly de Lotbinière, better known as Lobby, the man who changed the face of BBC radio commentary. (Getty Images)

Raymond Glendenning in one of the BBC's earliest radio cars. (BBC Photo Library)

Football commentator George Allison was also manager of Arsenal. (BBC Photo Library)

It was not always sport. Howard Marshall in 1944. He was one of the BBC War Correspondents who reported on the D-Day landings. (BBC Photo Library)

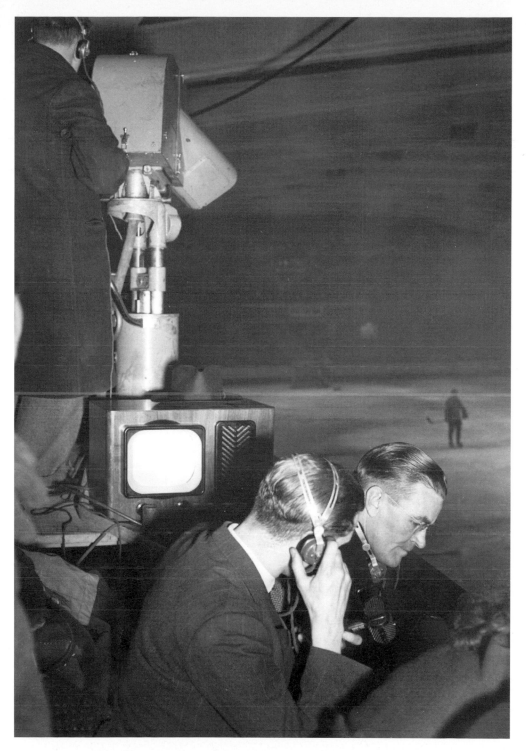

Stewart MacPherson with an engineer at an ice hockey match. (BBC Photo Library)

(top) Alan Allardyce on the haystack at Riccarton racecourse in New Zealand 1926 – "I could see with no trouble." (photo from Robin Allardyce)
(bottom) Peter Jones, Bob Burrows, Des Lynam, Cliff Morgan and Brian Tremble in 1973.
(BBC Photo Library)

Winston McCarthy making his final rugby broadcast in Wellington 1957
(Dominion Post Collection, Alexander Turnbull Library Wellington, New Zealand)

John Arlott at the microphone in 1967. (BBC Photo Library)

Three Test Match Special stalwarts. (from left) Henry Blofeld, Christopher Martin-Jenkins and Jonathan Agnew. (BBC Photo Library)

The BBC's main football commentators for many years, Alan Green (left) and Mike Ingham, at the 2006 World Cup in Germany. (BBC Photo Library)

IF GIVING THE SCORE is a priority, so is giving the result – especially at the end of a race.

In athletics it is usually the shorter races that pose the problem and of all the examples in this book, these commentaries transfer least effectively to the written page. The 60 metres sprint at indoor meetings is a challenge for any observer to follow, let alone describe. It allows the commentator some six seconds to construct a narrative. On this occasion Mike Costello found himself covering three false starts before the final and successful attempt to run the race. He saw immediately that one of the favourites (Kim Collins) was struggling, that another (Maurice Greene) was at the front, but spotted a third man coming through to win:

> *And would you believe it they are away and it's a fairly level break, Kim Collins has got work to do, Greene on the outside is coming good, but on the inside Leonard Scott has just snatched it on the line, I think.*

Costello was right, Scott did win.

The 100 metres allows the commentator the luxury of an extra four seconds to 'read' the race and give some structure to it. It is one of the most prestigious titles in track and field but Mike Costello described it as: '… close to being the most difficult thing in sports commentary. There is no easy way of getting across the technique of 100 metres commentary apart from just doing them, time and time again'.[12]

Taking on the women's 100 metres final at the 2005 world championships, John Rawling made the commentary on the race itself a small filling in a sandwich of anticipation and analysis. He set the scene, focusing particularly on the French athlete Christine Arron who had been the top runner on the Grand Prix circuit in the preceding weeks. While the competitors stripped down and went through the long process of preparing for the start Rawling discussed each in turn and placed them in the lanes, setting up the contest for the listener. Then they were on their blocks:

> *And away they go. A good start in lane six from Lauryn Williams and Arron not particularly well away. Sturrop's in front but here comes Arron closing. Is she going to be able to come through? She doesn't and it's going to be gold for Lauryn Williams of the United States.*

In the 400 metres the competitors compete from a staggered start because of lane advantage, and some commentators say position in the race is difficult to gauge. In addition, some runners may display intense fatigue in the final moments of a race. There were two athletes from Britain in the women's 400 metres final at the 2007 world championships, Christine Ohuruogu and Nicola Sanders. With some seven or eight seconds of the race left Mike Costello spotted that, although Novelene Williams and Natalya Antyukh were leading, the two British runners were in contention.

> Here come Sanders and Ohuruogu now challenging for the bronze medal. They've got SIXTY metres to run.

He saw too that the leader was struggling:

> Novelene Williams is tying up in the lead.

But like other watchers Costello was unprepared for what happened in the final strides. With less than five metres left, Novelene Williams was still in front, with Ohuruogu and Sanders just behind. Ohuruogu gained half a stride on Williams, who seemed somehow to draw her torso back from the tape at the vital moment. The only way Costello could capture Ohuruogu's victory was by shouting her name:

> Ohuruogu is challenging, Nicola Sanders is challenging. Over on the far side it's Novelene Williams from Sanders and ... Ohuruogu ... Ohuruogu wins the world championship gold medal.

Commentary on horseracing poses similar challenges, but here many listeners are betting on the outcome, which means there is an added responsibility on the commentator to get the result right. And racing provides a good illustration of how a commentator's rhythm of speech, mounting in urgency towards the finish, must reflect the underlying rhythm of the sport. New Zealand race commentator Reon Murtha stresses that this process must never be exaggerated:

> The skill in the commentary is identifying all the runners in the field, but also reflecting the drama and excitement unfolding naturally, without trying to falsely manufacture or invent it. Some races are quite mundane.[13]

Peter Bromley was BBC Radio racing correspondent from 1960 to 2001. He served for three years in the Hussars, rode as an amateur, worked for five years as a racecourse commentator, owned horses and became a consultant on horse breeding. But above all he had a remarkable voice, a rich, rounded baritone with great depth and assurance – 'all brandy and cigars', someone said. It must stand with that of the cricket commentator John Arlott as one of the most memorable in radio sport. It was a far more individual voice than that of the racetrack commentators in America and Australia who use a chanting 'drone' style which makes every race sound the same.[14]

Peter Bromley's first commentary for the BBC finished with two horses – *Deer Leap* and *Monet* – neck and neck as they came to the post. Bromley judged *Monet* the winner in a photo finish and then had an agonising wait for the judges to give their verdict. It was eight minutes before the judges confirmed that Bromley – in this first radio commentary of many hundreds – had got it right. 'I had a very soft spot for *Deer Leap* afterwards', wrote Bromley. 'His defeat by a few inches helped me on to a new career in radio.'[15]

Bromley sometimes found it impossible to recall – a few seconds after finishing a commentary – who had won the race. He brought almost all his commentaries to a perfect finish but he was one of those who had to be reminded immediately afterwards to which horses he had awarded the first three places. John Fenton spent many days alongside him in the commentary box and one of his jobs was to give Bromley what was called the 'you said' card – the names of the first, second and third placed horses, as Bromley had called them, set down in large clear letters.

Bromley got few races wrong. When he reflected on one notable mistake he attributed it in part to tiredness. He gave the Finch Decanter Stakes at Ascot to a horse called *Restive*, which by chance he had tipped to win in the preview programme. A few seconds later the commentator noticed the real *Restive* passing the post among the also-rans. It was a murky day but Bromley believed there were other factors that affected his performance that day:

> I think that after Royal Ascot, a twelve-runner sponsored sprint handicap simply did not get the adrenalin going fast enough. I was just exhausted after the Royal four days.

Bromley could reach for any gear he wanted, and knew when to deploy each one. The first stages of a race would be covered in a relaxed and languid way, the listener well aware that there was much in reserve. As the tempo of a race grew, Bromley would gently raise the speed, and, just fractionally, the volume. As the climax approached, he found the extra tempo needed to match the excitement of the race, but what was most striking was the controlled, effortless power. In his voice, there was never, as so often happens, a sense of strain. Even during the most thrilling finish there was something left in the tank. More than once a jockey paid Peter Bromley the ultimate tribute by asking for a copy of his commentary on a notable race.

John Hunt became the BBC's lead racing commentator after Bromley retired. Of course for big meetings he is backed by a team which for the Cheltenham Festival of 2007 included Luke Harvey – a former jockey and horseman – Ian Bartlett and the BBC racing correspondent Cornelius Lysaght. In longer races the experts like Harvey and Bartlett have time to talk while Hunt gets his breadth, but he never lets go of the main narration. 'I'm quite possessive of the race itself,' he said. 'My voice doesn't do a great deal for me (but) I find I slip into a rhythm quite well. Once the race starts I can absolutely guarantee that I'm thinking of nothing else at all.'[16]

Hunt's coverage of the Coral–Eclipse Stakes from Sandown Park in July 2007 showed the pressure a racing commentator may be under, even with a small field. The race pitted the 2007 Derby and 2006 Guineas winners, *Authorized* and *George Washington*, against each other but over an intermediate distance, ten furlongs. Also at stake in the race were the bloodstock ambitions of Sheikh Mohammed and John Magnier. To add to the complications 5 Live was also covering a Wimbledon semi-final that afternoon and Hunt went live on air fractionally after the start of the race, and had to create a sense of momentum immediately. Within thirty seconds or so he had set the scene, identified the favourite, mentioned each horse and taken the field through the first two furlongs:

> *Just under way here and the first furlong sees Authorized and Frankie Dettori, sent off red-hot favourite around 4-7, sitting in plum last position. Champery, his pacemaker, is doing the job early and he leads at a scorching early gallop here through the first quarter of a mile. He sits just in front of Yellowstone who's in second place and Archipenko, in third, but Champery's gone clear of those two. Notnowcato's in behind them, followed by Kandidate and then further back comes Admiral of the Fleet and the big two, George Washington and Authorized, the Derby winner, sit as the last pair here, and they've rather let this pacemaker go.*

Champery continued to lead the field until the horses swung right-handed with half-a-mile to go but the pace had been slowed. Now

Hunt spotted that jockey Ryan Moore was bringing *Notnowcato* over to the near stand side in search of drier ground, while Frankie Dettori kept the favourite on the far rail. (Moore had noticed when walking the course early that morning how much drier the ground was on the stand side.):

> *Champery, the long time leader, coming right back to them now, sits just a length and a half clear of Notnowcato, who's racing quite wide, wider than the others. Then we've got on the far side rail Yellowstone, Kandidate follows him, Archipenko under heavy pressure. No move yet from Authorized or George Washington, in behind Admiral of the Fleet. The runners are stretched right across the track here, with Notnowcato coming right over to the stand side, the other runners have gone on the far side led still by the blue cap run of Yellowstone, but Authorized moving into top gear now, he's gone past George Washington, Kandidate running a great race just in behind them.*

As the horses came down towards the final one hundred and fifty yards, Hunt raised the tempo and captured the moment when the favourite was beaten by Ryan Moore's clever riding:

> *Notnowcato the leader this side, Authorized the leader of the bigger group, over on the far side. It's George Washington finishing fast as well … but it's Notnowcato … he's beaten them, from in second Authorized, with George Washington close up in third. They were wide apart, but it's Notnowcato's Eclipse…*

It was a fine commentary, delivered by chance during the exact moments when there was a break between games at Wimbledon.

1–5	Interview with the author
6	Email to the author
7	Interview with the author
8	Email to the author
9	Rex Alston *Taking the Air* (Stanley Paul 1951) p 84
10	Harsha Bhogle, interview with the author
11	Email to the author
12	Interview with the author
13	Email to the author
14	K Kuiper and P Austin have studied the speech patterns of racing commentators and auctioneers and suggested that the drone-like speech is a linguistic device designed to maximise the memory

resources of the speaker. (*New Zealand ways of speaking* Victoria University Press 1990)

15   Peter Bromley *My Most Memorable Races* (Stanley Paul 1988 p xiv)

16   Interview with the author

PART THREE

RADIO, SPORT AND THE NATION

ELEVEN

NATIONAL VOICES

THE EARLY INTENTIONS of the BBC were clear: it wanted to position itself at the heart of the nation. Live commentary on sport was one of the ways in which it achieved this end. 'This Derby race belongs to all of us,' the BBC had claimed in 1928 when it mounted commentary on the event for the second time. By 1935 the BBC was able to announce in its Handbook that commentary was becoming easier because radio was 'securing its hold on the national life'.

At first an intruder into the home, radio quickly established itself as a presence in the lives of listeners, nestling in as part of the furniture. The best-known commentators were nationally-known voices, indelibly associated with the sport they described. Some major commentaries were landmarks in the calendar. They had the feel of ceremonial occasions, involving millions of listeners around the country.

IN AMERICA, radio quickly became an important part of everyday life, and something that the business community welcomed as an opportunity. As major sporting events were increasingly networked across America during the 1920s and 1930s, listeners scattered across the country were tuning in to the same ball game or the same fight. The connections between sport and the way people think about their country are complex but for an hour or two each week these listeners, born in so many different countries, shared in one part of the American dream.

During the hard times of the Depression, boxing, with its aggression and struggle for survival, assumed a metaphorical status in the USA. The fights between Jack Dempsey and Gene Tunney in 1926 and 1927 drew some of the largest early radio audiences. Then, in the 1930s, the emergence of Joe Louis created a new wave of interest, especially among black Americans, many of whom bought radios specifically to listen to his fights. When Louis fought Max Baer at the Yankee Stadium in New York in 1935, Buick Motors sponsored the radio coverage in order to launch their new model. There were 90,000 people present and the commentator Clem McCarthy captured every move in a ritualistic almost soothing chant. He took the listener close to the savage, closing moments:

> *Louis is backing away but he comes in on Baer and they're right above me now as I talk with Baer with his back to me and Louis gives him two left jabs on Baer once more. Louis leads with a left, Baer has got his hands close against him now ... and he straightens out, he ducks his head back that time, he got a good stiff left on the chin. Now he misses with a left. Louis ducked and went under, and Louis gives him a left full to the face and a left over the eye. Louis with another left, another left. Max went into a clinch, the referee orders them to break ... they're over here against the ropes, Max has got his back to me and* (gasps in the crowd) *he took an awful right, and then a left to the jaw and he's gone to his knees, he's gone down and the count is FOUR, FIVE, SIX – Baer is on one knee – SEVEN, EIGHT, NINE – Baer is not up – Baer is on his knees at the count of ten. Your fight is all over ... your fight is all over...*

There were some pockets of resistance to live sport – owners of the three major baseball teams in New York all banned live coverage for five years in the 1930s – but in general the growing radio networks brought sporting occasions to a widening audience, and helped to confirm the place of sport in American life. During the Depression, President Roosevelt used his weekly radio broadcasts to try and bring together people in a divided country. Radio commentaries and popular shows, as much as movies, provided entertainment and pleasure. By the late 1930s, ninety per cent of Americans had radio in their homes and there were already millions with sets in their cars. It has been estimated that as many as forty million listeners tuned in at weekends to follow the progress of the racehorse *Seabiscuit* at the height of a remarkable career.

Athletics also gained followers from the broadcasting of major meetings. Ted Husing, a renowned baseball commentator, recalled how Ralph Metcalfe, the great sprinter, responded to the attention of the medium. 'Let him know that a meet was being broadcast, that the whole nation was vicariously his audience, and he became capable of miracles.'[1]

By 1930, three major radio networks and many local stations were broadcasting a football game every weekend, dominating the airwaves on Saturday afternoons. The National Football League (NFL) was created in 1922 and during the next twenty years college football, helped by radio coverage, became a major spectator sport.

But *the* American radio sport was baseball. With one significant exception baseball bought together all sectors of American society, offering a shared experience for immigrants from diverse backgrounds. As early as 1924 the Chicago station WMAQ was carrying every home game of the White Sox. William Wrigley, the owner of their local rivals, the Cubs, wanted radio coverage: 'The more outlets the better – that way we'll tie up the entire city.'[2]

An essential feature of baseball was the attachment of commentators to specific teams, thereby providing for fans the voice of their club. Tom Manning spoke for the Cleveland Indians, Ty Tyson for the Detroit Tigers, Fred Hoey for the Boston Red Sox. Some owners even scouted for new commentators who they felt had the voice and personality to match the club's image and to project it for supporters. Across America listeners in unexpected places turned the dial and formed a loyalty with a club in a distant city, a loyalty that sometimes lasted a lifetime. The great baseball broadcasters, including Graham McNamee, Red Barber and Ted Husing, used gaps between the play to entertain their listeners with baseball talk, as others did later with cricket.

When technical limitations, or a ban, restricted live coverage, commentators recreated the games in the studio from telegraphic messages passed to them minute by minute. Among those expert at this technique were future president Ronald Reagan and 'Bull' O'Connor, who later became notorious as the police chief who set dogs on civil rights demonstrators in Alabama. So popular were these 'synthetic' broadcasts that people would gather outside studios or offices where the broadcasters were sitting with their array of sound effects to catch a glimpse of them at work.

By the middle 1930s, at a time when BBC live coverage of sport was almost at a standstill, the great American sportscasters were significant figures in the life of the nation. They exploited the opportunities presented by the new medium and became legendary figures with a huge following. When commentators moved clubs, some fans went with them.

IN OTHER COUNTRIES, TOO, radio established itself partly through live coverage of sport. This was often achieved by commentary on one particular sport, the sport that was developing as a national favourite.

Successful coverage often came to be associated with the voices of one or two broadcasters.

In France, the nation's greatest sporting event, the Tour de France, moved at speed around the country, sometimes through mountains and deep valleys. This great cycle race was the ultimate commentary challenge for early radio. The innovator, Jean Antoine, was a journalist who persuaded his paper to help him bring the story of the race to the radio station TSF.

In 1929 Antoine accompanied the race in a van carrying a short-wave transmitter which he tried in vain to link to the studio in Paris. As radio technology improved the transmissions became more successful and by 1931 almost one hundred were made in the course of the Tour. Then, in 1932, a purpose-built broadcasting van, which carried a recording facility and was capable of negotiating the relevant parts of the Alps and Pyrenees, came into use. From 1935 the radio-reporter rode pillion on a motorcycle, following the cyclists along the route and stopping from time to time to give the recordings of his reports to the broadcasting car which linked up to the radio station by telephone. The broadcasts won the TSF station its largest audiences, bringing the drama of each day's race into homes and workplaces.

Both sport and radio were important to the regime in Italy in the 1920s and 1930s. Sport was an important part of the school curriculum. The country was still a relatively young nation and Mussolini saw radio as a means of helping to create a sense of national identity. The sets were too expensive for many Italians at that time but Mussolini tried to ensure that there was one in every village. One of the responsibilities of radio commentaries was that of teaching the nation 'good Italian'. No dialects or accents were allowed.

The Italian commentator who became known as 'the first voice of football' was Nicolò Carosio. His broadcasting career began in 1933 and continued until 1970. Carosio brought hundreds of games, not least his country's World Cup wins of 1934 and 1938, to generations of Italian football lovers. He was 'the soundtrack of the idyllic years', said one writer:

> His voice would stir our imagination and create landscapes and games in a way that television has destroyed like snow in the sun… Everybody always said that he weaved in the commentary independently from what happened on the ground, so there were two matches going on, the real one and the one he described.[3]

Carosio was honoured in 2007, the centenary of his birth, by the issue of a postage stamp which pictured him in his favoured hat, alongside an old-style microphone and a stylised football pitch.

Soon after the state broadcasting organisation of Norway, NRK, was established in 1933 it began to seek ways of broadcasting the country's main winter sports. Its coverage of the winter Olympic Games in 1936 drew large audiences and two commentators – Finn Amundsen and Peder Christian Andersen – established themselves as national favourites.

Arne Porsum, former head of NRK Sport, recalled that period:

> For the people of Norway radio was a strange thing in the thirties. Many of them could not afford to buy a radio. During transmissions from big events like world speedskating championships and Olympic Games people travelled long distances to find good friends – who had a set – rather like people gather round a widescreen television today.[4]

When the winter Olympics of 1952 were held in Norway, NRK invested considerable resources in new equipment, there was very extensive coverage and the commentators became nationally known figures. Later radio developed its coverage still further in response to the growth of television, for instance by stationing reporters out on the cross-country slopes to give eye-witness accounts. Knut Bjørnsen, who worked in radio for a few years before becoming a senior commentator on Norwegian TV, said that radio remains uniquely placed to give live coverage of winter sports. 'It's not possible to get the best out of TV sport without listening to the radio simultaneously.'[5]

The man who described Norway's famous football victory over England in 1981 was Bjørge Lillelien, a commentator who, in the modern idiom, saw himself as much as an entertainer as a journalist. In his book about sports commentary on NRK, Arve Fuglum describes the scenes before the match on that memorable evening, and how, in a reversal of their usual roles, it was the commentator who gave the monarch an audience:

> Bjørge Lillelien never takes a taxi to the stadium; he travels there with everyone else, on the tube. The atmosphere, the people and the smells are to be sucked in, and saved. Up in the commentator's booth King Olav wants to come by and have a little pre-match chat. Mr Lillelien accepts; he

finds it difficult to say no to the monarch. He is anxious. King Olav takes the hint and leaves the booth after just a few minutes, wishing him good luck on the way out.[6]

The final moments of Lillelien's broadcast, from just before the blowing of the final whistle, have become among the best-known in the history of radio commentary:

> *Long English ball outwards, England attacks from the right! The referee adds more and more time! This is going towards British citizenship for him! There he whistles! Norway has beaten England 2-1 in football! We're the best in the world! We're the best in the world! We've beaten England 2-1 in football! It's absolutely incredible! We've beaten England! England! Birthplace of giants! Lord Nelson! Lord Beaverbrook! Sir Winston Churchill! Sir Anthony Eden! Clement Attlee! Henry Cooper! Lady Diana! We've beaten them all! We've beaten them all together! Maggie Thatcher, can you hear me? Maggie Thatcher, I have a message for you in the middle of your election campaign, I have a message for you: We have knocked England out of the World Championship in football! Maggie Thatcher, as they say in your language, in the boxing bars around Madison Square Garden in New York, 'Your boys took a hell of a beating! Your boys took a hell of a beating!'. Maggie Thatcher, Norway has beaten England in football, we're World Champions! It's Norway 2 England 1, what a fabulous night for football ...*

In Georgia, too, a football commentator once celebrated the success of his favourite team on air, but in this case he was detained by the police for so doing. Kote Makharadze had covered, from Düsseldorf, the success of Dinamo Tbilisi in the UEFA cup-winners' cup for radio stations across the Soviet Union, including those in his home state of Georgia.[7]

Makharadze was himself a Georgian, Dinamo Tbilisi was his home team and he could not refrain from an expression of provincial patriotism:

> *This is a great victory for the Georgian players, they will get the Cup they deserve. I can imagine what is happening in Tbilisi – and the whole country will be celebrating.*

But at Moscow airport, on the way back to Tbilisi, Makharadze was taken aside by the KGB and kept in custody for three days. His widow, Sopiko Chiaureli, remembered vividly her anxiety:

I went to the airport to welcome him back, but he wasn't there. No-one could tell me what had happened. Immediately I called all the family, thinking maybe he had come another way, but there was no news. We couldn't understand what was going on because we knew he hadn't planned to stay in Moscow. Finally, on the third day, he phoned. He said 'I can't say much, I'll explain when I get back.' When he did get home he told me the whole story. He explained that the Soviet authorities had been infuriated because he'd celebrated the team's success as a victory for Georgia. 'Why did you mention Tbilisi and not other cities?' they asked him. 'Why didn't you talk about the victory of the Soviet players?'[8]

For forty years Makharadze covered a wide range of sports, but was best-known, not just in Georgia but across the Soviet Union, as a football commentator. A warm and congenial man, Kote spoke expressively, using his hands, addressing his listener directly. His voice was deep and rounded, a little gravelly, but musical to the ear. He was a fluent speaker of Russian and Georgian, and broadcast in both languages – an educated man whose commentaries contained many references to events and ideas outside football.

Other commentators admired Kote Makharadze for his intuitive feeling for the way a game of football unfolded; his very fair, exact assessments. One listener recalled the pleasure of hearing commentaries by Makharadze and his special association with a period of success in Georgian football:

> I remember many times when we used to go to the country and listen to commentary together. Many of the families had small radios but we would gather round a loudspeaker in the centre of the village, so we could share the game together. This was especially in the 1960s and '70s when the Georgian team was improving. Even if you woke me in the middle of the night I could tell you immediately that it was Kote speaking. You absolutely did not need to be present at the game, his descriptions were so exact. Besides the accuracy he had a great sense of humour, a laconic style. He was incomparable – one among millions. He had a special flair, a gift for narration, you felt he was speaking to you individually. Kote was there at the right time. Such people are born when they are needed.[9]

Kote Makharadze's careers in commentary and in theatre ran in parallel. He played more than two hundred roles including major parts in Shakespearian plays. He also acted in films, wrote for the stage and directed plays. He delivered more than two thousand commentaries. It is difficult to find parallels except perhaps to imagine Laurence Olivier narrating Premier League matches on a regular basis.

Makharadze believed that although commentators could improve with practice, some aspects of the art could not be taught, and that his commentaries enabled him to give people great pleasure:

> Perhaps I have something which commentary requires, something that cannot be taught. If you have a talent, you have it, and that is it. There is an intonation there, a force which you use to touch anyone. I sometimes think that none of my parts in the cinema or the theatre have brought as much joy to the people as my commentary during that one game in 1981.[10]

On Makharadze's death in 2002, the then President of Georgia, Eduard Shevardnadze, led the tributes. Such was his reputation that he was buried in the Didube Pantheon in Tbilisi, alongside others who had made their name in science or culture and contributed to Georgian history.

Also in Eastern Europe, György Szepesi became the voice of a sport, and even a nation, during crucial passages in his country's history. Szepesi was born in Budapest in 1922 and grew up in a city where on every piece of waste land, and in every school playground, 'hundreds of children chased after a football from the afternoon to the evening.'[11]

He was only eight when football and radio came together and the commentary seed was planted:

> It all started with the purchase of a Philips radio. My father was a passionate radio listener and in 1930, with the European Championship final between Hungary and Italy coming up, he decided he would buy a large apparatus. The date was May 11th 1930 and it was a sunny and wonderful day. The match was played in the Ferencváros stadium and the Hungarian team unfortunately lost 5-0. István Pluhár, who was the pioneer of Hungarian sports radio, provided the commentary and it was at that moment, at the age of eight, that I decided that when I grew up I

would follow this path and that I also would like to stand before the microphone.

Radio was an important part of life in pre-war Hungary, especially for sports-lovers. György Szepesi's ambitions were nurtured by listening to commentary on the Hungarians' football team's victory over England in 1934 and their success in the 1938 World Cup in France where they reached the final. Szepesi recalled how restaurateurs exploited the situation. 'They set up radio sets in their gardens and charged extra money. By collecting ten or twenty fillér for each diner they could cover the monthly subscription charge and were able to buy quite expensive sets.'

Although Jewish, Szepesi somehow survived the war years in Hungary. In April 1945, at the age of twenty-three, and shortly after German forces had been driven out of Hungary, he was called to a ruined building in the battered main street of Budapest, Rákóczi út. There he made the test broadcast that was to start him on his cherished career. A few weeks later, he was asked to cover a football international between Hungary and Austria, only the third international match played in Europe after the war. Szepesi recalled the circumstances of life in Budapest at that time, and the fact that he was not alone in making an international 'debut' that evening:

> We got hardly any money for the commentary, instead we received some oil and beans. To get to the ground I used the trams, which cost twenty peng in each direction, and my fee for the broadcast was thirty peng, so the fee was not even enough to cover my return journey. These were the times of huge inflation in Hungary and the value of money went down and down daily, so that the fixed rates for commentary could not keep up with it.
> But the essence for me was that Hungary played Austria again after an eight-year gap. And in this game an eighteen-year-old was making his debut for the Hungarian team. His name was Ferenc Puskás and in the twelfth minute he scored the first goal.

Szepesi soon became established as the main football commentator on Hungarian radio. In 1953, Szepesi was so confident that the Hungarian team would beat England at Wembley that he persuaded the broadcasting authorities to schedule his commentary twice, once for those who could listen live in the afternoon and again in the evening. Despite this, the broadcast led to a rush by workers in factories to change their shifts so they could be at home to hear the commentary live. In mines, workers at the surface pinned the latest score onto the cages which went up and down to service workers at the coal-face. Szepesi recalled that special measures were taken by radio in Bulgaria, where there was also great interest:

> The Bulgarians did not have any money for a broadcast, but felt that they could not miss out on the match and the Bulgarian radio took the Hungarian commentary live. A man called Ede Kardos sat in a studio in Sofia and minute by minute translated what I said for the Bulgarian audience. I received several hundred telegrams from Bulgarian listeners thanking me for the broadcast.

Szepesi established his reputation in part because of the vital importance of radio in Hungary during the early part of his career. There was no television in the country until 1954 and it was some years after that date before ownership spread. Radio was a powerful instrument of propaganda and the prime means of communication. In 1949 the trial and 'confession' of László Rajk, the Interior Minister, mounted to assert the control of the Soviet Union over Hungary, were broadcast live. And in 1956 it was on Hungarian radio that Imre Nagy broadcast his appeals to the international community for help against the Russian forces.

Tibor Gold, who grew up in Budapest after the war, remembered the importance of radio, and of Szepesi, in those years:

> There was an all-pervasive control of our lives and radio was one of the few means of escape from this. My parents had it on almost all the time. Apart from propaganda, it brought us two things – classical music and sport. György Szepesi was my hero, he was like a god to me. During the 1952 Olympics, when the Hungarian team did so well, I listened to almost all his commentaries. He had that rare gift of conveying the sense of excitement, and anticipation, of sporting events, the sense that something was about to happen. That was so important, bringing a little colour and drama into a world where everything else was uniformly grey, drab and dangerous.[12]

For fifty years, through the years of Communist rule in Hungary and beyond, Szepesi covered every football World Cup and every Olympic Games – possibly an unparalleled record in commentary. He became a senior figure in FIFA and in the Olympic movement, while retaining a role as a commentator.

Szepesi covered many of the great matches that Ferenc Puskás played for Hungary. But Puskás left his homeland shortly after the failed uprising of 1956. In 1981 it was György Szepesi who helped to make the arrangements whereby Puskás was able to return to Hungary for the first time since 1958. And in 2007, more than sixty years after his first broadcast, and more than seventy-five years after he was first inspired by a radio commentary, Szepesi was still chairing a weekly sports programme on Hungarian radio.

In the Republic of Ireland the beginnings of radio coincided with the struggle for independence and the establishment of the Irish Free State. Radio provided an obvious vehicle for those looking for ways to affirm a particular sense of Irishness. The inaugural speech on the Irish radio station, 2RN, in January 1926 was given by Douglas Hyde, a university professor (and Protestant) who had once spoken of the need to 'de-anglicize the Irish People'.

'Eire is standing on her own two feet,' he proclaimed in his address. 'The Irish language being one and her culture, music and Irish sport being the other.'[13]

2RN quickly began to use sport as a means of identifying the new nation with traditional games.[14] The first commentary, on a hurling match at Croke Park, was broadcast in August 1926, some months before the first commentary in Britain. The commentator was PD Mehigan, an experienced and popular journalist, with a good knowledge of sport but no experience at all of broadcasting. Years later he recalled how he reported for duty at the old Croke Park stadium in Dublin and was ushered into a seat near the press box:

> A leather contraption was put around my neck with a yellow brass tube in front into which I was told to speak. It was all new to me. I had no voice test whatsoever. I had just the teams on a slip of paper in my hand.[15]

The broadcast was a success and within a few weeks Mehigan was covering the All Ireland Football Final, and its subsequent replay. These broadcasts caused the *Irish Radio Journal* to predict that commentaries would become 'one of the prime attractions of a wireless service.' A veteran of Irish broadcasting, Seán Óg, has recorded a story from those days:

I'm reliably informed that for the replay of the 1926 All-Ireland football final between Kerry and Kildare, upwards of a thousand people assembled outside Benner's Hotel in Tralee's main street to hear the broadcast of the game. At half-time and with things looking blue for Kerry, every man, woman and child in the crowd marched into St John's Church nearby and said the rosary for a good result.[16]

Kerry won.

PD Mehigan continued as a favourite for several years, until his career came to a sudden end. One version is that he had to be removed from the microphone mid-commentary, having had too much to drink before the game. Another is that he forgot to come back for the second half of the match.

In those early years wireless was a luxury in Ireland and people gathered at friends' houses to hear the big commentaries. Sometimes there was standing room only, and some people would stand outside in the yard and listen through the open windows. Others would crowd into the bars and kitchens of pubs to hear the main matches. The popularity of commentaries was such that they also provided an obvious opening for propaganda.

During a dispute between the Irish government and the republican movement in 1933, commentary on the All-Ireland football final was interrupted when a group of men burst into the commentary box. The commentator, Eamon de Barra, was told at the point of a gun to stop speaking and his visitors then broadcast an appeal to listeners to support those on hunger strike in Mountjoy Jail. When they left the box, commentary continued.

A major player in the development of radio commentary in Ireland was the Gaelic Athletic Association (GAA). The GAA was established in 1884 as 'an organization for the preservation of Irish games and pastimes'.

Many Irish politicians had been GAA members and played Gaelic games and the broadcasting of them was an obvious way of highlighting Irish distinctiveness. GAA activists saw other games, for instance cricket, football and rugby, as symbols of English power, disapproved of commentary on them and for many years banned fellow members from playing them. On a number of occasions in the 1930s, the Association banned commentaries on big games because Radio Éireann would not use their preferred commentator. But today GAA is a modern businesslike organization and its new stadium at Croke Park is one of the finest in Europe. Memorably, it hosted a rugby match between Ireland and England in 2007.

If Gaelic games were seen by some as part of the nation-building project in Ireland, so was the protection and spread of the Irish language. The occasions when most people have heard the language spoken in commentary were probably when a commentator broke into Irish during a Sunday afternoon commentaries in English on the main RTE station.

That man is Micheál Ó Muircheartaigh. Ó Muircheartaigh grew up in a village in County Kerry where there was no radio – the nearest was in a house a mile away. During a career that lasted more than fifty years, for much of which he had a full-time job as a teacher, he has become a much-loved figure. Many see him as the best hurling commentator the country has had, but he has covered many sports. He is authoritative but never pompous, investing all his commentaries with irreverent humour. Here he describes the Sligo team conceding a goal:

> *I saw a few Sligo people at Mass in Gardiner Street this morning and the omens seemed to be good for them. The priest was wearing the same colours as the Sligo jersey … forty yards out on the Hogan stand side of the field Ciaran Whelan goes on a rampage … it's a goal … (Pause) … So much for religion.*[17]

Michael O'Hehir, like Ó Muircheartaigh, had a lifetime's commitment to the work of the GAA. O'Hehir soon became a popular figure after he started in 1938 and continued as a national favourite until he suffered a stroke in 1985. He covered nearly one hundred All-Ireland finals but is perhaps best-known for his commentary on the one played in New York in 1947. In Britain O'Hehir became a member of the BBC's Grand National team taking the horses in his characteristic high-pitched voice from Beecher's Brook to the Canal Turn.

THREE COUNTRIES OUTSIDE EUROPE, Brazil, India and New Zealand, provide further examples of the conjunction of sport, radio and the way people feel about their country. The story of commentary in these countries is explored in greater detail in the chapters which follow. The stories have elements in common, but the cultural encounter between sport, radio and ideas of nationality is different in each, reflecting different histories.

Radio, said one historian, gave some people in Latin America their 'first chance of being a nation'.[18] Brazilian football is a world brand and so, some might say, is Brazilian radio commentary, which has often been as exuberant and inventive as the players themselves. Brazilian commentary is surely the most distinctive in the world, offering listeners a passionate and magical excursion onto the field of play. It played a major part in helping spread football in Brazil and capture the spirit with which it was played. As a result people throughout Brazil came to see in their national team an expression of themselves and their country in which they could take pride.

'An Indian game accidentally invented by the English.' Thus did the Indian sociologist Ashis Nandy attempt to capture the paradox of cricket's popularity in India.[19] The arrival of radio in what is now India, Pakistan and Bangladesh, coincided with the first home test match against England in 1933. At this stage the game was already establishing itself among the middle-class in urban areas – it was the 'vehicle of choice for several forms of Indian striving' said Indian journalist and author Mukul Kesavan.[20]

Despite cricket's imperial connections, radio commentary helped spread its popularity. But it was the development of commentary in Hindi and other vernacular languages which was most influential in spreading interest in the sport and helping it become in the eyes of many 'the national game'.

When the first radio stations opened in New Zealand in the 1920s they turned quickly to sport. The effect, said Patrick Day, the historian of New Zealand broadcasting, was 'to unite the population ... and to affirm a particular understanding of New Zealand as a nation'.[21]

This was when the country was beginning the process of establishing an identity separate from that of Great Britain. Radio commentaries, many of them during the night, on the great encounters with the British and South African rugby teams won large audiences and helped to confirm rugby as a national obsession. New Zealand's most famous commentator, Winston McCarthy, outshone his BBC colleagues in his passion at the microphone. But New Zealand rugby's cosy relations with apartheid polarised opinion in the country and presented a considerable challenge to commentators.

Radio (and TV) commentary in the USA has been the subject of several studies. The information in this chapter draws chiefly on: Curt Smith *Voices of the Game* (Simon & Schuster 1992); David Halberstam *Sports on New York Radio* (Master Press 1999). Michael Oriard *King Football*

(University of N Carolina Press 2001); Ronald L Smith *Play by Play* (Johns Hopkins 2001).

The Tour de France material draws on Cécile Méadel *Histoire de la Radio des Années Trent* (Paris 1994) and Christian Brochand *Histoire Générale de la radio et de la télévision en France* (Paris 1994).

Information about Kote Makharadze draws in part on Georgian newspaper reports at the time of his death.

The material on Ireland draws chiefly on: Seán Óg o Ceallacháin *Seán Óg His Own Story* (Calmac Publishing 1988); Micheál Ó Muircheartaigh *From Dún Síon to Croke Park* (Penguin 2004); M Gorham *Forty Years of Irish Broadcasting* (Talbot Press 1967); Richard Pine *2RN and the origins of Irish Radio* (Four Courts Press 2002); M Cronin *Sport and Nationalism in Ireland* (Four Courts Press 1999); Ed. N Garnham and K Jeffery *Culture, Place and Identity* (University College of Dublin Press 2005).

1	Ted Husing *Ten Years before the Mike* (Farrar and Reinhart 1935) p210
2	*Voices of the Game* p14
3	Franco Gabici *www.simonel.com/bollicine/gabici111.html*
4	Email to the author
5	Email to the author
6	Arve Fuglum was for many years head football commentator for NRK. His book is entitled *Magiske øyeblikk* (Magic moments) (NW Damm and Søn 2003)
7	Tbilisi, the capital city of Georgia, was at this point in the Soviet Union. Dinamo Tbilisi was for a period one of the most successful football teams in the Soviet Union and won the European Cup-winners Cup in 1981. Georgia gained independence in 1991
8–9	Interview with the author
10	Interview with Marina Vashakmadze (*www.magtigsm.com*) 1999)
11	Interview with György Szepesi (Budapest October 2005) conducted by Robert Sikos, translated by Tibor Gold
12	Interview with the author
13	Richard Pine *2RN and the origins of Irish Radio* (Four Courts Press 2002) p146 and 187-188
14	2RN later became Radio Éireann and then Radio Telefis Éireann (RTE). The Irish Free State became Ireland in 1937 and subsequently the Republic of Ireland. Hyde became the inaugural president of Ireland in 1938
15	PD Mehigan *Vintage Carbery* (Beavor Row Press 1984) p 31
16	Seán Óg took over the reading of GAA results on Sunday night radio in 1953. His predecessor had been his father, Sean Seán, who had undertaken the role since 1930. Seán Óg was still reading the results in 2007, making a total of 77 years, father and son
17	James McAllister, posting on Guardian Unlimited
18	J Martin-Barbero *Communication, Culture and Hegemony* (Sage 1993) p164
19	Ashis Nandy *The Tao of Cricket* (Viking 1989) p1
20	Mukul Kesavan *Men in White* (Penguin Viking 2007) p21
21	Patrick Day *The Radio Years* (Auckland University Press 1994) p54

TWELVE

GOOOOOO – OOOOOAL!

A STORY IS TOLD of people in Rio de Janeiro attending a play which coincided with an important football match in the city. They were anxious to keep in touch with the game and they brought small transistor radios and earpieces to the theatre. Then, when a goal was scored, they stirred so audibly that the male lead in the play stopped, looked out to the audience and asked 'What's the score?' Some of the listeners quickly gave the news. Satisfied, the actor resumed his role.[1]

Radio commentary came to Brazil in 1930. At that time the country's population was some thirty millions, the large majority living in rural areas.[2] São Paulo, ahead of any other South American city, had begun the process of industrialisation and was expanding quickly. During the previous decades the city had gained thousands of newcomers both from abroad (many of them from Italy), and from Brazil's rural hinterland, all coming to seek work. There was no public radio service initially but by 1930 a number of private broadcasting stations had established themselves. Football was about to move onto a professional footing. And in 1930, too, a new political regime, led by Getúlio Vargas and with ambitions to modernise the country, was seeking ways of establishing itself and giving the country a new sense of identity.

IN 1930 A YOUNG LAWYER won a competition to work at Rádio Educadora, a São Paulo broadcasting station. Nicolau Tuma was only nineteen, attending law school and supplementing his income as a journalist, mostly covering crime stories. Tuma was a great talker, fast and inventive, and it was friends, who admired his voice and his ability to improvise, who suggested he would make a good broadcaster. His father, a pioneer in radio advertising, may also have helped Tuma understand something about reaching an audience.

Rádio Educadora had been established in 1923. Two years later it began broadcasting football results, making use of loudspeakers set up in places frequented by the public. In 1931, a few months after he began working there, Tuma persuaded his managers that he should try a football commentary. The date was July 19th, and the match, between the home city and Parana, was for the Brazilian championship.

At that time players wore no numbers on their shirts and Tuma went to the dressing rooms before the game to meet both teams and familiarise himself with their physical characteristics. He used a simple technique for helping listeners envisage the pitch:

> Put a matchbox in front of you. Divide it in half, on your left there are São Paulo's players, on the right Parana's players.[3]

There was much to describe, the game ending 6-4 to Parana. Tuma was on his own and had to talk continuously for the whole game, relieved only by the commercial breaks taken by the sponsor. There were probably only a few hundred listeners scattered across the city but Tuma's fast-talking style made an immediate impact and soon there were requests that he describe more games. 'You really talk like a machine gun', someone said to him. The label stuck and Tuma was widely known in years to come as the machine-gun speaker. He always insisted that his speed derived from a desire to keep listeners fully informed. The priority was to be objective, 'describing the game thoroughly and without missing a single event':

> The commentator is nothing more than a photographer of what is going in, one who takes pictures with his voice and communicates exactly what is going on.

It was appropriate that the first football commentary in Brazil should have been in São Paulo, the city where the game itself first entered the country. It was there in 1894 that a young Englishman, Charles Miller, returned from studies in Southampton with two footballs in his luggage and began games with his fellow expatriates. The game was quickly adopted by all social groups. It could be played easily by the poor and rich alike; its very nature enabled it to be shared easily across social divides. By 1902 the city had its own football league. By 1910 it was the most popular game in Brazil and in 1919 the country won the South American championship. In 1930 Brazil reached the final stages of the first World Cup in Uruguay only to be eliminated in the opening round.

Tuma more than anyone laid the first foundations for commentary in Brazil, especially in São Paulo. Reception was not always good, and it was easily distorted during bad weather, but Tuma helped to create a good network of commentary facilities – broadcasting cabins in the major grounds, and telephone points in minor grounds for journalists to phone in with match reports. There were, as elsewhere, enthusiasts who loved to assemble the valve radios of the day and show them off to friends. But radios were beyond the means of most people and the majority could only listen to commentary on sets set up in roadside cafes and public places, where people would gather in large numbers to cheer on their teams. These were often emotional occasions and when a match between teams from Rio and São Paulo, with commentary from Rio, was broadcast over speakers in São Paulo, local supporters were so incensed at what they believed was the commentator's bias that they smashed the speakers in a number of locations.

Tuma began to diversify to other sports, including motor racing. His broadcasts caused a sensation as he and his colleagues captured the races from points around the course. But commentary on the Brazilian Grand Prix in 1936 came to a premature end. A crash between two cars in third and fourth place, in which spectators were caught up, led to some grisly scenes. Tuma kept to his habit of 'taking pictures with his voice': "There are limbs to one side, legs everywhere, blood squirting from the dead and injured.' Listeners who had friends or relatives at the race track became horrified and the station eventually went off the air to bring Tuma's description to a close.

By 1933, Tuma was working for Rádio Record, an innovative station which offered analysis of the match as an alternative to music during the half-time break in a match, using a second commentator or summariser to discuss the game. But, in Brazil, as elsewhere, there were disputes between radio companies and football clubs over the impact that commentary had on attendances at games. In 1933 newspapers began to carry reports to the effect that people would rather listen to the matches than go to the stadium. Soon afterwards Rádio Record was barred from commentary.

There were probably authentic concerns about the impact on gate receipts but it seems that a rival station, Rádio Cruzeiro, had made an exclusive deal with clubs. Like commentators in other countries facing a similar situation, Tuma and his colleagues were determined to evade the ban. Good quality binoculars became a necessity. The commentators followed at least one match on a long ladder erected outside the ground and described the game so effectively that most of their listeners thought they were watching from inside. Another practice was to rent a property adjacent to the stadium and use the roof as a makeshift broadcasting studio.

In addition to his pioneering work in radio, Nicolau Tuma was the first of a number of Brazilian commentators to be involved in public affairs. In 1932 he was one of three announcers who read news reports on Rádio Record when student demonstrators took control of the station in protest against the actions of the Vargas government. In later years he moved to Rio and was active in support of democratic movements. He coined a word that was to become part of the language for someone on low pay who combined work in radio with an element of idealism: *radialista*. Tuma continued as a commentator until 1942 and then became a director at Rádio Difusa. From 1947 to 1954 he was a member of parliament and was active in the drafting of reforming legislation. He died in 1998.

———————————————

RADIO COVERAGE OF FOOTBALL in Rio de Janeiro had begun to develop in 1933 primarily through the voices of Renato Mumi and Amador Santos. Mumi is reported to have been very calm, 'like an opera narrator' one writer put it. Santos, too, recalled the veteran commentator Luiz Mendes, had a quieter style than his São Paulo counterpart Tuma:

> Santos had no emotion, no feeling. He spoke very slowly. Amador created a kind of card in which the field was divided into small squares with numbers on them. So he said for example 'Player X has the ball in the twenty-fourth square', and the listener needed to have this card. He even mailed this card to listeners who requested it. This enabled him to get an idea of how many listeners he had. If he sent out five thousand, for example, he knew he had at least five thousand listeners.[4]
>
> Santos was merely descriptive. 'Player X had the ball in square thirty-three, crossed it to a player in thirty-five.' In São Paulo things worked in a different way. Tuma had the 'speaker' or machine-gun style. This is called the Paulista style and there are some commentators who still use it today. All the Paulista commentators studied in Nicolau Tuma's 'school'. Nearly all commentators from São Paulo are 'machine guns' in contrast to commentators from Rio who have a more descriptive style.

As technology improved, Rio and São Paulo stations could be heard more widely across the country and by the mid-1930s the number of radio receivers in Rio alone had reached fifty thousand. In 1932 the government formally allowed advertising on radio, opening the door to greater profitability and leading to greater US investment in radio. Important media groups, such as the O Globo chain, were established, involving both newspapers and radio, and they all gave football greater prominence.

During the 1930s, radio became an increasingly important part of daily life. Latin America generally was a fertile soil for radio, in part because of its strong oral tradition. One source puts the number of radio receivers in Brazil at 357,000 in 1939; another says that by 1940 there were one million, this in a population of approximately forty million.[5] The majority were in private homes but a significant proportion was in cafes and eating places where people could cluster. These were important not just in towns and cities but – in what was still overwhelmingly an agrarian society – in villages across the country.

Radio connections from Europe were not good enough to allow commentary to Brazil from the 1934 World Cup finals in Italy. But in 1936 a young broadcaster, Gagliano Neto, born in Recife but working in São Paulo, went to Buenos Aires for the South American championships. There he commentated direct to Brazil on his country's victory over Peru. As an experiment Neto took with him an assistant, Ary Lund, to analyse the match at half-time.

But it was the 1938 World Cup in France that formed a decisive moment for radio commentary in Brazil. For the first time a commentator, Neto, travelled outside South America with the team, sending back live broadcasts from Europe. Those who had by then invested in radio, or who gathered in the public squares in São Paulo and Rio de Janeiro where loudspeakers were set up, were rewarded with dramatic and controversial games.

A cluster of broadcasting stations, helped by sponsorship from a casino, formed a consortium to send Neto to France with the Brazilian team. Neto, still only twenty-seven, was now based in Rio. Radio manufacturers such as Philco launched special promotions to exploit the coverage and the broadcasting stations who were already promoting their commentaries of other sports such as motor racing now competed fiercely for listeners to the broadcasts from France.

This World Cup, the third, was taking place against the background of an ominous political situation in Europe. Argentina and Uruguay, who refused to take part in protest at FIFA's refusal to run the tournament in South America, were both absent. The English Football Association again declined to take part. But in Brazil the tournament was important and the country's mixed-race team of footballers carried the hopes of millions.

With the help of a telephone cable from Europe to South America, Neto gave live commentary on all Brazil's games. And it was these radio commentaries which first put a footballer's name on the lips of millions of Brazilians. He was Leônidas da Silva: born Rio 1913, first played for his country 1932, and Brazil's only goalscorer in the 1934 World Cup. Nineteen thirty-eight was the year that changed his life.

To cover Brazil's first match against Poland on June 5th, Neto travelled with the team to Strasbourg. This was still before the era of numbers on shirts and Neto had to familiarise himself rapidly with the opposition players, none of whom he had seen before. Brazil began the competition with a victory which even today stands among the tournament's most legendary matches. On a rainy Sunday afternoon, Neto had a busy first forty-five minutes: Brazil were 3-1 up at half-time. In middle-class homes of Rio and São Paulo, and in cafes and public spaces across Brazil, people – some of whom had never met before – embraced with elation.

The line from France was a little indistinct at times, but Neto had a measured, authoritative voice, which everyone could follow. If this was World Cup commentary, they wanted more. In the second half Brazil did indeed score again. But they conceded three goals: it was 4-4 at full time.

It was early afternoon in Brazil. Neto, commentating alone, should have been exhausted but the sheer drama of the occasion carried him on for another half an hour. The Poles, surprisingly, were more exhausted by the muddy pitch than the Brazilians and after extra time the game finished Brazil 6 Poland 5. Leônidas scored three of the goals – including the two crucial ones in extra time, one of them it seems in bare feet.

Could radio have wished for more? The first commentary in São Paulo in 1931 had finished 6-4; this, the first from Europe, had improved even on that. The Vargas government had taken new powers the previous year and was using radio to maintain its position. The upsurge of interest in a national team suited a regime which had been promoting the notion of unity between the races. Following the victory in Strasbourg, ministers in Brazil ordered extra loudspeakers to be put up in public squares.

Neto now moved on with the Brazilian team to Toulouse, where the opponents were Czechoslovakia. In Rio and São Paulo some shops and banks closed early while some of the bigger stores invited in their favoured customers to hear the broadcast. 'Where can I listen?' people asked each other and called friends to arrange which bar and restaurant to meet. 'Come to the shop – we have powerful speakers – listen to the Czech defeat' ran one poster. Crowds gathered in such places as the Parco Antonio Prado and the Parco de Patriarcha in São Paulo and in the Cruzerio art gallery in the capital, where large speakers had been set up to relay the broadcasts.

This time international football reverted to a familiar stalemate – the 1-1 draw – but there were many conflicts on the pitch and three players were sent off. The rules required a replay two days later and this produced a 2-1 victory for Brazil. By now Leônidas had scored two more goals. Neto described vividly to his audience at home the 'bicycle' kicks which Leônidas executed with such confidence and aplomb. French newspapers, he told listeners, were calling him 'the black diamond'.

Neto now faced another journey across France. The semi-final against Italy, only two days after the replay with Czechoslovakia, was in Marseilles. But it proved a disappointing afternoon. Leônidas did not play, rested for the final said his coach. Brazil lost 2-1, the victim they felt of a disputed penalty decision. Neto had one more match to cover: the third-place play-off against Sweden. The team gave him a victory to finish his expedition to Europe: 4-2, and two more goals for Leônidas da Silva.

No World Cup final then for Neto to narrate.[6] But he had established a place in the history of commentary and the team returned to Brazil in triumph. In the years that followed the popularity of football and radio grew in tandem, as stations across Brazil gave more time to the game. Thanks in part to the broadcasts of 1938 the hold of soccer on the Brazilian imagination deepened. In Europe word spread of the team's remarkable performances and of the gifts that Leônidas had displayed. All this gave, some would say saddled, Brazil with a reputation for audacious and creative play. Here were the origins of 'the beautiful game'.

And much of this was owed to Leônidas. 'I compare him to Pele', said Luiz Mendes, who had just started in radio work at the time. 'I don't think he had more skills than Pele but he wasn't inferior to Pele. The difference is that Pele had more media attention.' In later life Leônidas had mixed fortunes. He worked briefly as a radio commentator but in the 1970s he developed Alzheimer's disease. He died in 2004.

Gagliano Neto remained in the radio business, founding Rádio Continental in 1948, but finishing his career in São Paulo with a station which covered his favourite sport: horseracing. He died in 1974.

Through its history Brazil had strong connections to Europe. But the broadcasts on the 1938 World Cup opened them up in a new way. Listeners to the games talked for years afterwards of Neto's powerful and deliberate voice. He had described performances which made them – whatever their class or race – proud to be Brazilians, perhaps even briefly to experience what has been called 'an invisible national unity'.[7]

RADIO COMMENTARY DID NOT flourish in Brazil in isolation. The 1930s were an important period not only in the development of football and broadcasting but also of popular music and culture. The arrival of electromagnetic recording in the country in 1932 contributed to the emergence of a new generation of singers and composers, especially in Rio, and in the popularisation of the samba. Like football, samba was absorbing influences from all the elements of Brazil's racial heritage.

Alongside football, the burgeoning array of commercial radio stations embraced radio serials, comedy dramas and popular music. Commentators were part not only of a sporting culture but of a wider expressive lifestyle in which music and speech, often humorous and inventive, were a key part. And if any one individual personified these connections it was a man who combined these worlds, a popular musician and samba composer who also pushed back the boundaries of commentary style: Ary Barroso.

Barroso was born in 1903 and bought up in the small town of Ubá, in the north-east of Brazil. His father – a lawyer by profession but also a poet and singer – died when Ary was only seven, and the young boy was bought up by relatives. An aunt noticed that Ary had a talent for music and made him take piano lessons. By the age of twelve he was playing at the local cinema as an accompanist to silent films and at seventeen he moved on to Rio where he soon began composing and making music. Barroso made his debut on radio as a musician in 1933, just as the medium was expanding its role in popular music. His familiar figure, smiling and bespectacled, often standing in front of his samba band in their 'AB'-embroidered jackets, appeared on sheet music that found its way into thousands of homes. Barroso's best-loved composition, *Aquarela do Brasil*, is sometimes referred to as Brazil's 'second national anthem'.

Barroso began covering football in 1935 and for the next fifteen years or more was one of the most popular figures in football broadcasting. He was the fans' commentator: they loved his willingness to break the rules and his shameless bias towards Flamengo, his adopted team. He once marked a goal by leaving his microphone and rushing to the side of the pitch to celebrate. When Vasco threatened to score against Flamengo he announced, *'I don't want to look.'* Barroso carried a small mouth organ with which he would mark the scoring of a goal. He found the instrument in a little shop near the club's stadium and it became his trade mark: a short lament when Flamengo conceded a goal but emphatic notes of triumph when they scored. Barroso is also credited with inventing the idea of 'field reporters' – commentators at pitchside who could better capture the atmosphere of the game, and perhaps snatch a few words from a player, even a goalscorer, as play unfolded.

Barroso may have chosen Flamengo because it was the most popular team in Rio: 'Ary had an enormous audience because there were an enormous number of people who supported that club. He chose Flamengo and it helped him be recognized as a sports commentator,' said Luiz Mendes. By 1938, when the Brazilian team made its mark in Europe for the first time, Barroso was such a favourite that he was the natural choice to add commentary to films of the team's matches.

Ary Barroso spent a short spell in Hollywood, writing music for movies, and had a term as a city councillor in Rio. He presented a television show in which new singers presented themselves for the approval of the audience: Ary struck a gong whenever they went out of tune. He died in 1964 when only 62.

AFTER THE SECOND WORLD WAR radio commentary in Brazil assumed a new level of popularity, not least during the 1950 World Cup.

Barroso's popularity and that of other commentators in the 1940s had fostered the success of football. In his book on Brazilian football, Alex Bellos stresses the importance of radio in a large country where so many of the population were illiterate: 'Radio not newspapers was the vehicle that turned football into a mass sport.'[8] Political actions were also important. In 1940 the Vargas government took over the

Rio station Rádio Nacional and provided it with the resources to begin nationwide shortwave broadcasts. Radio, according to the media historian Elizabeth Fox, helped integrate the nation and 'imbue it with national identity'.

The station began to reach almost all parts of Brazil, including villages and rural areas far away from the main centres. In these areas listeners could not go to stadiums to see matches but, inspired by the matches they heard on radio, they began to choose teams from the big cities to support. Many of the best-known commentators made their names partly through their partisan coverage of individual teams, acting as the voices of the supporters. Commercial sponsors quickly saw radio's potential and commentators often wove the names of key products into their narrative. Individual stations became associated with the fortunes of different clubs.

Brazil was awarded the 1950 World Cup in 1946 and work began in Rio on a new stadium, popularly known as the Maracanã, and, with a capacity of 180,000, the biggest in the world. The fifteen teams that took part (including England, competing for the first time) were reduced in qualifying matches to four – and these played not semi-finals and a final but a mini-league to decide the overall winner. Radio audiences in Brazil grew steadily during the opening stage of the tournament as the home side beat Mexico and Yugoslavia, and then drew with Switzerland. And in the first two games of the final stage the Brazilian team swept the commentators and listeners along in an orgy of goals: Sweden were beaten 7-1 and Spain 6-1. World Cup victory was almost certain: a draw in the final game against Uruguay would suffice.

So parties assembled in houses across the country to listen to the final match against Uruguay, in the Maracanã. Rádio Nacional put out its strongest team including Jorge Curi and Antônio Cordeiro. Rádio Globo turned to Luiz Mendes. Only twenty-six, Mendes had begun working in Porto Allegre in the early 1940s while still in his teens but he had swiftly begun to establish himself because of his wide knowledge of South American soccer.

Hours before the game, the stadium was full. When Brazil opened the scoring the result of the tournament seemed beyond doubt. Then Uruguay equalised. But, with the game inside its final quarter of an hour, Brazil had only to hold on for victory. Jorge Curi was on the air for Rádio Nacional when the Brazilian centre-half Danilo made a crucial mistake:

My Omega watch with state-of-the-art precision tells me we are now on the 32nd minute … Jair pushes the ball back to Danilo, Danilo loses control of the ball to Julio Perez who delivers it immediately towards Ghiggia …

Luiz Mendes recalled vividly what happened next, and how he was stunned into repeating the news time and time again:

I described the goal with no exaltation: *'Ghiggia has the ball, dribbles past Bigode, he tries to recover the ball but is unsuccessful, Ghiggia dribbles past again, he is going to cross the ball'.* That's what everybody thought he was going to do, just like he did when Uruguay scored the first goal. But he did not cross the ball; he kicked it past the goalkeeper and scored the goal. I said *'Goal! Scored by Uruguay'.* After I said it I realized what had happened, became shocked and asked myself 'Uruguay scored?' I said *'Yes, ladies and gentlemen, Uruguay scored again'.* I said it nine times, with nine intonations. It was as if a bomb exploded inside of me like every Brazilian. The city was in silence. Today I would say this was the most profound silence in history, in which we could hear our own silence.

The sadness that enveloped the stadium was felt in thousands of homes across Rio. So quiet was Rio, someone later added, that even the dogs stayed silent. It was defeat, a humiliation even, from which Brazilian football took time to recover.

But the best days of Brazilian football, and commentary, were ahead. By 1954 such was the distinctive exuberance of Brazilian radio commentary that during the less interesting World Cup matches in Sweden an alternative spectator sport developed: watching the Brazilian commentators at work. Their sheer enjoyment and physical excitement as much as the passion in their voices made them a subject of wonder.

IT WAS REBELO JÚNIOR in the 1940s who first made use of the extended cry when a goal was scored, now the most imitated of all the trademarks of Brazilian commentary. Its advantage to some commentators in the early days was that, since players did not have numbers on their shirts, it gave a few extra seconds to find out exactly who had scored. But it became the motif of a passionate and unbuttoned style. From the days of Ary Barroso commentators developed an inventive language, sometimes enriched by elements of fantasy and magic. They chose not just to describe the football, but to capture at the microphone the elation and despair of fans, and the idioms of daily life.

Brazilians love to tell stories of the mistakes or escapades of their commentators and how they extricated themselves. Of how Pedro Luis, narrating a game between England and Scotland, realised when the teams took the field that he was not sure which side was which and how, midway through the first half, he found he had guessed incorrectly. Discreetly, he switched them round. And of how Anthony Garotinho, narrating a game using information supplied down a phone line, felt the line go dead, but continued with the 'commentary'. And how, when the line was restored at half-time Garotinho, finding that two goals had been scored during the 'silent' period, managed to weave the two goals into play during the second half of the match.

The individuality of voices, the bias, the deployment of catch-phrases and invented language, and sometimes the slang vocabulary of the street, have all been much-loved features of Brazilian commentary. The phrases or sayings which individual commentators adopt, and by which they come to be recognized, are known in Portuguese as *bordões*. They lose impact when translated into English but they fall somewhere between the catchphrase of the entertainer and the more literary illusions of Stuart Hall's match reports on BBC radio. Luiz Mendes introduced many *bordões* already in use in Argentinian radio like *'Pelotasso'* (from the Spanish word *pelota* for ball) to indicate when a goal was scored. Waldir Amaral's favoured *bordão* when a team scored was to say *'Há uns peixes na rede'* – 'There's a fish in the net'. Washington Rodrigues conjured affectionate nicknames for groups of spectators – *'Geraldines'*, for those in the 'geral', the area in the Maracanã stadium where people used to stand to watch, and *'Archibalds'*, for those in the arquibancada terraces.

With his inventive and playful language, Fiori Gigliotti of Rádio Bandeirantes in São Paulo won many listeners in the countryside, those unable to go to stadiums and see the big games. He loved to open proceedings in theatrical terms: *'The referee whistles, the curtains open and the game is rolling ... hold on, hold on, Brazilian supporters, there's too much emotion for your hearts'*. And, when the game ended: *'The curtains are closing and the show is over'*.

Osmar Santos brought a similar humour and metaphor to

commentary. *'The ball is on the avocado's stone'*, he would say as the players lined up at the centre circle to begin the game. The ball he called 'the little chubby one.' And after a goal: *'The little chubby one lies under the net and rolls about quite tastily'*. He brought a range of celebrities including politicians and musicians into the commentary box to join in the fun.

Santos also had a political voice. Between 1964 and 1985 Brazil was ruled by an increasingly repressive military regime, which, in its bid for popular support, exploited the success of the Brazilian football team. Osmar Santos was at the front of a number of rallies in the campaign for direct elections in the early 1980s. He used his status as a commentator to appeal for support and led the crowds in the singing of the Brazilian national anthem. But his commentary career was to be foreshortened when as the result of a serious car accident he almost completely lost the power of speech. But Osmar Santos, ever inventive, has developed a new and successful career as a painter.

Waldir Amaral, who gave his first commentary alongside Gagliano Neto in the 1950s, was responsible for several innovations in the organisation of commentaries. Edson Mauro said Amaral was another who led the way towards a more colloquial style of broadcasting:

> Amaral was the creator of simultaneous transmissions, with two journalists or reporters who observe the game from behind the goal. He brought a new approach, for instance commenting on something that is going on in the world or has happened a little time before, information from daily life. He introduced some adaptation of popular song lyrics, slang words, soap-opera text. Waldir started using the Portuguese of daily life on radio.[9]

Brazilian commentary styles have also been enriched by the influence of Spanish-speaking commentators. Luiz Mendes for example was influenced by broadcasts from neighbouring countries:

> I was in an area where Argentinian, Uruguayan, Paraguayan and Brazilian radio stations were popular. I heard Lalo Perichari from Argentina, Lalo's brother, Tchieto Perichari, from Uruguay, also Carlos Soler from Uruguay and of course Gagliano Neto from Rio, he was the most famous commentator at that time. I also listened to Odovaldo Cosi who worked at Gaucha Rádio before he went to São Paulo. With this I got the hang of what being a sports commentator was. Lalo Perichari in Argentina

had a very interesting way of narrating a goal. When I started working in Porto Alegre I mixed all these styles and after a while I became the most famous commentator in that city.

Some commentators have had spells in football management. Washington Rodrigues had two spells managing Flamengo, and in both periods the club's fortunes improved. He was called in primarily because the club – which has the biggest supporter base in Brazil – felt they needed a respected outsider, who was also a supporter, to see them through a sticky patch in their fortunes.

Rodrigues found that in his new post as a manager he could not maintain quite the same relationship with his former colleagues:

> When I became Flamengo's coach, I came to understand the big leap between the two job areas. The commentator relies on what happens in the match, and only someone who is in that position knows how hard it is to get information. On the other hand, you've got the players and the coach who have all the information but cannot really say much otherwise they will most likely help their opponents. I learned that a few things I said as a coach to commentators were actually working against us, by providing important information to our opponents. So I explained to my colleagues I would have to protect some of the information and not share it with them.[10]

In the days before television, when they could not see the match being described, many listeners expected their commentators to take liberties. Washington Rodrigues recalled his days as a young man listening in the 1950s:

> The commentators would create this magic picture; the shots would always go close to the post, the goalkeeper would always jump magically. It was actually a kind of fantasy football. When TV arrived we were forced to follow what happened with less fantasy, because people would watch the match on TV while listening.

Not everyone welcomed the impact of television. During the 1962 World Cup played in Chile little television coverage was available in Brazil and most of the population followed the tournament on radio. Commentators described a brilliant Brazilian team decisively beating England. But when the TV pictures arrived a couple of days later it was clear that the victory had been more prosaic. The playwright Nelson Rodrigues famously challenged the film version. The radio reports did contain an imaginative element, he acknowledged, but they were 'true'; the television pictures were wrong. 'Only idiots are objective, they don't understand that a game of football obeys the rules of excitement.'[11]

But if one role for commentary is to describe the game we want to hear, not the one on the pitch, then perhaps the best example comes from the journalist João Luiz. Alex Bellos tells how Luiz disliked the result of the 1950 World Cup final match so much, that he decided to change it. He made a film of the revised game. Ghiggia receives the ball, approaches the goal but fails to score, and the game ends as a draw. To add conviction to the production, Luiz Mendes kindly re-recorded his commentary, with the new ending. Brazil were champions after all.

THE IMPORTANCE OF both radio and football has declined in Brazil. Satellite channels have made it possible to watch the Brazilian team live wherever they play. Popular radio personalities from the past like Milton Neves – who began with Jovem Pan in the 1970s alongside Leônidas da Silva and Osmar Santos – now have TV shows.

Other sports such as volleyball and athletics are gaining ground on football, especially among women. Pedro Costa of the Rio Football Federation has noticed the change:

> The Olympics have started to have a bigger space in Brazilian culture. New generations still like football but they can appreciate other kinds of sport. And radio is weaker and less important than twenty years ago. Partly this is because fewer people go to the stadiums. In the future radio stations will have to pay in order to transmit matches.[12]

The globalisation of football has also impacted severely on soccer teams, with the majority of top players seeking careers in Europe at a young age. Poor and corrupt management has affected a number of clubs, and sometimes they have turned against broadcasters. José Carlos Araújo has been one of the most respected commentators in Rio in the last thirty years. Araújo suffered at the hands of Eurico Miranda, the dictatorial manager of Vasco, who banned him from matches at Vasco's home stadium São Januário as part of a campaign against reporters he said were too critical of the club's play. Araújo was subsequently shown by the press narrating a match while watching it on TV.

And commentators themselves have not escaped criticism. 'Some of them have a poor reputation,' said Fernando Duarte, a Brazilian journalist who has studied the football industry across the world. 'People feel that some are in the pockets of the clubs, or that they sometimes take bribes to mention products.'[13]

Adverts to be used during radio commentaries are written to sound like sports narrative so they can be incorporated as seamlessly as possible into the commentary. It is common for commentators to incorporate the sponsor's product into their account of play: '*What a great shot ... and a great shot deserves a great beer'.*

Radio in Brazil, said Alex Bellos, 'gave football a language of its own.' That language has survived partly because by the time television began to spread among the middle classes of Brazil in the late 1960s the transistor boom had taken off. Many Brazilians had portable radios to which they could listen on the move, and many took their sets with them to the stadium to follow the game they were watching and get news of other matches. Indeed, the terraces would sometimes be strewn with discarded cheap sets after fans had thrown them down in disgust when their team had lost.

In 1982 when *Globo* bought exclusive TV rights in Brazil for the World Cup in Spain the slogan adopted by the Rádio Record station was: 'Watch the game on TV, but listen with your heart on *Record*.' One supporter has described how even in the 1990s radio was part of the process of developing club loyalty:

> By the age of ten I was following my club's games on the radio. The radio turned the match into a whole day's event. There is usually a report every hour or so during the day bringing the latest news and then two full hours before the match full-time coverage begins. I would sometimes try to do my homework while the pre-match build-up began but I could never concentrate because I got so excited... Most games happen on a Sunday, just like religious events. Hardcore fans don't allow other people to interrupt them when listening to a match, a behaviour which resembles praying at church. The way club crests are mystified is in a way similar to the way we worship our saints and hold images.[14]

Radio's great asset is its pervasive presence – more than ninety per cent of households have sets – and its portability. The biggest clubs still have supporters all over the country and radio is the main point of contact for club news. Radio journalists were the largest group among the journalists who went to Germany from Brazil for the 2006 World Cup. Pedro Ernesto Denardin of RBS in Porto Alegre who was one of that group asserted the continuing place of radio:

> When the Brazilian players walk through the 'mixed zone' area after games where the media are lined up against a barrier hoping to ask questions, it is always the scrum of radio journalists who get the answers first. Radio still has lots of penetration in Brazil – I'd say that twenty per cent of our listeners are also watching TV, with a battery-powered radio clipped to their ear. The radio narration is much more exciting.[15]

Paulo Cezar, a Brazilian who moved to London, grew up listening to radio in Brazil and had played top-class football there. He lived and played football in London and listened to football commentary in both countries. He insisted that whatever changes had taken place, Brazilian commentators, with their love and passion for the game, were a special breed:

> English commentators commentate only with the mind. Brazilian commentators play the game as they talk, and commentate with the heart.[16]

Football in Brazil owes a lot to radio and Brazilians still treasure their great commentators because of their special way of celebrating the country's national game.

Here is Luis Penido of Rádio Tupi. It is 2000 and the final of the Copa Mercosul, an inter-club competition in South America, between Vasco and Palmeiras. The clubs have finished level after two legs and are playing a decider. Being runners-up in Brazil is a disaster, and there is everything at stake. Vasco go 3-0 down but then, despite being reduced to ten men, somehow claw their way back to 3-3. Each time they score the triumphal sounds of the Vasco anthem are played, drowning out the commentator's voice. Penido is shrill and hoarse from all the excitement and he knows he has to squeeze in one more mention of the sponsor's product. As the referee looks at his watch Vasco move forward into their opponents' half, with their star player Romario lurking on the edge of the box, but the ball goes out of play:

The throw-in will be taken by Jorginho Paulista. He gathers himself, and delivers the ball to Viola on the left-hand touch-line, takes it forward – let's choose the man of the match, the match sponsored by Guarani, the tastiest way of getting energy, the only gaurana powder drink that has a great flavour – there goes Viola taking Vasco's attack forward, dribbles past one player, passes the ball, Juninho Paulista puts the ball across, it takes a deflection off a defender (voices rises to a crescendo), Romario is there, Romario is there, Romario completes the move, the ball is in the back of the net!
CHAMPIONS !!! CHAMPIONS !!! CHAMPIONS !!! CHAMPIONS !!! Goooooooooooooooooooooooooooooooooooooooooo ooooooooooooooal! It's Vasco's goal! It's Vasco's goal! It's the miracle goal! It's the winning goal! It's the deciding goal! It's King Romario's goal! It's a fourth goal! It's a turnaround, it's incredible! I want to hear the champion Vasco's anthem (the band starts up). Let's sing really loud, let's sing for a long time, the result is four-three, not long ago the score was three-nil. Life changes minute by minute – it's the victory, the consecration. It's Vasco as champions. Well done, Vasco. I will sing this anthem all night long. Romario in extra time.

This account draws chiefly on: E Soares *A Bola No Ar* (Summus 1994); ed J A Mangan and LP Da Costa *Sport in Latin American Society* (Cass 2002); ed Elizabeth Fox *Media and Politics in Latin America* (Sage 1988); Elizabeth Fox *Latin American Broadcasting* (University of Luton 1997); ed L Bethell *Cambridge History of Latin America* Volumes 6,7 and 10 (CUP 1984-90); Alex Bellos *Futebol, the Brazilian way of life* (Bloomsbury 2002); Gisela Swetlana Ortriwano *França, 1938, 111 Copa do mundo, O Rádio brasileiro estava lá* (University of São Paulo 1998); *The Beautiful Game* (Gollancz 1998); Janet Lever *Soccer Madness* (Chicago 1983); E Galeano *Football in Sun and shadow* (Fourth Estate 1997); ed J Arbera *Sport and Society in Latin America* (Greenwood 1988).
Newspapers consulted for 1938 and 1950: *O Estado de São Paulo, Jornal do Brasil* and *Correio da Manhã*.

1   Tony Mason *Passion of the People?* (Verso 1995) p 99
2   The population of Brazil are descendents of indigenous people, Portuguese colonial settlers, slaves from Africa and diverse waves of immigration including many from Italy.
3   This and later quotations from Tuma drawn from *A Bola No Ar* Chapter 1
4   Interview with the author
5   Daryle Williams *Culture Wars in Brazil* (Duke University 2001) p 285
6   The Cup was won by Italy. *The Times* of London sent no reporter and

covered none of the matches. The day after the final, among four pages of sports news, it printed a one-sentence report from Reuters giving the result at the foot of a column.

7   R Pareja writing about the impact of radio in Colombia, quoted in J Martin-Barbero *Communication, Culture and Hegemony* (Sage 1993) p165
8   *Futebol, The Brazilian way of Life* (p239–240)
9–10   Interview with the author
11   *The Beautiful Game* p 114
12–13   Interview with the author
14   Interview with Frederico Aragao 2005
15   *Guardian* June 26th 2006
16   Interview with the author

THIRTEEN

INDIA AND THE TRANSISTOR

COMMENT BLENDED WITH REPORT. Technical details mixed with actual performance. Reading of the wicket, its gradual wear, incidents which may contribute to the ultimate result of the match. A little natural humour here and there. The crowd reactions. Mannerisms of the players. Now and then a comparison, a dip into the pages of *Wisden*. An easy natural chat about the play as if one is sitting among friends. Is broadcasting cricket such a difficult task after all?[1]

'As if one is sitting among friends.' This is the recipe for cricket commentary of 'Bobby' Talyarkhan: outspoken journalist, man-about-town, the pioneer of commentary in India, a man with 'a hell of an ego'. And perhaps the only person in the history of radio to commentate alone on one event for five days without a break.

British India: a swathe of peoples, languages and religions, largely controlled, at the time radio arrived, by a small European elite. A country half the size of Brazil but, in 1930, with some 350 million people, most living in villages.

Cricket was brought to India by the British in the 1780s. During the second half of the nineteenth century it was taken up by other groups, providing some well-educated Indians with an opportunity to meet, and beat, the British at their own game. Its popularity grew steadily and in 1906 a Hindu team beat a team comprised of the best European players in India. Bombay[2] was always one of cricket's main centres, so much so that by February 1930 *The Times* (of London) suggested that the game was very popular in the city and its environs:

In any of the fishing villages near Bombay one is almost certain to find men and boys engaged in cricket … all towns of any size have cricket teams and in a city of such size as Bombay there must be hundreds of clubs…

At this time radio was just getting established in India. The Indian Broadcasting Service had stations only in Bombay, Calcutta and Madras and they broadcast very limited programmes. Bombay was a crowded, hectic city with more than a million inhabitants. In the previous decades it had expanded rapidly to become India's leading commercial centre. Thousands of people arrived each year, many to work in its growing industries – more than eighty per cent of those living in Bombay in 1930 had been born outside the city. Writer Boria Majumdar has argued that social change on this scale provoked a demand for leisure pursuits and that during the 1920s sport, especially horseracing and cricket, emerged as significant sources of entertainment in the city.

The scene of the first live sports broadcast was the Bombay Maidan, that large expanse of open space at the southern end of the city. Since the 1870s the Maidan had been the centre of European sport in the city. It was here in the 1880s that the English polo players had famously resisted the attempts of local cricketers to establish their own ground. It was here that the Hindu team had claimed their famous victory in 1906. And it was here India's first domestic Test was to be played.

On December 15th 1933 a broadcaster took up position in a makeshift commentary box on the boundary. Additional seating had been built to cater for the large numbers expected and the broadcaster found himself among a crowd of 30,000 spectators. Several thousand others clung to nearby vantage points – trees, walls and roofs of neighbouring buildings.

The sense of expectation among cricket-lovers in the city was high. The Government closed all public offices for the first two days of the game and ticket concessions were offered by the railway company to those travelling to Bombay from other parts of western India. In October of 1933 *The Illustrated Weekly of India* had revealed that arrangements had been made for the match to be broadcast and gave assurances about the quality of the coverage: 'A competent critic has been appointed who will give a running commentary during the game.' It is unclear who the broadcaster was – it may have been Colonel Sethna, Director of Bombay Radio – but the names of commentators were not included in the broadcasting schedules released to the press.

The Test match was not without controversy. This was a time of growing resistance to colonial rule and a proposed tour by England in 1930–31 had been cancelled because of disturbances in India. There was also some political opposition in Bombay to the 1933 tour, but since there had been little top-class cricket in the city during preceding years, many cricket-lovers were keen for it to take place. The first full Indian team to tour England, in 1932, had enhanced the reputation of Indian cricket and there were high hopes that England could be beaten. As a piquant extra, of which much was made on public occasions, the English captain, Douglas Jardine, was returning to the city of his birth.

English-language newspapers of the time suggest that there was considerable interest in the game but it is difficult to assess how many people followed these first broadcasts. It is not even clear whether the broadcasts included actual commentary, as opposed to score updates. As there were little more than 10,000 licensed sets in the country as a whole at the time the commentary would only have been accessible to a few thousand listeners at the most. However, this was an important innovation – the first sporting broadcast – and in one Bombay company at least the management installed the latest Pye Radiogram so that staff could follow the progress of the Indian team. England won comfortably soon after lunch on the fourth day, but the match was distinguished by a brilliant century by Lala Amarnath, the first by an Indian in a Test.

There were two subsequent Tests that season, in Madras and Calcutta, but there seem to have been no live reports from them, though the Calcutta station broadcast a fifteen-minute report each evening at the close of play. A year later, however, a lengthy period of live commentary was broadcast in Bombay on all three matches in the Quadrangular tournament between communal teams – Hindus, Muslims, Parsees and Europeans.

This was when that the young journalist, AFS Talyarkhan, 'Bobby' to his friends, made his debut. Talyarkhan not only covered the cricket matches of the Quadrangular tournament, but the boxing commentaries from the Cooperage Halls a few days later. It was the beginning of a versatile career as a commentator, covering many sports.

Talyarkhan's early efforts did not escape criticism. With the radio commentary came the letters to the press, in this case the *Bombay Sentinel*:

> The people responsible for the broadcasting arrangements made a mess of things. The man behind the microphone was evidently a tyro and was unable even to identify the players. In England and the Continent broadcasting of major sports is entrusted to experts. Surely in a big city like Bombay, the proper men could be found for the job?

Another letter was equally cutting: 'What with the many asides and 'ahems' of this gentleman the listeners could hardly make out whether he was broadcasting a Cricket Match or telling a bed time story.' The writer complained that, having invested in a four-valve set: 'I felt as if a couple of hundred rupees had been wasted ... it is a pity that in a big city like Bombay the Radio should be so much neglected.'

But either these critics were in a minority or Talyarkhan quickly got the measure of the commentary business. He soon began to establish himself as a cult figure. His stamina was legendary. In that first year, 1934, he commentated alone for several hours a day, and for nine days during an eleven-day period. His sporting columns in the Bombay press were witty and outspoken. He became one of the most influential figures in Indian sports broadcasting and journalism.

Ardeshir Furdonji Sohrabji Talyarkhan was born into the Parsee community in Bombay in 1897.[3] Members of the community were active in commerce, business and the growing nationalist movement, and they were also cricketers. They formed the first non-English cricket club in India and in 1886 sent the first team from India to tour England. Anyone born into that community at the end of the 19th century was born into cricket.

Talyarkhan spoke in later life of his dislike of study at school and his early love of sport. From the age of ten he followed horseracing, and began to watch races from outside the Poona course. His father was a lawyer, part of an upper-class family and managing director of a big commercial house. Bobby was sent to England to learn the cotton trade, but he was not cut out for business. He recalled that there were futile attempts to master arts, commerce, law and insurance, and even go into the antique trade. He soon branched out into journalism. He became something of a social figure, 'a natty dresser', who drove sporty cars, one favourite being an open-top English Riley with leather seats.

How and why he secured his first opening as a commentator in 1934 is not entirely clear. It seems likely that managers at the radio station, like Colonel Sethna, knew the elder Talyarkhan and that provided the crucial link. Writer Ramachandra Guha, who has written a history of cricket in India, offers another explanation:

> His Parsee origins may have been a factor – he could appeal across the religious divide, at a time when Bombay had large Hindu and Muslim populations. Some nationalists

– of all persuasions – would not work for British-run radio stations so this may have opened a gap for him.[4]

Whatever the explanation, Talyarkhan took his chance. He quickly became the best-known commentator in India. The numbers owning radios were very small, but they were growing among the educated classes in the cities. AD Bhogle, father of Harsha Bhogle, was born and brought up in Hyderabad and went on to become a respected university teacher. He listened to Talyarkhan throughout his teens:

> I remember the quality of broadcast as very poor (with atmospherics claiming an almost equal share with signals) and it was made worse by the distance. But such was the attraction of cricket that listeners were prepared to put up with it. For cricket broadcasts AFST was the sole attraction in the late thirties and early forties. AFST popularised cricket and cricket popularised him. He had a partiality for certain cricketers, and he did not try to disguise his personal preferences. When SH Sohoni scored his first run he would say: 'Ah, he's just 99 short of a century.'[5]

Like John Arlott in Britain a few years later, Talyarkhan had a presence, and an influence, within sport which went beyond commentary itself. There are significant differences between the two men but, like Arlott, Talyarkhan helped to secure for radio a legion of cricket listeners, who tuned in not just to get news of the game, but to hear the commentator.

Like Arlott, he was renowned not for his tactical understanding of the game but for his command of language and the pleasure he found in sport. Like Arlott, he took part forcefully in debates around sport. And in these debates he asserted a particular view of his country and its future.

Talyarkhan's early fame derived in part from one episode, probably without parallel in the history of commentary: he loudly and publicly campaigned against the very tournament which his own commentaries helped to promote. That tournament was the knock-out competition held between teams from different communal groups.

When Europeans established sporting clubs in Bombay (and the rest of India) they were closed to other races. In due course, first Parsees, then Hindus and then Muslims did the same. The first cricket competition between teams from the four communities, the 'Quadrangular', was in 1917. The tournament became increasingly popular, a focus of rivalry and the occasion of large displays of partisan support. In due course it became the highlight of the sporting year in Bombay. In 1937 a fifth team ('The Rest') joined the tournament, henceforth called the Pentangular. Bombay's communal cricket tournament was the apex of the cricket year.

But for many nationalists the notion of communal teams became increasingly unacceptable. Most were campaigning for a free India undivided by religion and in this respect key figures of the nationalist campaign in the 1920s, Gandhi, Nehru, Jinnah and others took the lead.[6] A combination of political unrest and pressure from nationalists resulted in the suspension of the Quadrangular tournament in 1929.

When the tournament was revived in 1934, letters appeared in the press calling for it to be replaced by a territorial competition like the county championship in England. By 1938, leading writers, especially those committed to the idea of a unified, independent India, were calling not just for the abolition of the tournament but of the communal clubs themselves.

Talyarkhan was a leading protagonist in this debate. He took up the invitation to commentate on the matches and did so for several years. The very fact of his commentary helped to sustain interest in the tournament. But he grew increasingly vociferous in his attacks on communalism in sport – an 'evil that I have made more noise about than any other man.' He was scathing about the failure of nationalist leaders to condemn communal facilities which were not open to other groups. Talyarkhan told a students' conference that it was the Pentangular cricket tournament itself which bred communal enmity. 'The time has come when you should forego the pleasure of seeing particularly interesting cricket in order to show to the world that you are no longer prepared to tolerate communalism in cricket.'[7]

The main vehicle for Talyarkhan's attacks was his newspaper column *Take it from me* published in the *Free Press Journal*. Here Talyarkhan developed a three-way dialogue between himself as writer, himself as broadcaster and 'all my sporting friends, men and women' – he was a keen advocate of sports participation by women. The column was quite unlike most of the material around it. It was conversational, chatty, humorous, and occasionally scurrilous, but at the same time trenchant. It always ended with an appeal to Steve, the writer's imaginary friend: *Do you get me Steve?* This was the first sports column in Indian journalism and the most talked about. But the resolution that Talyarkhan and others sought – for the communal tournament to be replaced by a zonal one – did not finally come to fruition until 1947.

Although Talyarkhan covered the communal tournament regularly from 1934 onwards, the published radio schedules for the early 1940s show no listing of cricket commentaries for the event. By now All India Radio (AIR) had been established – the station's name, and acronym, had been skilfully chosen in 1936, at a time when there was no Indian state. It may be that AIR decided not to cover the matches. It is just possible that Talyarkhan took his opposition so far as to withdraw from commentating (as Arlott was to do over a proposed South African tour to England), and that this influenced the decision of AIR. Or it may be that the arrival of a new director at the Bombay radio station led to Talyarkhan being 'stood down' for a period because he insisted on airing his views on communalism during the commentaries. However, he covered other matches at this time and won many devoted listeners.

This was the time of some historic cricket games involving Indian state and national sides, and some historic performances. It is his association with these that helped to underpin Talyarkhan's reputation. Somehow the unbroken, epic qualities of his commentaries matched the great feats that he described. He covered every ball of the unique Ranji Trophy game at Poona in 1940 when a match scheduled to last three days was extended to five in search of a result and then abandoned as a draw.[8]

He talked his way through several great innings by VM Merchant and VS Hazare and discussed their competing claims to be the leading batsman of the day on the radio and in print. Talyarkhan knew the top players well. He was willing to criticise them, some thought unfairly, and his interventions in disputes between them could sometimes be influential. But one feat was surely unique in the history of radio commentary: he commentated alone on all five days of the Test between India and West Indies in Bombay in December 1948, with the assistance of only a scorer.

The venue for that match, and much of his commentary, was the Brabourne Stadium in Bombay. Built in 1937 at Churchgate, a mile or so from the old Gymkhana ground on the Maidan, the stadium was the product of an alliance between the Governor of Bombay (after whom it is named) and the Cricket Club of India, with some financial contributions from a number of Indian Princes. In its day it was rightly counted among the best sporting complexes in the world, for in addition to providing a fine arena it offered all the facilities of a private club.

Dicky Rutnagur, himself a commentator on All India Radio and for many years a cricket writer for the London *Daily Telegraph*, was taken by his father to see Talyarkhan in the commentary box:

> He thought he knew more than he did but he was a very good descriptive commentator. He captured the atmosphere. The whole set-up was pretty incestuous and he knew all the cricketers personally, so he could really bring out their characters ... it was interesting, very interesting, very good diction, he spoke beautifully.[9]

The head teacher at Rutnagur's school had no wish to miss Talyarkhan's commentaries. When big matches were on, and Talyarkhan was holding forth, he arranged for all the boys to sit in front of a speaker listening to the description of play. During breaks the head would discuss the progress of the match, while the girls were sent out for other activities.

Talyarkhan provided live commentary on a wide range of other sports, including football, hockey, boxing and racing. When the Indian Games were staged at the Brabourne Stadium he was whisked by car to the Mahalaxmi racecourse to cover the Eclipse Stakes (the biggest race in the country at the time) and then rushed back to the stadium to cover a 10,000 metres cycle race.

At football and hockey matches he was generally seated at a table at ground level, in front of the crowd and directly opposite the halfway line. He was smartly dressed, open-faced, a moustache, hair combed back. Cigarettes and a drink would be close at hand. Those who knew him, and who listened to his commentaries, recall the richness of his voice. Some describe the style as authoritative, almost gruff.

Talyarkhan's career in cricket commentary came to an end during the season of 1948–49. He took on the whole of the second Test of the West Indies series, played at the Brabourne Stadium. But then, when the West Indies returned for the fourth Test later in the season, there was a conflict. 'It got very political,' recalled Dicky Rutnagur:

> All India Radio wanted the Maharaja of Vizianagram, popularly known as Vizzy, to be one of the commentators.[10] The Cricket Club of India, who owned the Brabourne Stadium, said this was not acceptable. Their chairman Vijay Merchant had had a big row with Vizzy on the 1936 tour. But Vizzy had pull with ministers and others in Delhi and so Bombay commentators suffered. Bobby said 'I'll do it myself, or not at all.' And that was the end of it.

It is not surprising that Talyarkhan would not give way to the Maharaja. According to Narrotam Puri, whose father was a contemporary, 'Vizzy's commentaries were as poor as his playing skills – he often told cricketing stories while play was going on and the listener after three minutes would be startled to hear India were 16-2.'[11]

'Bobby had a short fuse, a hell of an ego,' recalled Rutnagur. 'He would get obstreperous when he had a couple of drinks. He would really start shouting ... he was a bullshitter, but I liked him and I got on well with him.'

'He could be infuriating,' recalled the veteran journalist KN Prabhu, but 'one accepts him, even in his most aggressive moments, as one who made sport, through the medium of the radio, a live force.'

'Countless boys of my generation would have given anything to be Bobby,' Prabhu wrote.[12]

Talyarkhan returned to live commentary only once more, when Pakistan Radio invited him to help cover the first Test between India and Pakistan in 1955. Given the history between the two countries, and Talyarkhan's record on communalism, it was a significant gesture. In 1979 his admirers arranged an event to celebrate his achievements and presented him with a purse. 'I will continue to be a nuisance to the public as long as I can,' he announced.

Talyarkhan spent his final years living at the Cricket Club of India, from whose lovely stadium he had given so many commentaries. He remained a great talker, with strong views and a sharp sense of humour. His eyesight was failing but he continued to compose his daily articles, ready to be collected by a courier from the newspaper offices. He went on with his writing and broadcasting to the end of his life. The 'man with iron lungs', as one cricketer called him, died in 1990 at the age of ninety-two.

———————

TALYARKHAN WAS A CENTRAL FIGURE in establishing the potential of commentary in India but his listeners constituted a small proportion of the population. In 1939 there were only 92,000 radio licences in the country and by the time of independence in 1947 radio transmissions still reached only about ten per cent of the population.

Cricket was not the only sport to be covered. The Calcutta station had begun football commentaries in June 1934 (before Talyarkhan's first cricket commentary). Other sports, including racing, hockey and boxing followed. But in his final report to the government of India in 1939 the director of All India Radio, Lionel Fielden, struck a fairly pessimistic note and provided a downbeat assessment of interest in sport:

> In England a large staff of experienced commentators has been built up and plenty of funds are available for the employment and travelling allowances of commentators … In India the case is a very difficult one. Occasions of wide and general interest are not so common. Interest in football or cricket for instance is generally limited to a comparatively small area. Lines over great distances are apt to prove inadequate.[13]

However, after 1947, facilities for linking stations improved and this provided the opportunity for matches of national interest to be heard by listeners across India. There were always those in India who opposed cricket. Ramachandra Guha quoted BV Keskar: the nationalist politician who was later to become Minister of Information and Broadcasting wrote in 1946: '[Cricket is]… but a sign of our utter slavery, our tendency to copy blindly the habits of English civilization, and ape the likes and the preferences of the English gentleman.' But Keskar eventually gave way to the interest in cricket. At the time of the West Indies cricket tour of 1948–49, ball by ball commentary on Tests could be heard in all the major cities, covering the entire play each day in four of the five matches. This was ahead of BBC practice by several years.

Those who had radios listened at home but others had to find sets elsewhere. AD Bhogle remembered:

> A radio was not yet a ubiquitous presence in middle-class homes, not in our home in any case. And I had to devise many ways of being within earshot of the radio: go to the teachers' club of the school where my father was the chief, go to the students' hostel or stand in front of a teashop for hours on end and hope the commentary would filter through the atmospherics, street noise, what have you.[14]

Pavement shops were an important listening point for people who could not afford their own radios and some helpful shopkeepers posted up the latest score on blackboards. All India Radio also began to transmit relays from the BBC in England. The veteran commentator Suresh Saraiya recalled:

> Before transistors came along, we would order Irani teas (dhosa and a cup of tea) in a hotel lobby and listen.

We would just keep ordering so we could hear more commentary. At the age of fifteen, during the 1952 Indian tour of England, I remember going to a local doctor's house and standing outside listening to his radio.[15]

During the 1960s new networks extended the range of AIR, and radio ownership began to grow. From approximately two million in 1960 the number of licence holders grew to around twelve million in 1970 and over twenty million by 1980. By then transistors were popular. Mukul Kesavan remembered:

Portable transistor radios became affordable and the respectable urban poor, wobbling on cycles could be seen carrying largish sets, with their antennae extended, and their speakers crackling with Vividh Bharati, Radio Ceylon or cricket commentary.[16]

Millions were listening on that August evening in 1971 when India won their first Test Match in England, and children garlanded the radios with flowers. In 1972 the sports writer Kishore Bhimani described what he called the 'transistor syndrome' during big matches:

In tea shops by the wayside and in posh restaurants, in Government offices and in sedate board-rooms, in passing cars and aboard trams and buses, the monotonous drone of the wireless will obliterate all else. So overwhelming is the pre-occupation that the Railways might consider inscribing on the walls of carriages: *Please do not talk if it disturbs the transistors of your fellow passengers.*[17]

Transistors soon became de rigueur among spectators at the big games. Suresh Saraiya estimates that up to a third of spectators may have taken them to matches at one stage. Commentators at Indian grounds could hear their voices coming back from the crowd as they spoke and Chadra Nayadu, the daughter of India's first Test captain CK Nayadu, recalled what happened when she began her first commentary: 'The moment I came on they raised the volume.'[18]

Not only was it possible to get the commentator's 'take' on what was happening but listeners could voice their approval or disapproval of the commentators' asides. Sometimes players could pick up what was being said about their performance.

Occasionally remarks by commentators unintentionally inflamed spectators who were disgruntled by an umpire's decision. At the Brabourne Stadium in Bombay in 1969 during a Test match between

India and Australia, many thousands of Indian spectators were listening to commentary. With India struggling to avoid defeat one of the last Indian batsmen, Venkataraghavan, was given out caught. There was a short delay before the umpire raised his finger, and Venkat stood his ground briefly. To add to the uncertainty one radio commentator cast doubt on the fairness of the decision, thus fuelling the feelings of spectators. Bottles and chairs were hurled onto the ground and fires were lit. Play was delayed for some time. Although there is disagreement as to how much responsibility for the disruption rested with the broadcasters, neither commentator on duty that day was selected again by All India Radio for Test match duty. Transistors were subsequently banned from some Indian grounds.[19]

GRADUALLY, ALL INDIA RADIO built up a team of commentators who created a large following for cricket among those who understood English. They included Berry Sarbadikari, a journalist who was said to have been the only Indian sportswriter at the 1948 Olympics; Dev Raj Puri, a former Test fast bowler; Dicky Rutnagur; Ananda Rao from Madras who made his first broadcast in 1943 and subsequently covered fifty-seven tests; and Pearson Surita from Calcutta. The former Indian captain Vijay Merchant was popular as both commentator and summariser.

These commentators were to be followed by another generation which included Raj Singh, manager of an Indian team to England and president of the Cricket Club of India; VM Chakrapani, a former newsreader remembered for the quality of his spoken English; Anant Setalvad, admired for his elegant and calm voice; Suresh Suraiya, who covered more than ninety Test matches between 1965 and 2005 and liked to begin each spell of commentary with the phrase with which he had completed the last; and Narrotam Puri, who had his introduction by sitting in the commentary box with his father, Dev Raj. Between them father and son Puri covered a period of almost fifty years.

Harsha Bhogle began his commentating career in the early 1990s while still a teenager. When growing up in Hyderabad, he was helped into commentary at the age of eighteen by the encouragement of his father. He recalled the impact of radio in his youth, when Sunil Gavaskar was his hero:

> Through school and through college, the transistor was our best friend. Inevitably it was switched off when

Gavaskar got out. Often we took it to bed and it is there we heard Suresh Saraiya announce India's Test win at Auckland in 1976 (of course Gavaskar scored a century). It was there too that we heard the dulcet tones of Anant Setalvad announcing the start of another century.[20]

Radio certainly helped in the spread of cricket but how far it spread, and how far it became part of Indian life, has been much argued over. The *Times of India* was a little premature perhaps in 1937 in talking of 'the great hold which cricket ... has on the people of India'. But in the post-war years the game grew in popularity and followers who understood English accessed BBC commentaries as well as those on All India Radio. Mukul Kesavan remembered the voices on the BBC: 'I listened, entranced by the marbled perfection of their accents.' Kesavan made a link between his acquisition of English and his love of cricket:

> It wasn't a coincidence that the first Test series I followed was played the same year that I became fluent in English ... It was also the year that I acquired enough English to follow All India Radio's Test commentary. English consolidated the place of cricket in my life ... Cricket helped me practise reading English and reading English helped me fall deeper into love with cricket. For me, as for many Indian boys of my class, English was an inseparable part of the romance of cricket.[21]

As interest grew it became quite common for cricket to be referred to as 'the national game.' All India Radio claimed that in some areas more than seventy per cent of licence holders listened to commentaries on the 1978 tour by the West Indian team. It was this scale of interest which later prompted the Indian diplomat Shashi Taroor to argue that cricket has seized the imagination of Indians like no other sport:

> Everything about the sport seems suited to the Indian national character, its rich complexity, the infinite variations possible with each delivery, the dozen different ways of getting out, are all rather like Indian classical music, in which the basic laws are laid down but the performer that improvises is gloriously unshackled by anything so mundane as a written score. The glorious uncertainties of the game echo ancient India thought.[22]

Others, though cricket-lovers, have counselled caution about claiming too much for cricket's popularity. Mihir Bose, in his book on the history of Indian cricket, argued that if that strand of Indian nationalism rooted in Bengal had won out in the struggle for power rather than the cricket-loving Bombay, football might well have taken the lead among Indian sports. Certainly the numbers following cricket before the 1960s must have been a small proportion of the population because almost all the commentaries were in English. Something more was needed to spread interest in cricket.

At Independence in 1947 the people of India shared a nation, but not a language. English had been the main language of broadcasting before independence and almost the only language of commentary. It was the language of the colonial power and, to some extent, of the educated classes. Before 1946 there had been only a few commentaries in vernacular languages.

The great majority of Indians spoke one, or more, of the many local languages of India, twenty-two of which are recognized in the Indian constitution. At that time Hindi was the most widely spoken of the local languages, and as such was recognized in the 1947 constitution as the national language. But there were large parts of the country where it was not widely spoken or understood.

Radio had obvious potential during the process of building a new nation and in the years following independence, AIR considered ways of spreading the Hindi language. There were those who sought to use AIR to promote 'true' Hindi, and who promoted formal lessons in the language over the radio. Others took the view that Hindi could not be foisted on people but had to grow organically. It took a number of years before a major initiative was taken in relation to the use of Hindi in sports commentary.

A senior official at All India Radio, HR Luthra, recorded how in 1962 a formal decision was taken about the languages to be used:

> The Directorate instructed the stations that for cricket test matches … running commentaries in regional languages, either on a separate channel or in short chunks interspersed with the English commentary, may be arranged as a matter of course by all originating stations. However running commentaries on the final of major tournaments in hockey, football and tennis were to be given in English but stations were told that it would be

desirable to give a short summary of the game at the end in Hindi or the regional language of the stations. Sports events of regional or local character were to be covered in regional languages.[23]

There had been some commentaries in regional languages before 1962 but with this decision came the possibility that cricket, in particular, might be broadcast more widely across the country. All India Radio now developed cricket commentaries in a number of languages, for instance in Bengali for listeners around Calcutta, Tamil for the Madras area, Hindi for the city of Bombay and Marathi for state games in Maharashtra outside of Bombay. Commentators began to emerge who specialised in vernacular languages.

The earliest Hindi cricket commentator to become nationally known was Ravi Chaturvedi, who began his career with All India Radio in 1962. He covered international matches for more than forty years, including more than one hundred tests, and developed a large following.

These developments greatly increased the amount of radio time devoted to cricket. AIR was committed where possible to commentary in both Hindi and English, so if a local station organised a broadcast in the language of its region, there would be three simultaneous commentaries. Individual stations throughout the country then decided which commentary or commentaries to take; in northern and central India most of the smaller AIR stations took just one channel, normally the Hindi one. Thus it was that the audience for cricket was no longer restricted to those who could understand English.

One broadcaster who did much to popularise commentary in Hindi had been inspired to take up broadcasting by listening to Melville de Mellow's commentary (in English) on Gandhi's funeral in 1948. Jasdev Singh was then a sixteen-year-old college student. He attended school near his home in Chaksu but at the age of sixteen won a scholarship to college in Jaipur:

> About six or seven one evening I was attending a lecture given by the Indian High Commissioner to Australia. As I remember someone comes into the hall and whispers into his ear. He seemed stunned, pale-faced and we all knew something had happened. He or the Principal comes to the podium and announces with great sorrow that Gandhi was dead.

I took my bike, it was one and a half miles to my home in Jaipur and the whole market was shut, every building, it seemed no-one was alive. We had recently bought a radio and on January 31st me and my mother and sisters sat, ears glued to the radio. Melville de Mellow sounded like Mellow de Mellow. I couldn't follow the heavy English words but I and my mother both followed his sentiments and also a bit of the language but not everything. It sounded to us as though the whole nation was weeping tears, and that was true. I told her in Hindi: 'Byi, mein, Hindi men commentator banunga' – 'I'd like to be a commentator, I will be a Hindi commentator'. That was the day and moment.[24]

It was to fall to this young man, whose mother-tongue was Punjabi, to give voice to his nation's emerging national language, Hindi. His voice, said one eminent Hindi writer, was 'a sweet mixture of Hindi-Urdu and Punjabi'.[25]

In the years that followed Gandhi's funeral, Jasdev Singh took every opportunity to practise and develop the skills of commentary and announcing. He became a familiar figure at local social events, ceremonial dances and processions. Eventually in 1955 he joined the Jaipur station of AIR as an announcer. He moved to Delhi and in 1962 came his first important national assignment: the annual Independence Day celebrations.

In 1964 – when All India Radio decided there must be Hindi commentary alongside English at the Olympic Games – he accompanied Melville de Mellow to Tokyo. Later that year Jasdev led coverage of Nehru's funeral. Like Howard Marshall and others at the BBC, Jasdev Singh was to combine commentary on both ceremonial and sporting events. In addition to cricket and hockey he covered nine Olympics, and forty years of Independence and Republic Day parades. The Padma Bhushan award, conferred on those who have given distinguished service of a high order to the nation, was conferred on him by the President of India in 2008.

There was one major public event when Jasdev Singh stayed at home. When Indira Gandhi was assassinated by Sikh members of her own bodyguard in 1984 All India Radio decided they could not risk asking a Sikh to describe her funeral.

Jasdev remembered a key moment when All India Radio was developing coverage of cricket in Hindi at all venues, so that commentary could be relayed across the country. Madras was a Tamil-speaking area where there was still some opposition to Hindi:

> My boss, BC Chatterjee, said: 'You must face the music. You must be the first Hindi wallah in Madras'. So I went to Madras, remembering my parents and my God, and we started double commentary on one channel. After fifteen minutes the commentary was passed to me. I knew that many people were listening in the stadium on transistors in Tamil. But in the town all the Hindi wallahs were listening. I was sweating there in the air conditioning. I did not hear any noise in the stadium and when I came out I spoke to the station director and he said 'everything is OK'. Then the local manufacturers came to me and said: 'We like your commentary, we can follow your Hindi, but can you give the numerals in English?' So that is how it started.

Among Jasdev Singh's best-remembered commentaries are those on India's hockey successes, especially those of 1971. India was then a dominant force in world hockey and the game was followed widely in the country. When the World Cup was held in Kuala Lumpur in 1971 there was great public interest.

India met the home side, Malaysia, in the semi-final. Jasdev remembered the tension, and the feelings it aroused in the city:

> With some ten minutes to go Malaysia were leading 2-1. It was do or die ... I remember saying that Aslam was running like a deer, with a stick in his hand. 'I feel Aslam may bring luck to India', I said. I used the Hindi characterisation 'the maker of someone's luck.' As chance would have it within two minutes he had taken a penalty corner and India scored.

India went on to win. The final, inevitably, was against Pakistan. Millions were listening throughout the subcontinent. Work stopped, as it does in all countries on these occasions. The story is widely told in India of the Prime Minister, Indira Gandhi, berating cabinet colleagues, who had transistors in their pockets: 'Go back to your offices until the game is over. You're not listening to me'.

It was India's greatest victory, the winning goal scored by Ashok Kumar, who went on to become a commentator himself. Not long afterwards, Jasdev Singh was present when the team attended a function with Mrs Gandhi. Her security officer introduced Jasdev to the Prime Minister. 'Madam, you must meet the voice you've been listening to,' he said. Mrs Gandhi complimented Jasdev on his commentary: 'You increased the beating of our hearts,' she said as she greeted him. Jasdev Singh later recalled that he met many people who told him of their prayers during the game and how 'they had kept a photograph of their God or the holy book on the radio set.'

But it was cricket where Hindi commentary had its most significant impact. 'It was commentary in Hindi which really helped to accelerate the growth of the game,' said Ayaz Memon, for many years sports editor of the *Times of India*.[26]

Sushil Doshi, who has been a popular commentator in Hindi over many years and still covers important matches for Indian radio, shared this view: 'With the advent of Hindi commentary the game reached the farmers, the housewives and the commoners who otherwise would never listen to English commentary'.[27]

Most AIR cricket commentaries began to follow a standard pattern: fifteen minutes of Hindi alternating with fifteen minutes of English. In part this reflected the growing acceptance of Hindi, but it also stemmed from financial constraints which made it difficult to resource a third, local language broadcast. Only those All India Radio centres with more than one primary channel provided commentary in a regional language. Anant Setalvad explained how things have changed:

> We began with English then Hindi and then the local language. So at one time we used to have three separate booths in Bombay – English, Hindi and Marathi. In Calcutta it would be Bengali, and so on. It's no longer that. In the old days English and Hindi were not very popular but if you go to these places today most people speak Hindi and definitely understand it.[28]

Another aspect of cricket commentary which provoked discussion among commentators was that a specific cricket vocabulary developed in English, especially to describe field placings. Commentators in Hindi and other Indian languages had to decide how to handle these terms, many of which had no natural equivalent in the vernacular. Some speakers of Indian languages were keen to find Hindi or Bengali equivalents for phrases like 'deep square leg' or 'cover drive'. In his autobiography Jasdev Singh argued against this:

In sports commentary I have never been in favour of translating technical words as the translated words do not necessarily convey the same meaning as the original. 'LBW' or 'wicketkeeper' are technical words. A common man, a housewife or a grandmother, or a shopkeeper will never use these words. The simple question will be: 'Sir, who is batting and who is bowling? What is the score?' One can understand using the Hindi translation for 'batting' and 'bowling' but there does not seem to be any need to change other technical words.[29]

Increasingly English technical terms became part of Hindi commentary. There was movement the other way too, with English commentary in India adopting some Hindi words, such as 'Maha' (a great innings).

Commentators, cricketers and listeners have spoken of the importance of Hindi commentary in the spread of cricket and of the pleasure it has given. The great Indian batsman Sunil Gavaskar has acknowledged its importance:

I have been taught all my life in English. I find it much easier to speak in English but with Jasdev I always speak in Hindi. He asks me a question in Hindi and I request him to explain it to me. He always explains the question with a smile. My confidence grows stronger by this. It is only because of him that I have been able to establish contact with thousands of Hindi-speaking cricket lovers. It is because of commentary in Hindi and other local languages that this game has become so popular.[30]

Testimony was also supplied by Indian cricket supporters around the world exchanging stories of the great commentators, their inspired moments, and their mistakes. Blogs like *Men in White* contain a host of fond memories:

As a South Indian, the commentary of Doshi and Setalvad completed my Hindi education, especially numbers. To this day, you can wake me up in the middle of the night and ask me what 'ninyaaanave' and 'chouraasi' translate to and you will get the correct answers (ninety-nine and eighty-four resp).
I live in US. I grew up listening to Hindi commentary by

Murali Manohar Manjui – it was melodious music to my ears.

Those who follow in both languages enjoy the alternating vocabulary:

> I was driving to work in the morning with the radio commentary on, listening to cricket in Hindi and English alternately. Jaywardene went from being a batsman to being a 'ballebaaz', while Zaheer bowled in English and threw in Hindi.[31]

But it is perhaps the pairing of Sushil Doshi and Anant Setalvad on the 1977–78 tour of Australia which is most remembered. In the final moments of the series, they could resist the temptation no longer and described alternate balls, one in Hindi and one in English. Thus they gave voice to the paradox of the Indian cricket heritage.

FROM THE EARLY 1980s the effects of globalisation and privatisation changed the face of sports broadcasting in India. The period in which radio was the main companion for cricket fans faded. In 2008 the population was more than 1.1 billion and All India Radio put radio ownership at more than 110 million sets. Television coverage had expanded rapidly and key one-day matches attracted millions of viewers.

The drift away from cricket some thought they detected in the 1970s was halted when India won the World Cup in 1983. Indian cricketers became superstars and the Indian cricket authorities were able to strike lucrative deals with cable and satellite TV companies. All India Radio retained exclusive rights to commentary on big matches but the desire to maximise advertising revenue affected the coverage, as Harsha Bhogle has observed:

> You will be amazed at the amount of commercial time there is on it. You definitely miss an average of a ball an over. They've fallen in love with the idea of generating revenue, but they haven't fathomed that you need to provide a service for the revenue you're receiving. They've gone very blatantly commercial in the last two or three years because they've been combining advertising on TV and AIR. If you buy time on TV you must buy a certain amount of time on radio. As a result every time there's a

boundary hit, a commercial comes up because someone is sponsoring a boundary.[32]

Pradeep Vijaykar, who became one of AIR's leading English-language commentators, confirmed the pressure: 'There is a fixed quantum of ads to be squeezed in, whatever the duration of a match.'[33]

This meant an advertisement after every over, sometimes more often. The commentators' attempts to make the broadcasting interesting were frustrated because they were constantly interrupted.

Bhogle went on to do extensive radio and TV work around the world and became particularly popular in Australia. He epitomised the modern media professional and developed a career outside commentary. But he was convinced his chances of getting into commentary in 2008 would be much reduced:

> There's a feeling in India that if you're a non-cricketer you have to earn the respect of the cricketer. The sad thing is now that the bar for the cricketer is much lower than it's ever been, especially on TV, and the bar for the non-cricketer is higher. A very ordinary broadcaster who has played ten Test matches is more likely to get the job than the outstanding broadcaster who hasn't played. I fear that's happening around the world.[34]

In February 2006, the thread of continuity whereby all Test matches have been covered live on radio for more than seventy years was broken. All India Radio could not reach an agreement with advertisers and the first match of the series against England at Nagpur was not covered. Fortunately the deadlock was resolved and commentary was back on air for the second match. It has been estimated that some twenty-five million Indians now listen to coverage of international matches on radio, at home, in shops and in cars.[35]

This is a small proportion of those watching on TV, but it remains one of the largest radio commentary audiences in the world.

Radio made a unique contribution to the spread of cricket in India, especially once commentaries in regional languages were adopted. The early morning broadcasts from Australia, and the evening commentaries from the West Indies or England had a special flavour. They enabled millions of Indians to follow the progress of their teams around the world, during a period when India was establishing itself as a modern nation. That Indian cricket is now a world brand, and the largest source of revenue to the game, owes much to this process. Radio helped make cricket in India, as it helped make football in Brazil.

India and the Transistor

Main sources: GC Aswathy *Broadcasting in India* (Allied 1965); VL Baruah *This is All India Radio* (1983); Mihir Bose *A Maidan View* (Allen and Unwin 1986); R Cashman *Patrons, Players and the Crowd*; (Orient Longman 1980); PC Chatterji *Broadcasting in India* (Sage 1991); Boria Majumdar *Twenty two yards to Freedom* (Penguin Viking 2004); Ramachandra Guha *A Corner of a Foreign Field* (Picador 2002); Mukul Kesavan *Men in White* (Penguin Viking 2007); H R Luthra *Indian Broadcasting* (1986); M Masani *Broadcasting and the People* (National Book Trust of India 1976); S Tharoor *The Elephant, The Tiger and the Cell phone* (Penguin Viking 2007); AFS Talyarkhan *On with the Game* (Hind Kitabs 1945). Newspapers consulted: *Bombay Chronicle; Times of India*

1 AFS Talyarkhan *Times of India* October 5th 1964. As far as can be ascertained this was before Brian Johnston compared commentary to 'talking among friends.'

2 Now known as Mumbai. Cities are referred to by their names at the time.

3 Followers of Zoroastrianism, mostly living in the Bombay area, were called Parsees because they were expelled from Iran (Persia) in the 7th century. Among Test players belong to the Parsee community have been Polly Umrigar and Farokh Engineer.

4–5 Interview with the author

6 Jinnah subsequently campaigned for a separate state (Pakistan) but in the 1920s supported the idea of one nation and spoke of cricket as a 'unifier' for Indians.

7 Speech to Bombay Students Conference November 1941. Converted by author to direct speech from the reported speech in the *Bombay Chronicle*.

8 By this time Maharashtra had made 675 and Bombay 650 but neither had started their second innings. One captain commented to the *Times of India*: 'The wicket isn't giving much help to the bowlers.'

9 Interview with the author

10 The Maharaja captained the England team on the tour of England in 1936. His batting average on the tour was 16, fractionally below his career average of 18. During the summer he was knighted.

11 Narrotam Puri *The rise and decline of radio commentary* (*www.cricketnext.com* 2007).

12 These comments from Talyarkhan Souvenir Brochure 1979 and Obituary, *Times of India* July 15th 1990

13 L Fielden *Broadcasting in India* 1940

14–15 Interview with the author

16 Radio Ceylon had been a popular alternative to All India Radio for listeners who wanted more popular programmes including music. Vividh Bharati was an All India Radio station designed to counter the attraction of Radio Ceylon.

17 *Statesman,* Calcutta December 12th 1972, quoted by Ramachandra Guha

18 Interview with Peter Baxter, BBC Sound Archive

19 The story is told by Richard Cashman in his book *Patrons Players and the Crowd*.

20 *Rediff on the Net*: the cricket special

21   Mukul Kesavan *Men in White* (Penguin Viking) 2007 p15
22   BBC Radio 4, March 2006. Shashi Tharoor was at the time an
        Under-Secretary General at the UN
23   *Indian Broadcasting* p 362
24   Interview with the author
25   Hindi writer Kamleswar quoted in *South Delhi Live* May 2001
26–28   Interview with the author
29   Jasdev Singh *Autobiography* p 81
30   *Dharmayng* May 5th 1987
31   Posted by Soundar, Puneet and Mukul Kesavan respectively on the
        Cricinfo blog *Men in White* February 2007
32–34   Interview with the author
35   David Hopps, *Guardian* March 4th 2006.

FOURTEEN

LISTEN TO McCARTHY

IT WAS ON A warm summer night in January 1925 that rugby and radio came together in New Zealand for the first time. In Cardiff the touring New Zealand team were playing the last match of their tour of Britain. A small private radio station in Wellington remained open until nearly three o'clock in the morning, waiting to receive the final score, and those listeners who stayed up heard the news within three minutes of the end of the game. On hoardings around the city, at railway stations, and even on street pavements, the result was chalked up for all to see. The All Blacks had won.

When radio arrived in New Zealand it was a country of just a million and a half, occupying a land area slightly larger than that of Britain. More than ninety per cent of the population were of European, largely British, heritage, many of them deeply attached to their country of origin.

Broadcasting began with private stations operating under licence and the Wellington station which broadcast the 1925 rugby result was one of these. In 1925 the Radio Broadcasting Company (RBC), a private company, was given the brief by government to develop stations in the four main cities.[1] A key feature of the agreement was that the RBC would receive income from licences, thus giving it an incentive to devise programmes that would help increase the sales of radios.

In April 1923 a group of sea scouts had succeeded in broadcasting to a few amateur radio enthusiasts a description of a sculling event in Nelson harbour. But the first live commentary in New Zealand to be formally organised by a broadcasting station took place in May 1926.

An enterprising sports announcer, Alan Allardyce, persuaded the Christchurch broadcasting station that there was an opportunity to interest people in radio. The annual rugby match between Christchurch and the High School Old Boys, played at Lancaster Park, was a popular event and the venue was not too far from the broadcasting transmitter. Allardyce talked the radio station into the idea that a commentary would get people interested in radio; and he persuaded the rugby authorities too, confiding to them that the broadcast would get people interested in rugby. And so the commentary went ahead, and was deemed a success. Few details survive but one enterprising resident, living at the edge of the ground, gave the event an unexpected twist. He placed a loudspeaker connected to his radio on his garden wall, with the result that players and spectators alike could hear every word.

Alan Allardyce was the man who did more than anyone to get commentary started in New Zealand. Over a period of some twelve months in 1926 and 1927 he led a series of audacious experiments which established live coverage of sport as a key feature of New Zealand radio. Allardyce had grown up in Christchurch, a sedate town serving the farming communities of Canterbury province. He had played a little sport, went to the races with his parents, and began studies in marine engineering. But in 1914 his life was changed by the Great War. Allardyce was a corporal in the ambulance corps and a stretcher bearer at Gallipoli. He returned from Europe in 1918, to a country disillusioned by the war, and tried to make a living on a re-settlement farm.

Allardyce would listen to the twice-weekly broadcasts of the Christchurch station, transmitted from a loft in the farmers' sale yards. He had developed a number of sidelines, one of which was selling radio sets, so when the local station began broadcasting sports news Allardyce would put a set on the bar of his favourite Christchurch hotel within the hearing of his fellow drinkers. Pubs were big centres for racing conversations and betting so punters heard the race results on Allardyce's radio long before the local bookmaker knew them. They rushed out from the hotel to place their bets in good time.

Early in 1926, Allardyce secured some part-time work as a radio announcer. He later recalled that at that time radio was regarded as little more than an esoteric hobby but he could see that New Zealanders' interest in sport could be connected to a growing interest in radio.

From the start it became clear that Allardyce was a natural commentator. In the weeks following the broadcast from Lancaster Park he covered three other popular sports – trotting, boxing and hockey. The first hockey commentary was on an international between New Zealand and the visiting Indian army team. With his assistant at his side operating the controls Allardyce sat in the open on a balcony of the pavilion and described the game, almost certainly the first hockey match ever to be broadcast.

Thus, well before the BBC had begun live broadcasts on sport in the UK, listeners in Christchurch had heard commentaries on several sports. The audience was small of course – there were barely five thousand licences across the country at that time, and Christchurch had a population of little more than 100,000. But the RBC had set up a main office in the city and its managing director saw sport as a means of gaining public acceptance of the new medium. Allardyce soon extended his commentary repertoire to soccer, cricket and athletics and the city began to establish itself as a centre for sports broadcasting.

Allardyce's most daring experiment came in August 1926. The RBC needed to get the racing and trotting authorities on board and Allardyce was given that task. He persuaded both the Trotting Club and the Jockey Club to let him cover a major meeting from the Riccarton racecourse, their condition being that he worked from out in the open, and not in the stands. The only vantage point he could find was the top of a haystack. It was cold and damp after recent rain and poorly located on the far side of the course, near the nine furlong post, but he made it work.

The man who drove Allardyce to the course helped him carry the batteries and gear to the top of the stack and then disappeared, leaving him with a microphone and amplifier, and a diagram showing him how to connect them. But Allardyce insisted that this was no problem:

> I borrowed a telephone which was connected to the microphone on the haystack and I was along all day. There was no talkback to the studio so I didn't know whether listeners were hearing me or not.
> I could see with no trouble. I didn't make one mistake all week. I knew all the colours, I knew most of the riders. I knew Riccarton very well. I'd been going there since I was eight years old.[2]

Allardyce recalled that after each race he had to slide off the haystack and dash three hundred yards to the finish to see if he had got the result right. He went through the whole card that day, and the next two, describing each race in turn.

A year or so later came an important landmark. The new Wellington station was due to open on July 16th 1927 but was ready to transmit from the morning of July 9th. It was the day of New Zealand's biggest domestic rugby match – the Ranfurly Shield Challenge, to be played at Masterton some sixty miles from Wellington. Allardyce persuaded the station to test the system by covering the game, even though the commentary would have to be broadcast on a landline at a far greater distance than had ever been attempted before.

Allardyce had chosen well. The game between Wairarapa and Hawkes Bay brought in ten thousand people, some on a special train from Wellington, and the match was full of incident. Allardyce was placed among the crowd on one of the open banks and had to work under some difficulty but this added to the authenticity of the occasion. As the crowd around him moved to and fro, he tried to remain in place, clutching his microphone. At times they crowded down to the touchline, impeding his view. 'I've just had a fight with one man, I'll get my breath back in a minute,' he reported.

This was an important breakthrough, perhaps the day when for some people the habit of listening to rugby began. It was one of the first broadcasts in New Zealand to be heard quite widely across the country. People in many townships stood around public loudspeakers to hear the broadcast. In the small town of Fielding hundreds of people assembled in the main square and heard the sounds of the game and the shouts of the crowd as if they had been present at the match.

By August, Allardyce had done some fifty commentaries. In November 1927 he broadcast all seven days of the Canterbury race meeting at the Riccarton track, covering every race. His only respite came when a female announcer was put on air to describe the dresses worn by women spectators.

Allardyce was soon appointed sports editor for the RBC and oversaw a steady increase in live coverage. In the year ending June 1928 there were on average eleven hours of commentary a week, more than the BBC was offering. But when the control of radio changed hands in 1932, Allardyce fell from favour, left the company, and never broadcast again.

Briefly Allardyce was a voice known across the country, especially when in September 1928 Charles Kingsford Smith and his crew in the *Southern Cross* attempted to fly across the Tasman from Australia for the first time. Broadcasting stations stayed on air throughout the night to report news of the flight and Alan Allardyce was dispatched to Wigram airport at Christchurch to join the waiting crowds. From the roof of the main hangar Allardyce described the plane's arrival and its welcome by a crowd of thirty thousand. All four main broadcasting stations took the Allardyce commentary and people across New Zealand, some gathering in the homes of neighbours, shared proudly in a great achievement.

MUCH HAS BEEN CLAIMED for the place of rugby in New Zealand society. 'A large part of the country's emerging identity would be invested in this particular sport' was the assessment of one leading historian, writing about the impact of the 1905 tour of Britain, on the role that rugby would play in New Zealand.[3] Others have argued that the game embraced egalitarian values; that following rugby was the great common denominator men of all backgrounds could share; that virtue attaches to pastimes which demand physical endurance and in which one is liable to get hurt. In the first years of the 21st century challenges were made to the prevailing views about the origins of New Zealand's love affair with rugby, suggesting that the game had quite practical origins in the desire of public school teachers arriving from Britain to provide a vehicle for expanding sporting rivalries amongst white-collar young men in Christchurch.[4]

It does seem that the tour of Britain by the All Blacks in 1924–5 gave the game impetus in New Zealand. Radio was just appearing on the scene. At the same time New Zealand was being invited to re-think its relationship to Britain and in 1926, under the Balfour Definition, the country was offered much greater autonomy. It was an offer received with mixed feelings as some New Zealanders had no desire to loosen their ties with Britain. The issue of what it meant to be a New Zealander was becoming an increasingly live one.

A few years later, when the British & Irish Lions toured New Zealand in 1930, commentaries helped to cement the place both of radio and of rugby in New Zealand life, and encourage the belief that the two were good for each other. The broadcasts had many of the trappings of modern media coverage. All four Tests were broadcast simultaneously on the four RBC stations, with the exception of local coverage in Christchurch. In addition some stations took relays, for instance the Southlands Radio Society at Invercargill carried the Dunedin commentary down to the southern tip of the country. National coverage, the beginnings of a national audience, the emergence of a national game – these were important broadcasts for the future of radio, and indeed the future of New Zealand.

During the first Test at Dunedin in 1930, loudspeakers were put up at the main stadium in Wellington so that spectators watching a local game could listen to the broadcast. Interest in the tour mounted as New Zealand took the second and third tests. Relays were set up in the Empire theatre in Dargaville (north of Auckland) and in the

Winter Show building at Wellington, where some six hundred people crowded in to hear the broadcast. At moments of drama many joined in the cheering with those watching at the ground.

The newspaper *Radio Record*, in which a weekly schedule of programmes was published, served as something of a propaganda vehicle for radio commentary on sport.[5] The paper attributed considerable influence to the radio commentaries, one the rugby authorities could be pleased about:

> ... in their record attendance on Saturday the Rugby Union was certainly reaping the popularity evoked by the steady broadcast by radio throughout recent seasons. The influx of country visitors from far afield has shown the hold that Rugby has upon the whole country, and indicates that radio has built a Rugby audience far beyond the confines of the cities primarily concerned.

The commentaries undoubtedly aroused enthusiasm and the commentators, who included Charlie Lamberg and Gordon Hutter, received many plaudits. They did their preparation well, attending team practices to ensure that they had no problems with the identification of players during a game. The commentaries were noted for moments of sentiment and humour, and local touches. 'There are many Taranake farmers here, guess some of their wives and children will be milking the cows tonight.'[6] Some listeners sent messages to the commentators by telegram during the broadcast and these were read out on air, anticipating by more than seventy years the commitment to 'listener involvement' favoured by modern broadcasters.

At the end of August, the British team visited the Wellington studios to make their farewells. The moments when the British team left Wellington docks for the journey to Australia en route to the UK were covered live. Each member of the team was asked to make some final remarks to the microphone and 'not a few young ladies were thanked for their hospitality'.[7]

There were several disputes between New Zealand radio authorities and sporting bodies at this time, deriving largely from fears similar to those expressed in England, America, Brazil and elsewhere. A ban on racing and trotting commentaries lasted for several years but was resolved when the New Zealand Broadcasting Board (NZBB) agreed to make an annual payment for commentaries.[8] The New Zealand Rugby Union (NZRU) also enforced a partial ban and tried to prevent coverage of the 1930 tour but they were forced to give way, largely through public pressure. No real rugby enthusiast, argued *Radio Record,* would stay at home when there was a live match to watch nearby.

The broadcasts of the 1930 tour helped to lead to a change of opinion among both broadcasters and rugby authorities. By 1934 the NZBB was paying the rugby authorities £500 to broadcast matches under its control. The Broadcasting Board had covered rugby league matches in Canterbury during the ban on rugby union but it now abandoned the former, arguing that it was 'committed to the broadcasting of the national game'. In 1937 the South African Springbok tour received even wider coverage, with every match broadcast live, and heard throughout the country. By now 'Whang' McKenzie, the ex-teacher from Dunedin, had become a favourite commentator. Broadcasters had successfully used sport to create a nationwide audience. Radio had a firm partnership with rugby and the sport's position in New Zealand life seemed unassailable.

BEFORE TAKING THE STORY of rugby and radio further, a diversion is necessary: in the direction of the wrestling ring. It was in its coverage of wrestling events, as well as rugby, that New Zealand radio won national audiences, and the man who did this was Gordon Hutter.

Hutter was the most versatile and best known of all the pre-war commentators. He broadcast racing, rugby and many other sports, but it was wrestling that he did most to popularise. Wrestling evenings had long been an attraction in the larger New Zealand cities but it was Hutter's radio commentaries which did much to win a country-wide following for the sport.

Gordon Hutter was born of Austrian and Jewish parents in Auckland in 1901. His first broadcast was in 1923, his speciality being the performance of humorous recitations. But he was also a compulsive games player, excelling in many sports, and in 1927 he was asked to try a live broadcast on cricket. This was the start of a career lasting into the 1940s, one which brought him a considerable following. Almost always in a suit, and wearing a trilby, he was a familiar figure at outside broadcast events.

Hutter started to cover wrestling in the late 1920s when the Canadian George Walker was one of the sport's main attractions. Auckland Town Hall would be packed, with many prominent locals in the best seats. The ring was placed about a metre and a half above the floor and Hutter stood beside it, his microphone level with the canvas floor.

Listeners waited keenly for the familiar refrain when Walker applied his 'back-loop slam': *'He can't get out of it … he can't get out of it … he's out of it.'* Hutter and Walker between them, it was said, did more to sell radios than anyone at that time. Listeners could follow every move through Hutter's calm and authoritative descriptions, heard above the raucous shouting of the crowd, some of whom had come straight from the local pubs. And Hutter was renowned for getting from the ringside to the studio, just under a mile away, to read the evening sports bulletin in just the time it took to play two records.

Later the star of many of Hutter's wrestling commentaries was New Zealander Lofty Blomfield. Here is Hutter, meticulous as always in capturing the details of a fight, describing from Auckland Town Hall a British Empire heavyweight title bout between Blomfield and his Canadian rival Earl McCready in 1939:

> *Blomfield's holding McCready with a side twisted headlock and forced him over into this corner. McCready's trying to get his knee into the middle of Blomfield's back and he's taken Blomfield up and right back into the corner and he holds on tight with that side headlock on McCready. The referee's going in between the pair of them and he breaks them out.*
>
> *Blomfield's climbed up the ropes to get extra pressure but the ref broke them out and back into the centre. Back they come and this time McCready gets the inside position to force Blomfield's head back. He forces Blomfield back against the rope and then forces his head over with the yoke hold. Blomfield's trying to swing round, Blomfield swinging round suddenly, but McCready beats him to it, and McCready bringing Blomfield down over his own knee and holding on tight. Some of the crowd are calling it a stranglehold, but the referee puts his fingers underneath McCready's arm and says it's all right …*[9]

Hutter was often accompanied by a 'comments man'. His name was Peter Morelatos but he was universally referred to as 'Blind Peter' – he had lost his eyesight in a boating accident in the 1920s. Like Wakelam's 'assistant' at Twickenham in 1927, Blind Peter must have been quite a spur to Hutter's descriptive powers. He also acted as the voice of Blomfield's fan club, shouting encouragement for the local favourite to embroider Hutter's commentaries. After a few violent thumps, recalled one listener, you would invariably hear Morelatos's gruff encouragement: 'Go it, Lofty'.

Radio Record regularly printed letters from Hutter's admirers – 'a glad smile comes over our faces when your voice is heard' said one admirer in Nelson. An Auckland woman testified to how much the commentaries meant to people in poorer accommodation:

> You little know the joy and gaiety you are giving to hundreds of back-block people. I am a white-haired mother, but I look forward always to your sporting news. I go with you to the races, football, wrestling, etc and enjoy every minute of your company.

These were hard times for many New Zealanders. The country had gone into recession in the 1920s and some estimates are that in 1929–30 perhaps forty per cent of the male workforce was unemployed. Wages and salaries were cut by ten per cent. When relief camps for unemployed workers were established in the countryside, the Toc H organisation donated radios to entertain the men at night. *Radio Record* sent a journalist to an isolated camp in Otago to ask about their listening habits and discovered that the men chose Gordon Hutter as their favourite broadcaster.

When the economy began to recover the arrival of car radios boosted listening figures for Hutter's broadcasts on wrestling and the races. *Radio Record* noted in 1933:

> The latest craze in Auckland is to have a radio set installed in your motor-car… Passing the Town Hall a few nights ago while a wrestling contest was in full swing I saw five taxi drivers seated in one car on the rank outside the Civic Theatre all enjoying the broadcast by Gordon Hutter.[10]

And one listener recalled that wrestling had a big following in rural areas:

> Farmers had the old radio sets in their cowsheds. The milking didn't finish until Lofty or Earl had won their bouts and tea was often not on the table until after ten p.m. The two men brought untold pleasure to many New Zealanders who lived in country areas and couldn't be at the weekly fights.
> The radio years were the great years for me personally, and I couldn't wait for nine o'clock to come round on wrestling nights. Monday was Auckland and Dunedin, Tuesday was Christchurch, Thursday was Wellington and some of the smaller clubs and cities had Saturday night … I was always in trouble for listening in on too much wrestling and my parents often checked at the door to see

if I had the radio going. Luckily I could usually hear them coming and managed to switch the radio off in time.[11]

Gordon Hutter would receive up to five hundred letters a week from listeners, some from as far away as Australia, with comments about his coverage or questions about the sport, and he would deal with some of these in the intervals between rounds. He was a qualified wrestling referee but from time to time he would visit the gym at the Hotel Auckland and ask about a particular hold, often requesting that it be applied to him so he could better understand it.

It seems likely that Hutter did collaborate in some of the 'scripted' moments in fights. He occasionally refereed wrestling bouts at out lying towns and he once disqualified the American wrestler 'Thunderbolt' Jack Patterson for 'gouging and hair-pulling'. Patterson clamped a headlock on Hutter, who had to be rescued by the other contestant. The police eventually entered the ring and brought proceedings to a halt. It was good publicity.

Hutter's stamina and versatility seem to have matched that of Bobby Talyarkhan in India. During week-long race meetings over the Christmas and New Year period he would regularly describe fifty-six races in seven days, while continuing his wrestling commitments in the evenings. At least once he described hockey and football matches played consecutively on the same afternoon. Like Alan Allardyce before him he was ingenious in finding solutions to commentary problems. On one occasion, during disputes with the racing authorities about access for commentary, he broadcast eight races from Green Lane Road outside the Auckland racetrack: he used stepladders from the footpath, then a motor lorry parked nearby, and finally the back of a vegetable cart operated by a Chinese trader. During that day his technical gear and telephone line had to be moved six times.

Attempts by Australian stations to lure Hutter away were unsuccessful but in the early 1950s he was cited in a high-profile divorce case and left New Zealand, returning later in life to be reunited with his wife. Hutter and Peter Morelatos died within a month of each other in 1968.

Hutter had worked through over a decade of increasing growth in radio ownership. Sports coverage grew steadily but it remained a male preserve with little attention to women's sport. Licence numbers grew rapidly during the 1930s, from just over fifty thousand to nearly three hundred and fifty thousand, and this represented a fivefold increase in the number per head of the population. More and more people were listening to the same programmes.

The government elected in 1935 was led by Michael Savage, who doubled as Minister of Broadcasting and who believed that radio ownership was an indication that an ordinary family was gaining access to the better things in life. In 1936 his government established a fully-fledged New Zealand Broadcasting Service (NZBS); by the outbreak of war eighty per cent of households had licences and commentaries on major sporting events could now be heard in almost every home.

THE MAN WHO WAS TO BECOME the most influential person in New Zealand sports broadcasting, Winston McCarthy, was born in 1908 and grew up in Wellington. He was to give New Zealand rugby its distinctive voice, and many New Zealanders felt he was their voice too – not the disembodied BBC-style voice of many announcers, but conversational, plain-speaking, and passionate about the game.

His father was a salesman, a great story-teller and entertainer. The young Winston could mimic anyone at an early age – Harry Lauder was his special turn. McCarthy calculated that between the ages of seven and ten he performed at nearly four hundred concerts, mostly fund-raising efforts to raise money for the troops going to Europe for the Great War.

He played a fair amount of rugby and knew the game well. He had many jobs after leaving school, none of them for any great length of time, and his opening in broadcasting did not come until 1934. A chance meeting at a party with a broadcaster led to an offer to take character parts in radio plays on a freelance basis. It was an opportunity to perform again. Three years later McCarthy joined the 2YD station in Wellington as a programme organiser.

It took him a few more years to get into sports commentary, a job he much coveted. His first microphone trial was unsuccessful. The Director of Broadcasting at the NBS was Professor James Shelley, who saw radio as a force for improvement, rather in the Lord Reith mould. McCarthy described his own voice as 'more Cockney than Oxford' and Shelley would not put him on air as the voice of New Zealand radio. (Shelley read the main news bulletins himself during the war, not trusting the announcers to do it with sufficient gravity.)

In 1942 McCarthy finally persuaded the station to let him cover a local college game in Wellington:

> I ... stood on a table with the crowd all around me and got

cracking. I didn't know some of the players from Adam
– they had no numbers on their backs ... But I'd found out
their names and recognised one or two. The backs were
easy, but, as usual, with the forwards I had to concentrate
a good bit. But I got through it all right.[12]

A year later McCarthy was in the army and there he soon began
broadcasts on inter-services games.

Early in 1945, the idea was conceived that a New Zealand army
team should be formed from troops in Europe and North Africa and
should tour Britain before the players returned home after the war.
The team was officially the 2nd New Zealand Expeditionary Force
team but they were more widely known simply as 'The Kiwis'. The
players won thirty-two of their thirty-eight matches and brought to
the game open and fast rugby which often excited similar qualities
in the opposition. And they played with what New Zealand's greatest
rugby writer, Terry McLean, called 'staunch and bewilderingly laconic
comradeship', reflecting perhaps the experiences they had shared as
soldiers.[13]

The idea that McCarthy might be sent to Europe at public expense
to cover the matches had to be cleared with the Prime Minister, Peter
Fraser, himself a rugby enthusiast. Fraser was approached at a suitable moment, while he was watching a big match at Athletic Park.
He was in no doubt what these commentaries might mean to New
Zealanders in the first months after the war. 'Yes, certainly. He *should*
go,' said Fraser. On the back of this instruction, McCarthy wangled
himself a commission and caught the next available flight to the UK.
McCarthy travelled almost everywhere with The Kiwis and was often
photographed with them, everyone in army uniform. He was one of
the squad.

The BBC had consented in principle to co-operate with their visi-
tor but they had no idea who was being sent. Fortunately perhaps
they identified in George Looker just the right person to act as an in-
termediary. Looker, an Australian by birth, had worked for some years
in the BBC Pacific section. McCarthy reported to him the day after arriving in Britain – his journey from New Zealand had taken seventy-
two hours – and it was clear immediately that the two men could do
business with each other. At their first meeting they worked out all
the details of what was to be a historic sequence of broadcasts.

'International' games were to be broadcast live on short-wave to New
Zealand. Commentaries on other matches were to be recorded and the
recordings flown to New Zealand. In addition, edited highlights would

be broadcast a few hours after each game. No one in New Zealand had been able to hear a commentary on anything resembling a national team for six or seven years. Now they could tune into McCarthy twice a week.

So McCarthy settled into his hectic routine of broadcasts, travel and editing, growing in confidence and in the impact he made both at home and in Britain. To undertake nearly forty commentaries and match reports, as well as the travel, in four months, spoke of a man of enormous physical and vocal energy. He worked regularly alongside Raymond Glendenning, Rex Alston and, occasionally, Howard Marshall, different voices but all polished to BBC standards. At first Glendenning always did the commentary for home listeners. McCarthy was told early on that his voice, set beside the rounded tones of the BBC men, sounded too much like a cockney to go out to British listeners. Then, recalled McCarthy, Looker broke the news that it had been decided that the home audience might after all be exposed to the commentator's broad and gravelly voice:

> We've been listening to your recordings and we've decided that even though you do sound like a cockney we don't notice it while we're listening to the game. We wondered if you'd mind doing half the match for us.

And so it was that, for the princely sum of twenty-five guineas, McCarthy's voice went out on the BBC.

There were many great games, not least the two matches at Cardiff Arms Park. Damaged as it was by bombing, and reduced in capacity, the atmosphere at the stadium was unique. The game against Cardiff on Boxing Day was McCarthy's first visit, the first time he heard the singing of the Welsh crowd, the first time he had commentated directly to British listeners. 'He created quite a sensation,' recalled one of his British colleagues, Rex Alston, years later, 'and in Wales they thought he was the best commentator they had ever heard.'[14]

A few days later came the 'international' match against Wales at the same stadium. The station in Wellington came on the air at 2.15 a.m. and all over New Zealand small boys were woken by their parents so they could listen.

But it was at Twickenham not Cardiff that McCarthy first used the phrase by which he is most remembered. Herb Cook, the short, bulky New Zealander, prepared for a penalty kick on the halfway line, less than a yard in from touch. McCarthy told his listeners:

There will be a terrific roar if it goes over. I'll let you judge for yourselves how he goes. Here he is moving into the ball. He has kicked it and, LISTEN (the roar from the crowd swelled and swelled). *It's a goal.*

His voice seemed to soar with the ball. Throughout his career he would now call *'listen'* whenever a kick was taken.

George Looker proved a valuable source of advice. He told Mc Carthy not to try and keep the tension going even when the ball was in touch, to bring in more light and shade. McCarthy recalled later:

That's how I came to force myself into that habit. You bring your listeners up with the excitement of the play to the goal-line, and then you drop your voice and say, 'Now, the ball's in touch, Jarden is going to throw it in. In it goes, and up goes White, he's taken the ball, he's whipped it back', bringing up the excitement gradually. And off you go again.

McCarthy's great skill and insight was to involve his listeners. This he did both in his short scripted match reports and in his live commentary. Some of his match reports remain, scribbled in pencil on foolscap paper, the written words with the same rhythm as his speech and always with the personalised opening: *'Hello, New Zealand'*.

New Zealanders had been starved of sports news. Their national team had not played since 1938 and the Kiwis carried all their hopes. The commentaries carried more than the usual magic of radio, they carried the hopes of a return to normality, after the hardships of the depression and the losses of war. McCarthy brought better news, and he brought it before the newspapers did, in a language New Zealanders could recognise. Within weeks he had become a household name.

To some it seemed that New Zealanders had won not just the rugby but the commentary stakes also. McCarthy certainly impressed Rex Alston. The two men could not have been more different: Alston (Trent College and Cambridge) and McCarthy (Marist Brothers' School, Wellington and veteran of 'the halls'). But Alston took an instant liking to him when they met in London:

Still in army uniform ... broad shoulders, the build and figure of a scrum half, which position he had filled with distinction in his own country, with the friendliest face in the world. He greeted me with a charming smile ... and

I knew from that moment that working with him would be easy.

Alston also came to admire McCarthy's commentary:

> I was amazed at the speed of his commentary and the wealth of detail that he packed into it. I had often heard Raymond Glendenning and he went fast enough in all conscience, though there were moments of comparative quiescence. But McCarthy was on the top note the whole time. He made everything sound exciting to the listener – even when a man was lying on the ground and the ball was some distance away ... his voice seemed as strong at the end of the match as at the beginning ... Not only did he know the game thoroughly, but never, on all the occasions I was with him was he at a loss for a word, never once behind the play and here and there he would interject little touches of humour to lighten the occasion.

It was an opinion echoed some years later by Bill McLaren who, as part of his early training, was sent to watch McCarthy at work in 1953. He stood behind him in the commentary box at Cardiff. 'He was really like a verbal typewriter, a machine gun and he was as knowledgeable of tactics as you would expect of a New Zealander.'[15]

After the war, McCarthy returned to full-time work with the NBS, covering various sports. In 1953 he left full-time employment with the broadcasting service and took a job as an auctioneer, continuing as a commentator on a contractual basis. He was the voice of New Zealand rugby until 1959, as well known, better known perhaps, than the All Black players themselves. He bought the great series of 1949, in South Africa, and 1953–54, in Britain, to New Zealand listeners who would otherwise have had to wait several days for filmed coverage. And then came perhaps the peak of his fame as a broadcaster, the home series of 1956 against the Springboks.

Some snippets of McCarthy broadcasts remain. The descriptions are vivid. Moves of some intricacy are recalled in detail immediately after the event. But what still gives the commentary its distinct appeal more than fifty years later is the character in the voice, the raciness, informality and warmth. Here he is at work in the third Test of the Springboks tour of 1956, played at Lancaster Park in Christchurch before a crowd of more than fifty thousand. It was a fine day, the ground firm and the rugby at the highest level. With New Zealand leading 11-7 South Africa scored a vital try which kept them in the game. McCarthy's rich, urgent voice follows the play with a natural authority, and the rhythmic phrases vividly captured the intrinsic pulse of the game:

> *It's got by Gentles again,*
> *He's coming around left*
> *Looking for business*
> *Still coming left*
> *Still coming left*
> *Inside he gets it to Ackerman*
> *Ackerman's caught by Clark*
> *Now it's gone out*
> *And it's got by Bekke*
> *He's trying to throw it down*
> *There might be a try to Claassen*
> *There's Rosenberg coming in now for a try*
> (McCarthy pauses to allow the cheering to subside)
> *It's a try for South Africa*
> *A try for South Africa by Rosenberg*
> *Twenty minutes gone*
> *Rosenberg, a try*

McCarthy certainly had his critics. They alleged that he over-egged the excitement in matches. Stories were told of people leaving their armchairs after fifteen minutes of a commentary to rush to the ground only to find that the dramatic game McCarthy was describing was a run of the mill encounter. Chris Laidlaw, a distinguished All Black himself, who listened to McCarthy when he was growing up, recalled a conversation in the 1960s:

> I remember talking to him about the job of the commentator – that it was to recreate something for the listener. He freely admitted that he would sometimes make an unexciting match much more exciting than it was. But for the rugby purist that was not a major problem because for them it was exciting anyway, even when nothing much seemed to be happening, but all sorts of things are happening.[16]

Iain Gallaway, who commentated on rugby for more than twenty-six years and was respected above all for his accuracy, thought that

McCarthy made sports broadcasting 'compulsive listening' but made this reservation:

> His style could not have survived in the present day, when sports spectators listen to the game through transistors as they watch it. For Winston was a law unto himself, and from time to time he improvised when he thought it would enhance the game … that style wouldn't be acceptable today, when detailed factual accuracy is required.[17]

No doubt McCarthy's childhood experience as an entertainer gave him an edge, a touch of theatricality and showmanship. He knew about the relationship between performer and audience, and the link he provided between players and listeners. He could switch subtly from the role of narrator to that of excited spectator. Those cheeky, personal inserts – *'Someone's going to get into trouble, you know'* – *'I reckon this boy's a little beauty'* – helped warm the nights of his listeners thousands of miles away. The sportswriter and historian Ron Palenski linked McCarthy to New Zealanders' sense of themselves:

> I guess you could liken his commentaries to New Zealand players. New Zealanders shaped the game in their own fashion; McCarthy's commentary did likewise and reflected how we saw ourselves.[18]

Winston McCarthy died in 1984. In later life he was always ready to hold forth, his conversation full of stories of the old days, the people he liked, and the people he did not. He gave freely of his opinions. In the *Auckland Star* Peter Devlin described visiting McCarthy in retirement:

> The prediction was made that Winston, the time being noon, would be sitting in the pub, having a quiet jug and talking to anyone who would listen. He would look up at our entrance, miss hardly a beat and say: 'Gidday, son. Sit down and have a beer'. And go on talking. Through the bat-wing doors – we were out west – and into the bar. There was Winston as predicted. He said: 'Gidday son. Sit down and have a beer'. And he went on talking.

THE 1950S WERE PROBABLY the peak years for radio commentary in New Zealand. Sports participation was growing among men and women. In 1955 there were seven hundred and twenty-two live commentaries, of which two hundred and thirty-nine were on rugby and one hundred and seventy-seven on racing, far more than in Britain. The big events were often from overseas and shared with the BBC. Night-time listening became an important part of life. Jonathan Hunt, who has been a minister of broadcasting and the New Zealand High Commissioner in London, recalled that when he was a child 'my father would take me into his bed to listen with him to John Arlott and Rex Alston'.[19]

It was rugby most of all which got people up in the small hours. In the 1960s, Bob Irvine took over from Winston McCarthy as lead commentator and Grant Nisbett, who was to be a radio commentator himself for many years, remembered listening to him on his transistor as a boy. 'The match might not have been until 3 a.m. but I didn't sleep before the game.'[20]

Commentary interfered with work and with holidays. David Lange, Prime Minister of New Zealand between 1984 and 1989, recalled that his father, a GP, would sometimes check out the scores between patients at the afternoon surgery. Writer Joseph Romanos remembered holidays as a child when he spent 'most of the day in the car with the key turned on'. 'Everybody listened', said Chris Laidlaw:

> Radio was institutionalised in peoples' lives – there was no alternative. Many of the big matches were played in the middle of the night and this gave it all a kind of Halloween quality – as if the broadcast was disembodied and from the other ends of the earth. That gave it a cachet which you would not get in the immediacy of a TV broadcast. With radio it was privilege, a privileged flow of information a long way off.

If rugby had a rival as the first sport of New Zealand radio, it was racing. And in the 1930s it acquired a radio commentator and trackside caller, who, like Winston McCarthy, became the voice of his sport. David Clarkson started his radio career as a twenty-four-year-old in 1937 and continued until 1971. The rhythm and unfolding pace of races, and their short duration, enabled Clarkson to evolve a technique, a patter presentation some called it. Each race seemed to be sung to almost the same seductive tune. His admirers would stand within a few metres of him in the crowded stands at the Addington track as he talked the race through. The writer Harvey McQueen remembered how Clarkson kept him company when he was ill at home as a boy:

> ... Pop and I would pick winners from the paper, and I would tune in to see how my choices got on. Race books became part of my reading mania. I cut them up and devised my own races, imitating Dave Clarkson, the caller. 'Good for his lungs', the doctor said.[21]

One of Clarkson's youthful admirers became his successor. Reon Murtha would try out his commentary skills as a boy by dropping tennis balls, each coloured to match the horses of a particular stable, into a stream and then telling his imaginary audience about their progress.

Murtha left school in 1959 at the age of eighteen and joined the New Zealand Broadcasting Service at Greymouth. Within a year he was doing course commentaries over the PA at Reefton, standing on a beer crate out on the steps at the foot of the grandstand. In 1961 he did his first radio broadcast on the local station at Greymouth and in 1969 he was sufficiently established to take over Clarkson's position as commentator for Canterbury Jockey Club at Riccarton. Over his forty-seven years, he developed a formidable reputation for accuracy and reliability. Reon Murtha won the affection not only of listeners and race-goers but jockeys and drivers too: they lined up to thank him when he did his last New Zealand Cup in 2006. He called the last of his estimated 50,000 races on his 'home ground' of Reefton in January 2007.

If Winston McCarthy's delivery matched the fast and colourful rhythms of rugby, that of another Scot, Iain Gallaway, was distinctly more urbane. In forty years of commentary, on rugby as well as cricket, between 1952 and 1992 he covered more than one thousand matches, many of the cricket matches in harness with the equally respected Alan Richards. Gallaway's unique position was that he combined experience of international matches with excellent knowledge of the local context of the game, and a continuing legal practice. This gave him a much stronger grounding in the audience to whom he was speaking than for many. Perhaps too the legal training and practice contributed to the quiet, assiduous and accurate commentary style.

Peter Montgomery was one of the latest in the line of New Zealand radio commentators to win a national audience, and this in an unexpected field: sailing. It was the commercial station 1ZB which spotted the possibilities of live coverage in the 1970s. Montgomery acknowledged that he had to invent a new approach because he had no predecessor in the job:

> It was an interesting time when I started because there was a mix of cultural cringe and Kiwi brashness. Some thought the British way was the only way. There were others who tried to connect with the audience as they would in a pub conversation.
>
> My broadcasts began with commentaries on fleet races for sailing boats and the style I used was similar to athletic or racing commentaries but I started to develop my own style and delivery.[22]

The success of New Zealand sailing grew in the 1970s and 1980s and Montgomery's reputation grew with it. During the 1977 Round the World race he learned from Clare Francis that she was reporting back to Capital Radio in London three times a week and he set up similar arrangements with New Zealand yachtsman Peter Blake and others. These reports became compulsive listening for many who had not previously followed the sport.

Montgomery then moved on further, sailing in some of the ocean classic races including the Sydney to Hobart and Fastnet races:

> It was my version of Hemingway at the bullfight: getting as close to the action as the matador but seeing it from a different perspective. During the 1984 Sydney to Hobart race when life was lost for the first time and two thirds of the contestants withdrew because of the conditions I reported that it was like driving an eight-ton truck off a three-storey building every five minutes. It was then that we saw what I called 'liquid Himalayas'.

With the growing success of New Zealand in Olympic sailing and the America's Cup, Peter Montgomery's reports became part of broadcasting folklore, just at a time when television seemed about to monopolise live sport. He drew many listeners again during the 2007 America's Cup. He often quotes the words of his mentor Bill McCarthy: 'Never forget you're talking to the little old lady with blue rinse hair and white tennis shoes in Riverton'. His ability is to capture, for many who have never been sailing as well as those who have, the thrills and the dangers of a special sport.

In the 1960s and '70s the issue of sporting relationships with South Africa created a sharp challenge for New Zealand commentators. During the tours to South Africa of 1928, 1949 and 1960, no Maori players were considered for selection. The New Zealand rugby authorities explained their position by arguing that it was in the interest of those Maoris concerned since they would be 'humiliated' if they went on the tours, and would be treated as second-class citizens. It was perhaps because of all this that the author Ian Wedde, writing of the ability of people of both Maori and European origin to support the New Zealand team together, wrote: 'This great national ritual was also the occasion of profound forgetting. The occasion was not so much about remembering who we were as forgetting who we are.'[23]

What did commentators have to say? In the months leading up to the 1959 tour Winston McCarthy supported the right of the New Zealand Rugby Football Union (NZRFU) not to send Maori players to South Africa. He argued that it was not the job of the NZRFU to 'interfere with politics', nor was the Union 'morally bound to show a lead to the world'. He argued that the existence from time to time of Maori teams in New Zealand from which whites were excluded was precedent for a whites-only team. Another of his arguments related to the impact that the performance of Maori players might have, for instance, if one of the star Maori players such as Pat Walsh or Bill Gray were to run through and score a try. 'The natives would go mad: we would have riots there and we can't be responsible for that kind of thing.'

McCarthy later acknowledged that in deference to South Africa's racist laws, 'some mighty players' had been omitted. In 1970, however, the South Africans, desperate to keep their sporting ties with New Zealand alive, announced that they would accept Maori players. McCarthy felt this was sufficient reason to tour. He was critical – aggressively so – of those who argued that to play in South Africa was to condone racism.

It was the 1981 tour of New Zealand by the Springboks which caused deep and bitter rifts in New Zealand society and required commentators to ask themselves some difficult questions. Some New Zealanders were already exploring their country's own racial history in new ways. Protestors saw it as an invitation to New Zealanders to declare where they stood on racism not only in South Africa but in their own society. The largest police operation in New Zealand history was required to deal with the demonstrations against the tour. The sport which seemed to have united New Zealand was now dividing it.

The commentators themselves were certainly divided. Some took the view that if a match was played it was their duty as journalists to be there to describe it, demonstrations and all. Some felt they had to take a stand with the protestors. And some could not make up their minds. Brendan Telfer, echoing John Arlott's position in England over a cricket tour, chose not to broadcast:

> I found apartheid so deeply and morally offensive that I did not wish to have anything to do with the tour ... I had been to South Africa and witnessed with my own eyes the essence of apartheid at work so that experience was crucial in helping me reach the decision not to work on the tour.[24]

Keith Quinn had not at first felt deeply involved in these issues. But a visit to South Africa in 1976 revealed to him the subjugation of black South Africans. The 1981 tour therefore presented him with a dilemma:

> I remember saying to the boss: 'I'll broadcast the games, but don't ask me to do background stories, don't ask me to interview the Springboks, just don't ask me to do this ...'[25]

In the end, the divisions in New Zealand society, and among broadcasters, were so deep that the Broadcasting Corporation took the unusual step of allowing staff a vote and there were meetings all over the country. The majority decided in favour of covering the tour. Keith Quinn was to play an important role in broadcasting not only about the rugby but about the reactions of those opposed to the tour, thus presenting to New Zealand a picture of itself as it reached a moment of choice in its history.

Although the tour took place, New Zealand society, and New Zealand rugby, changed as a result of the debates of 1981. The All Blacks did not play South Africa again until the ending of apartheid and no commentator ever again had to decide whether to cover a match involving a whites-only South African team.

There was however a postscript to the 1981 debate five years later. An unofficial tour to South Africa, involving a majority of New Zealand's leading players, was organised without the backing of the rugby authorities. The head of Radio New Zealand, Beverley Wakem, like her television counterparts, said there would be no commentaries. The grounds given (by Hugh Rennie, chair of the Broadcasting Corporation) were that the 'corporation would not validate or encourage an unauthorised event'. Broadcasters had a duty 'to respect the New Zealand and international structure of organised amateur rugby'. Others argued that since many people wanted coverage, it should be provided.

Beverley Wakem recalled that, in respect of radio, the decision was a pragmatic one: 'As this was not an All Blacks tour and it was not supported by NZRU it was felt that the public interest was served by news coverage of the matches and associated events.'[26]

Broadcasting historian Patrick Day took a different view. He described the interpretation taken by the Corporation of their duties as 'unusual', judging that 'The corporation came to an ethical decision and chose the anti-apartheid side'.[27]

RADIO'S HOLD ON LIVE COMMENTARY in New Zealand could not last. During the 1970s and 1980s television established itself and won much bigger audiences. Rugby became as important to television in New Zealand as the Premier League football is in England.

Much radio coverage migrated to the commercial network which was privatised in the 1990s. In 1989 'public' radio in New Zealand was entrusted to a state-owned enterprise, Radio New Zealand. It offers only limited live commentary while Radio Sport, part of the commercial company 1ZB, offers most of the coverage. General manager Bill Francis, himself once a commentator, was sure radio has a place:

> Radio can still hold its own. It's the mobility factor. Cricket commentary is still very popular – people listen when they are gardening or painting – and it helps our ratings lift. The advent of new media is enormous but people have the desire for familiarity.[28]

The top sports for Radio Sport in 2008 are rugby – which is a long way ahead of the others – cricket, rugby league and netball. A dedicated network called Radio Trackside, owned by the New Zealand Racing Industry Board, now has exclusive rights to broadcast all race meetings.

During the 2007 Rugby World Cup in France, many New Zealanders listened in the early hours to radio coverage from Europe. A number of 'alternative' commentaries were also on offer, aimed at those who wanted to follow the sport in a more light-hearted manner. Some New Zealanders, including people who like the game, have welcomed the fact that rugby has lost what Chris Laidlaw once called its 'vice-like grip' on the country's national identity. But radio played a key role in the process whereby rugby became an important part of New Zealand life and it will still be there providing its own unique 'pictures' when the rugby World Cup comes to New Zealand in 2011.

Main sources: *The Oxford History of New Zealand* (OUP 1962); Michael King *The Penguin History of New Zealand* (Penguin 2003); *An Encyclopaedia of New Zealand* (R E Owen 1966); *New Zealand Memories* (annual publication); Winston McCarthy *Listen! It's a goal!* (Pelham 1973) and *Broadcasting with the Kiwis* (Reed 1947); Patrick Day *The Radio Years* (Auckland University Press 1994) and *Voice and Vision* (AUP 2000); Chris Laidlaw *Rights of Passage* (Hodder Moa Beckett 1999); Terry McLean *Great Days in New Zealand Rugby* (Reed 1959); Iain Gallaway *Not a Cloud in the Sky* (Harper Collins); Bill Francis *ZB* (Harper Collins 2006) and *Inside Talk Radio* (Darius 2002); Warwick Roger *Old Heroes* (Hodder 1991); John H Hall *History of Broadcasting in New Zealand 1920-54* (Wellington 1980); *New Zealand Yesterdays* (D Bateman 2001); ed D Vanitz and B Willmott *Culture and Identity in New Zealand* (GP Books 1989); ed R Palenski *Between the Posts* (Hodder and Stoughton 1989); Ken Collins *Broadcasting Grave and Gay* (Caxton 1967).

Newspapers consulted: *Auckland Star*; *New Zealand Herald*; *New Zealand Listener*; *Radio Record*.

1   Auckland, Christchurch, Dunedin and Wellington – all established in the 1840s.
2   *New Zealand Herald*, April 7th 1979
3   *The Penguin History of New Zealand* p281
4   See *Tackling Rugby Myths* edited by Greg Ryan (University of Otago Press 2005).
5   The *Radio Record* was originally launched by the RBC. It served some of the purposes served by *Radio Times* in Britain, including that of defending the broadcasting authorities against criticisms from sporting bodies.
6   *Radio Record* August 1st 1930
7   *Radio Record* August 22nd 1930
8   The NZBB was set up by government in 1932 to replace the RBC and run New Zealand Radio.
9   *50 years of Sports Broadcasts* (Radio New Zealand 1975)
10   *Radio Record* September 13th 1937
11   Dave Cameron in *New Zealand Memories 2003* p54
12   This and other quotations from Winston McCarthy are taken from *Listen! It's a Goal* and *Broadcasting with the Kiwis* – see above
13   *Great Days in New Zealand Rugby* p114
14   This and other quotations from Rex Alston are taken from *Taking the Air* (Stanley Paul 1955)
15   Bill McClaren *Talking of Rugby* (Stanley Paul 1991) p55
16   Interview with the author

17   Iain Gallaway *Not a Cloud in the Sky* (Harper Collins) p177
18–20   Interview with the author
21   Harvey McQueen *This Piece of Earth* (AWA Press 2004) p191
22   Interview with the author
23   Ian Wedde *Living in Time: A Day at the Footie* (New Zealand Electronic
        Poetry Centre website)
24–26   Interview with the author
27   This and quote from Hugh Rennie: *Voice and Vision* p 332-33
28   Interview with the author

PART FOUR

THE CHALLENGES OF
DIFFERENT SPORTS

FIFTEEN

RISE OF THE SUMMARISER

ONE SIGNIFICANT CHANGE in radio's coverage of sport started in the late 1970s, one which would surprise the pioneers of commentary. A new dimension has been added to the commentary process. The original dilemma – whether to use a sporting expert or a broadcaster to do the commentary – was resolved by having both, side by side.

No commentary became complete without the voice of the experts, who summarise and analyse the action.

For many years the commentator's narration, if it was interrupted at all, was supplemented by occasional contributions from a summariser. Although practice varies in detail from sport to sport, the summariser became a central figure in the commentary process. Commentators may be in the lead but the broadcast is no longer a monologue. It is almost unbroken conversation. The idea is not only to provide expertise but to ensure good *talk*, and *opinion*, both seen as essential ingredients of popular broadcasting. It is perhaps no surprise that in one magazine poll in 2007 to find the best 'commentator' on cricket it was an articulate summariser – Geoffrey Boycott – who won.[1]

The forerunner of today's commentators, Teddy Wakelam, had a second person in the box with him for his first commentary from Twickenham in 1927. Back-up staff were also provided for football and racing commentators. In general Wakelam, however, disliked the idea of sharing the broadcast with an 'expert', especially for tennis:

> Sometimes the Americans work a double turn, a man like Tilden for instance coming into the box, and being cross-questioned and drawn out by the ordinary commentator. This has never struck me as being a very efficient method, but of course it means a lot from the point of view of name.[2]

But during the 1930s sporting experts first began to play a part in BBC commentaries, especially in boxing and football. They were given a limited role. In 1939 de Lotbinière advocated using the 'expert summariser' only at half-time in a football international. In the years after the war the practice of bringing a former player into the commentary box developed across almost all sports. The format initially – and it lasted until the 1980s – was one where commentator and summariser gave largely separate inputs: the summariser was 'invited' to comment between rounds in boxing, at the end of the over in cricket, between games in tennis, during pauses in the flow of play in football and so on. Vic Marks, the former Somerset and England off-spinner who joined the *Test Match Special* team in 1984, remembered:

> If you summarised next to Brian Johnston, technically there would be an over of BJ, and at the end of the over the summariser would say something – it wasn't a conversation.[3]

But the format changed. In 2007, during forty-three minutes of *Test Match Special*, the summarisers and the statistician spoke forty-six times; during a set of the men's singles final at Wimbledon lasting fifty-five minutes three summarisers spoke a total of ninety times; and during forty-eight minutes of commentary on a Champions League match the summariser spoke forty-five times. This is a random and unscientific sample but it illustrates the point: that a steady dialogue in much commentary became the norm.

Many broadcasters who learned their trade in an earlier vintage were not reconciled to the conversational approach. Tony Adamson, for example, felt that the pendulum had swung too far. 'We use the summariser far too much now, every time the commentator takes a breath we use the summariser'.[4]

Christopher Martin-Jenkins, who began covering cricket for the BBC in the early 1970s, attributed the change in part to the influences of other radio stations and he remains unconvinced the balance is right. If the summariser talked too much, he called him into line:

> It's local radio and the Radio 5 approach that has changed all that and, dare I say it, some commentators not having quite the confidence to see an over through on their own and therefore feeling the need to converse a bit. I feel it's gone a bit too far. Generally I work with sympathetic people and they cut their cloth to suit the commentator. For example Phil Tufnell – I worked with him in Sri Lanka – and he was talking all the time. He soon got the message that I didn't want him to …[5]

WHAT MAKES A GOOD SUMMARISER? Commentators themselves are fairly united in who they would pick. It would be someone who: has been at or near the top of their sport; is insightful about how that sport works; can talk fluently and succinctly; is familiar with the minds of current players but is not too close to them; and will easily adopt the style and dynamics of the commentary box. Knowing when to talk and when not to is perhaps the bottom line. And a decent microphone voice is needed. It is a formidable set of requirements. Such a combination of skills is quite rare in the general population: there is no reason to suppose it's more common among sportsmen and women.

Surely what the listener wants from the summariser is something that adds value to the commentary. Not 'that was a great shot', but an explanation of why the shot was good; not 'both sides are keen to win this one', but an explanation of why the match is of particular importance; not 'she's not having a very good day today', but an analysis of why this player is not performing well.

Summarisers gain their initial authority from having been at or near the top of their sport. 'A boxing summariser,' said Mike Costello, 'must bring boxing credibility with them. To have a world champion at ringside is absolutely key'.[6]

Jonathan Agnew, who took over as the BBC cricket correspondent upon the death of Brian Johnston in 1994, believed that for *Test Match Special* you must have someone who has played Test cricket.

But experience and authority on its own is not enough. Summarisers must be able to offer technical insights, and explanations of why something has happened. It might be former Junior Wimbledon winner Annabel Croft explaining the reasons why a drop shot by Maria Bartholi didn't work; or the former England cricket captain Graham Gooch, at the end of an over by Andrew Flintoff, taking us through it ball by ball, explaining how the bowler changed his pace and direction six times to undermine the batsman; or Terry Butcher on what makes a good cross to the goalmouth. Here Graeme Fowler, former Lancashire batsman turned top coach, explains why early in his innings a batsman may go out and tap the pitch:

> *Well you go and check and see what sort of a mark it's left, what line it is and you get your eyes used to it so you can see where it's bounced and what height it's come past you so it*

helps all your judgement and builds yourself into understanding how the wicket's playing.

Graham Taylor, who managed Watford, Aston Villa and Wolverhampton Wanderers as well as England, spoke of bringing to the game something the commentators lack, and of having a different approach to the business of watching:

> The commentators haven't played the game. Neither have they sat in the dugout. That is experience I can call on. They may be quite critical of play at times but I can see the angle a player receives the ball and the difficulty that causes. I'm doing what I've been doing most of my career. I don't take my eyes off the pitch but I don't follow the ball all the time.[7]

Summarisers also need to be able to get their points across. They need to be good communicators, good at explaining. 'An ex-boxer who can't talk is no good,' said Des Lynam, who began his career in radio before moving to television in the late 1970s.[8]

Richie Woodhall, WBC super-middleweight title-holder in the late 1990s, knew this was what he has to do:

> I've got a good eye and I can get things over to people who don't follow the sport. It's not like the Sky Boxing channel where people pay a sub and follow boxing closely. The radio commentary is going out to people who may not be regular followers and you have to explain things to them.[9]

In some sports, such as football, there are quiet periods of play where there is scope for the summarisers to say more. But when there is more action, succinctness often works best. The specialism of Trevor Bailey, the cricket summariser, was the concise judgement. Asked once by the commentator what he thought of Peter Roebuck's batting, the reply was immediate: *'Very strong on the leg side, good cutter of the ball, very watchful, rather ugly stance'.* In similar vein Geoffrey Boycott, asked about Harmison's recent bowling figures, said simply: *'They don't win Test Matches'.* When Daren Powell slogged Harmison for four and the commentator asked: *'What do you call that?'* Boycott gave a simple reply: *'Contempt'.* Former Wimbledon champion Pat Cash would give an immediate take on a tactical point in tennis – for instance Amelie Mauresmo's serving to Lindsay Davenport: *'It's crucial – if you're getting somebody who's attacking you, serve volleying or going for big shots – to serve to the body'.*

Experts also need to 'call' mistakes by top players, like former PGA Tour member Jay Townsend on Chris DiMarco at The Masters:

> *That's a big mental mistake. He had that back board behind the pin. He had a good thirty feet behind the pin to go ahead and sling it into the middle of the green and let the slope bring it back. He should have never, ever brought the front edge or short interplay in. Big mistake.*

Mike Ingham stressed that the summariser not only needs to know how to communicate but when:

> The best analysts dovetail naturally into the pace and heartbeat of a commentary, sensing instinctively the right moment to interject with some tactical insight. And they have the economy of words to be able to hand back as soon as there is significant action to describe.[10]

Not all international sportsmen and women can develop this expertise. Many famous footballing names have been tried as summarisers and then released. Ron Jones recalled:

> There are lots and lots of guys I've sat alongside, and they've won caps for England or whatever and they bring absolutely nothing to the commentary because they don't have the words ... and some of them surprisingly don't know as much about football as you might think.[11]

Summarisers are often expected to have access to the inside world of the players and to maintain social contact with them, while letting go of personal loyalties. BBC Radio tennis correspondent Jonathan Overend stressed how important it was to have at Wimbledon a player like Michael Stich who has 'good links with the locker-room'.[12]

Those links, friendships even, inform the judgements a summariser makes but they must not inhibit them. Angus Fraser, the former England pace bowler, acknowledged how well he knew some of the English players but added that when he became a journalist and a broadcaster he had to cut back on mixing with players. 'I don't really feel I belong in the dressing room. I've had my time in there, it's not my place any more'.[13]

Rob Nothman felt that most summarisers need time before they really begin to speak about the game objectively:

> They need to do the job for several years before they can let the handbrake off. At first they are close to the game,

they keep the handbrake on. When they're one step away from the game they can tell the truth more.[14]

Summarising of course is not just about what is said it is about the relationship with the rest of the commentary team, and with the listener. Producers are on the lookout for people who have the kind of personality that suits the ambience of the commentary box and communicate to the listener that they are good company. Commentators often stress that by socialising with summarisers outside work they strike a personal relationship which makes collaboration much easier. Ron Jones:

> It's also a matter of getting to know each other off the field as well. You have a meal with someone when you take a trip abroad, and you build up a friendship as well. You do get to know each other. If I was doing a match with Jimmy Armfield tomorrow, we would just take it up, even if we hadn't done a game for some time. We've been doing it together for fifteen years or so and I know instinctively when Jim wants to come in, and equally he will know when I'm going to stop, break off commentary, and ask him to come in.

As the commentary process became so conversational commentators and summarisers faced an obvious trap. Much sports talk has to be repetitive and unoriginal, commenting in an obvious way on what has been seen. (*'If they don't win this one, they're in trouble.'* – *'They'll have to play better in the second half.'*) This is the natural chatter of the fan. It is part of the fun of watching sport with friends. It is bound to make its appearance in the commentary box but if it gets in the way of the commentary it is infuriating. Listeners want more than what they can say to each other.

Commentators must be able to turn to the person at their side and hear something many listeners could not provide. Boxing provides an example. Mike Costello described the sport as 'almost a secret world'. He believed that if his summariser was excited by a fight it might help ensure that what the listener heard was an insight from that world:

> You want the listener to be taken as close to those (secret) places as you can and that's why I try and get as much of Richie Woodhall the boxer as I can. Because they're working for the BBC summarisers are under pressure to sound more fluent. I say to them: 'Just tell it as it is, tell

me as if you're standing next to me in a pub without the swear words. Tell me what you're seeing, let it go from the heart, as if you were there with them'.

At ringside they move into a different persona once the bell goes. Because they're only a few feet away, because they're doing something once again that's challenging them in the same atmosphere, they almost revert back to being a boxer, they really do get on fire.

In most sports the summariser became an essential part of the commentary process. This placed a new responsibility on commentators. Their duties included managing a conversational process in the commentary box, and ensuring that their summarisers added to the commentary without being intrusive. And, because the collaboration must sound friendly and seamless, the commentator and the summariser must get on well.

GIVE THE LISTENER A RINGSIDE SEAT. This has always been the mantra of commentary. How do commentators do this today? How do they deploy their summarisers?

In the following chapters contrasting and distinctive examples of the art of commentary are explored. Boxing (along with baseball) established live commentary on American radio in the days when the medium was first being developed. Its explosive and unpredictable nature gave it a powerful impact. One of its main challenges to the commentator is that there is no public display of which competitor is leading the contest. Football has always been a popular radio sport in Britain though plagued by contractual difficulties for many years. It has long been Britain's most popular sport, enriched by competitions in which the world's best players were on display. The Premier League dominated BBC 5 Live sport from its birth in 1994 and Alan Green became one of the country's best-known commentators.

Golf, most thought, was never going to be a subject of radio commentary – it was too slow and too drawn out, with few moments of excitement. Those assumptions were overturned, as the facility to place commentators at several holes enabled radio to maximise the tension and drama of major tournaments. Tennis was a favourite on BBC radio from the initial broadcast from Wimbledon in 1927. Radio coverage from the tournament was inventive, and set the pace for television, helping the sport maintain its place as a ritual in the

English summer. Tennis provides an example of a broadcasting station absorbing and showcasing a tournament as part of its wider brand.

Commentary on cricket is explored in greater detail. After many early difficulties it gained a special place on radio. It attracted, sometimes in a rather uneasy co-existence, those listeners who wanted to follow cricket, and others who wanted to hear the commentators talk – plus others who liked both. *Test Match Special* is arguably one of the most remarkable programmes in the history of broadcasting.

1   *Wisden Cricket Monthly* September 2007
2   HBT Wakelam *Half-time* (Nelson 1938) p 291
3–14   interviews with the author

SIXTEEN

BOXING'S CHALLENGE

The astonished stars gaze down upon ... the Yankee stadium, bursting and bulging to its farthest walls with ninety thousand human beings, crowded elbow to elbow and rib to rib. They've paid one million dollars in the primitive hope of seeing two young men, Max Baer and Joe Louis, batter each other into insensitivity. Farewell depression if this million dollar bout is any criterion of the time...

... The incredible thing is that here on the heels of the hardest time that America has ever had, we have ninety thousand men and women wildly eager to see madcap Max Baer smack young black Joe into dreamland or to scream with primitive savagery if young black Joe knocks the Levermore playboy clear out of the ring and back to the glittering lights of the great white (unintelligible). There are fifteen thousand women in this gigantic crowd ... sisters beneath the skin going back a million years to cave-women days when they looked on with flashing eyes as their men fought for them with stone hammers and stone-tipped spear. The well-known gentler sex, if you please, but as savagely eager for the kill as any male in this monstrous assembly. Admiration for physical strength and skill can't be educated out of the genus homo, creased out or reformed out. Not only here in the Yankee stadium but all over the earth the sons and daughters of old Adam wait for the bulletin to climax. They wait to hear whether the jungle man has smitten down the jester.

FROM THE EARLY DAYS OF RADIO, boxing commentary, more than any other sport, has allowed access to a gladiatorial and violent world. The speaker above is Ed Hill, setting the scene before the coverage of the 1935 fight between Joe Louis and Max Baer in New York. Hill, and the commentator Clem McCarthy, knew they had an audience of many millions and Hill's introduction – not live commentary of course – was carefully scripted to evoke and even celebrate the deepest of prejudices. The rhythmic cadences of his prose carefully warmed up the listener for the ritual violence that was to follow.

In the first decades of broadcasting, boxing and radio seemed to be made for each other. In particular, the big championship fights in America, especially those between the world's greatest heavyweights, provided listeners with some of their most memorable moments. Indeed, you might hear a man being battered senseless.

Here Joe Louis meets Max Schmeling in New York in 1938:

> *Max backed away and missed a right. Louis then stopped him with two straight lefts to the face and brought over that hard right to the head, high on the temple. And Max (*unintelligible*) a clinch and broke ground. He's back against the ropes now again, not too close to the ropes. And Louis missed with a left swing but in close quarters brought over a hard one to the jaw and again a right to the body, a left hook, a right to the head, a left to the head, a right. Schmeling is going down. But he held to his feet, held to the ropes, looked to his corner in helplessness. And Schmeling is down. Schmeling is down. The count is four. And he's up and Louis, right and left to the head, a left to the jaw, a right to the head, and Donovan is watching carefully. Louis measured him, right to the body, a left up the jaw and Schmeling is down. The count is five. Five, six, seven, eight. The men are in the ring. The fight is over – on a technical knockout. Max Schmeling is beaten in one round. The first time that a world heavyweight championship ever changed hands in one round – in less than a round.*[1]

This was a much heralded contest, a return bout from that day in 1936 when the German first met Louis and knocked him out, the American's first defeat. The commentator Clem McCarthy had no warning of what was to happen but how powerfully he captures it, not least the desperate Schmeling looking to his corner 'in helplessness', and the chilling prospect when 'Louis measured him'.

There were commentaries in four languages that night: English, German, Spanish and Portuguese. An elderly New Yorker, Ludwig Stein, recalled that as a young boy in a Jewish boarding school in Germany he and his friends had asked to be woken up to hear the fight. 'I have never forgotten the German announcer's plea *'Get up, Maxi, please get up – oh no, oh no – stay down – it's over.'* We applauded Louis's victory as a ray of hope for us.'[2]

Stein's account undermines a widely-held belief that Goebbels instructed German radio to stop the transmission when Schmeling was first put down.

THE BBC OPERATED in a different environment to American broadcasters but it also recognised that boxing and radio commentary were well matched. Boxing offered short and well-defined periods of activity, and the prospect of fierce and uncompromising action; there was always the possibility of the knockout blow; and the breaks between rounds provided the commentator with regular opportunities to recover from three minutes of non-stop description. To add to the excitement, the narrator literally has a ringside seat, within hearing of each blow, and is surrounded by a passionate, baying crowd. Des Lynam has covered the sport on radio and TV:

> Boxing is very conducive to being on radio. It has great atmosphere and excitement both in and around the ring. All you get is two guys slugging it out so you have to explain what is happening. You can't just describe each blow. It's not like TV where people can see what's happening – you are the eyes of the listener.[3]

But the BBC faced a number of difficulties in making a success of boxing broadcasts in the early years of commentary. There were problems in finding the right commentator, in striking an agreement with promoters, and in selecting a fight or fights that reasonably guaranteed a good evening's listening. When de Lotbinière came on the scene these difficulties persisted and there were periods when the BBC reverted to amateur matches because they could not get agreement with the main promoters. In 1938 de Lotbinière, always focusing on the need for a good narrative, wrote to the Army's Eastern Command about a Services tournament that the BBC was going to cover:

> I hope you will be able to give us a good bout for this not only because it is better entertainment for the listener but it is also a better advertisement for the sport. I mention this point because we had to take what we could get during the Police boxing and all we got was two gentlemen who stood with their arms round each other's neck and kissed one another. I nearly turned burglar.[4]

The first great boxing commentaries heard by British listeners came when the BBC relayed transmissions from across the Atlantic. Tommy Farr's fight with Joe Louis in New York in 1937 attracted the biggest audience. The Welsh boxer fought bravely through the fifteen rounds but lost on points. Despite being broadcast during the early hours it won a huge audience in Britain.

So close was commentator Bill Bowman to the ring that listeners could hear the referee talking to the boxers: *'Keep moving, keep moving'*. Well before the last round Joe Louis knew that this would be no knockout and, to the excitement of British, and particularly Welsh, listeners, Bowman captured how uncertain the outcome was: *'Farr drives the coloured boy back. Farr's going right after him ... He can't hurt Farr and Farr lets him know that'*.

One of those listening to Bowman's commentary was Harold Pascho. Born in 1912, Pascho recalled that he had just got married and set up house in Bournemouth. He had recently purchased an expensive new radio from the local department store for thirteen guineas, but saved three guineas by trading in an old set. His mother-in-law came to stay for her first visit to the new home and she stayed up with Harold and his wife until the fight came on at one o'clock in the morning. They cheered for Farr through every round.

IN THE YEARS AFTER THE WAR, in the hands of Stewart MacPherson and Raymond Glendenning, assisted by W Barrington Dalby, radio covered a great cluster of fights, involving Don Cockell, Freddie Mills, Randolph Turpin, Bruce Woodcock and others.

Another member of the commentary team, Eamonn Andrews, was from Ireland. In 1938, then only sixteen, Andrews wrote to Radio Éireann in Dublin: 'I am an expert on boxing and have studied elocution. Please give me an audition.'[5]

Although initially unsuccessful (Michael O'Hehir, all of eighteen, got the job,) Andrews was soon working at minor jobs in broadcasting and then branched out as a quiz-master, touring Ireland with the show *Double or Nothing*. He was a keen amateur boxer and once distinguished himself by winning an Irish title and then commentating on later bouts from the same tournament in the evening.

But his ambition was to work for the BBC. Andrews obtained a job with the Joe Loss orchestra, touring England and compèring a nightly quiz while the band took a break, and finally managed to make an appointment with de Lotbinière, playing him recordings of his work. Lobby made him listen to MacPherson and Glendenning and advised him to be patient – his chance would come. When Stewart MacPherson went back to Canada, Eamonn Andrews was invited to audition for *Ignorance is Bliss*. He was soon given commentary work and by 1950 he was presenting *Sports Report*.

Andrews was fast and fluent at ringside, able to capture the rhythm of the punching, raising and lowering his voice as the excitement ebbed and flowed. In 1955 he was sent to San Francisco to cover the fight between Don Cockell and Rocky Marciano – and told by the BBC to 'have a look at the American television programme *This is your life* while you're there.'[6]

Despite Cockell's relatively modest record, great expectations had been built up in Britain about his prospects and the commentary was keenly anticipated. It was another early-morning affair, with many thousands staying up late or setting the alarm for 3 a.m. Andrews felt the tension:

> I was always nervous before a radio or TV broadcast but that night I was screwed up more than ever. The awareness that my voice would be winging out across the Atlantic and into British homes at three o'clock in the morning suddenly hit me and gave me a heightened sense of thrill. My nerves vanished, of course, the second the bell went for the first round.

This extensive radio coverage in the decade after the war was not arranged without difficulty. In 1948 the BBC held a long meeting with the British Boxing Board of Control, who had become concerned that big fight commentaries were detracting from paying attendances at smaller venues. An agreement was reached whereby no more than five big fights would be covered between March and December each year and the BBC undertook to do a minimum of ten broadcasts from smaller promotions. The boxing nights of the forties were major events in the radio sports calendar. One listener remembered:

> The broadcasts started around 9 p.m. My routine was to have my bath and come downstairs in pyjamas and dressing gown to be given a chocolate biscuit and a mug of Ovaltine as the opening bell went. For me Bruce Woodcock and Freddie Mills were the big attractions.[7]

The successors to MacPherson, Glendenning and Andrews included Des Lynam and John Rawling. Lynam boxed as a schoolboy and was a keen follower of the sport but originally established himself on radio primarily as a sports news reporter. Interviewing Harry Levene one day the promoter suggested that Lynam might try commentating:

'You know your boxing. Why don't you become a commentator? You've got a good voice and bigger fools than you have done it'.[8]

At this time Bob Burrows, head of BBC Radio sport, was looking for someone to add more character and pace to boxing commentaries. He had done the voice tests on applicants – including Lynam – who came before a recruitment board in 1972 and had been impressed with him from the start. 'The great thing about Des,' recalled Burrows, 'was that he was fast, his diction was good, he was accurate – and he could read a fight well'.[9]

Lynam's first big assignment in boxing was the 1974 Commonwealth Games where he sometimes covered fifteen fights in one day.

TO FIND AN APPROPRIATE NARRATIVE STYLE, boxing commentators have to cope with some exacting demands. The action of a fight is neatly confined to three-minute bursts at a time, but it is fast and it is also repetitive. The narration has to capture the rapid details of the action, whereby ten or twelve blows may be exchanged in less than half a minute. In the case of lighter boxers the speed of the blows may be too fast for any speaker to match. In addition the commentator must be alert to the impact of a single blow, a blow which may determine the outcome of a fight. And the listener needs to be anchored in some general sense of the underlying momentum of the contest and who, if anyone, is 'in front'.

Des Lynam probably covered more championship and world titles for BBC radio than anyone. His approach was to record the key blows which were landed by each boxer but to weave them into a more general narrative which captured who had the initiative. He generally knew who his listeners were rooting for and he took care to tell them how their man was doing. But most of all, he could tell a good story.

Here is Lynam describing a European Championship title bout in Milan in 1977 between Alan Minter and Germano Valsecchi. Minter had had a series of wins, including a British title fight with Kevin Finnegan, during the previous two years to take him into the world's top ten. Valsecchi was fighting in front of a home crowd in Milan but early in the second round he took a standing count and Minter began to take control of the fight. Lynam gives the referee and the crowd their place in the story:

> *Maybe Alan Minter will win this one early. He's being held once again there and Valsecchi nearly went down there from a*

punch, and he's a got a cut underneath his left eye, the Italian, now, and the referee steps in and separates them. Alan Minter going in for the finish it seems to me, on the ropes on the far side of the ring. The Italian catches Minter with a good left hook. Minter gets caught (crescendo of cheers) *and you can hear the Italian crowd get behind their man there. Valsecchi is in desperate trouble and then came in with a big left hand and Minter really had to back off. But Valsecchi's on the ropes again and he's getting caught, Minter catching him to the head and then to the body but the Italian is desperate and throwing punches wildly now. And the referee's got to step in here and break them up.*

Just a few seconds left to go in this second round, what an incredible round it's been with Valsecchi taking a standing count. Minter's going after him again, now Valsecchi's on the ropes on this side, gets caught with a left hook to the head, eventually runs away from Minter, turns his back and runs into the centre of the ring. Minter goes after him again, but he's got to be a little bit careful from those big counter punches. Minter going after him, two good punches to the head once again, and Valsecchi still on the ropes, and still Minter's right hand is being held and if the referee isn't seeing that – well I wonder where he's looking. Valsecchi all over the place, Valsecchi all over the place and Valsecchi is cut and it seems to me that he's being helped onto that stool.[10]

John Rawling and Mike Costello followed a similar approach. Rather than offering an unending list of punches, the listener is given a story with a theme and underlying direction. Costello described how he developed a way of dealing with the speed and frequency of blows that were struck, and the element of repetition:

> Especially in a twelve-round fight, you have a lot of action that is exactly the same. The real challenge is to avoid repeating the same sentences over and over again, for example 'that was a good left, followed by a good right'. When I first started I did try and describe every punch in a combination but with someone as fast as Amir Khan the eye can't track all the punches that he throws, you have to group them into a combination or a flurry, or you pick up one that had a particular significance.[11]

BOXING POSES ONE UNIQUE CHALLENGE to the commentator. Whereas in other sports there is some sort of score, or the contestants are in some sort of order, in boxing the verdicts of the judges or referee are not made known to the spectator. This places a premium on the commentary team to read a fight correctly.

After some early difficulties, including one occasion in which a commentator tried unsuccessfully to read a fight from a position at the back of the Royal Albert Hall, the BBC began seating commentators next to the press desk at ringside. But it was not easy to 'call' all the fights correctly. Raymond Glendenning wrote about some of the difficulties faced by the boxing commentator in *Radio Times* in September 1947. He was responding to letters complaining about commentators getting it wrong. Even at ringside, he pointed out, you do not get the same view as the referee:

> He is actually in the ring. He gets the best and indeed the only view that matters. He can move round so that there are no obstructions in his way. He is in a position to see every blow. That is very important, for decisions often depend on hair-breadth measurements. A boxer's head suddenly shooting back may be caused by riding an attempted hit just as often as it is the result of a sound scoring jab... Frankly all we can do is to give you – the listener – an accurate idea of what it looks like to us and would seem to you if you were there.

Glendenning and Barrington Dalby caused some controversy in 1951 with their coverage of the world title fight between Randolph Turpin and Sugar Ray Robinson at Earls Court. The fight was a big event. 'Rarely have I ever sensed such an atmosphere of expectancy, of impending crisis, as I did that evening', recalled Glendenning later.[12]

He knew that Robinson was capable of a decisive attack at any stage but that, during the second half of the fight, Turpin's courage and skill was making an impact. Equally important, Turpin was rousing the home crowd to believe he was winning.

In his comments after the penultimate round Dalby suggested that with a good final round Turpin 'could just *snatch* it', the implication being that he was not ahead. Describing the closing minute of the fight Glendenning left the verdict wide open:

Well, whatever happens the English boy's got a grandstand fin-
ish, whether he can overcome the points deficit at the start I
don't know. In he comes again, he drives Robinson back over
the far side, clouts him with a left and right to the face, he's
got the champion in trouble now, in comes Turpin – the last
few seconds – left and right, the champion fights back with a
battery of left and rights to the body and they're milling away
– twenty seconds to go now – right up in the centre of the ring,
the centre of attraction to eighteen thousand people.
Robinson's eyes are a bad picture now and Turpin is still look-
ing completely unmarked, he's dancing round now ... in comes
Robinson, trying to throw his left-hand. Last ten seconds –
Turpin fights him off with a left hand, Robinson comes in try-
ing to get that right hand in, Turpin gets in at close quarters,
now they're milling on the ropes just above us here – which way
will this championship go? It all depends on Mr. Eugene Hend-
erson. Turpin scores the last punch of the round.
And who has won? Mr. Henderson is following the boys across
to the corner – everybody's running across the ring, photogra-
phers there ...

Turpin did win and there was a storm of protest from those who
felt the commentary team had under-estimated Turpin's performance
and thereby been guilty of bias against the British fighter. Unusually
the BBC chose to repeat the commentary a day or two later in an
attempt to demonstrate that the coverage had been even-handed.
Some but not all of the protestors were assuaged. Barrington Dalby
later said that he had made a slip of the tongue and had meant to say:
'Turpin could *clinch* it'.[13]

Des Lynam believed that, the more you commentate, the better
you get at calling a fight, and that listeners like you to do it. 'I became
very good at scoring the rounds, because I was commentating all the
time. If you don't call the fight you become very boring.'

But working into the broadcast some feeling for who is ahead is not
an easy task.

Costello agreed that the more fights he saw the more he could
judge, but he stressed that it was never simple:

> When you hear a commentator give his assessment of a
> fight – unless it's overwhelmingly one-sided – you have to
> remember that the commentator is spending all his time
> describing punches, and using up his thought processes.

It's very difficult at the same time to be judging objectively. It is a significant part of boxing commentary on the radio to let people know how the fight is going, even if it's to say 'This is very close'. Ultimately the credibility of the team depends on getting that right.

AFTER THE TURN of the millennium, boxing experienced something of a revival in Britain, helped by the success of fighters like Joe Calzaghe and Ricky Hatton. Radio scheduling of the sport was made easier by the fact that major events were often on Saturday evenings when there was no Premier League football. The BBC coverage of fights involving Amir Khan in 2007 provides an example of how boxing commentary works today and some of the issues that the commentary team faces.

Khan was then still in the early stages of his professional career after winning a silver medal at the 2004 Olympics and the promoter Frank Warren had put together an agreement with ITV for a series of fights designed to give the Bolton boxer more experience before he took on serious international contests. For the first bout the BBC had to decide whether the opposition lined up against Khan was sufficient to merit coverage. Commentator Mike Costello knew that Khan had already had some fights against lesser opposition and he recognised that there can be a problem if a boxing team want to bring fights to the media which are not truly competitive:

> We're constantly at loggerheads. ...last year (2006) we had a very strained relationship with Frank Warren, we didn't say it was cheating but... What we say on air has to be fair comment but I would only say on air what I would say to their face. We have to reflect what's been felt across the world of boxing. It's more difficult for ITV because he's part of their commercial package. There have been a couple of times when I've said to the editor: 'Do we really want to take this fight?' And he's rightly said to me: 'Look, if by chance this happens to be the one where's he's knocked out, we couldn't afford not to be there'.

That is indeed the view taken by Jim Hollis, boxing producer at the BBC. 'Amir Khan is a household name and there's plenty of interest in how he gets on.'[14] Hollis was convinced that the fight merited air time.

The summariser working on the Khan fights was Richie Woodhall. He was still active in the sport, training young boxers, when he was first approached by the BBC in 2005 to work as summariser and he has fitted fairly easily into the ringside dialogue:

> It's like a big conversation really, people talking about boxing ... It comes easy to me. I say what I see. As a summariser you've got to know when to speak and I just know. I've been in the ring and I can see things that others don't.[15]

Steve Bunce, an experienced boxing journalist, was also part of the commentary team – he sat behind Costello and Woodhall. Bunce knows Costello well. 'We grew up and boxed together as kids'.[16] His was a third voice, especially before and after the fights and, occasionally, between rounds.

Khan's first fight of the series, in May 2007, was against Steffy Bull, someone who many thought had retired from the boxing game. Mike Costello did his usual preparation:

> I looked at his list of opponents and I got in touch with Martin Watson's people and asked what sort of fighter he was. At that stage it was a familiar theme with Amir Khan's opponents, they were quite tidy opponents but couldn't punch with any significance. We all knew pretty much that it wouldn't be much of a test.

In the first round Costello began to give his listeners warning signals, indicating that Khan was trying to please the crowd rather than produce the kind of fight that was needed. Round two was not much better, but Costello did what he could to give the fight some significance:

> *Clearly Khan's watched tapes of Steffy Bull and clearly there'll be more difficult nights for Amir Khan but its all part of the development process. He's got to work out how to cut the ring off here, because Steffy Bull at times is virtually running away here ... it's all been a bit rushed from Amir Khan for a lot of the first six minutes here, as Steffy Bull finds his confidence to stand his ground in centre ring and throws a neat punch, a neat left hand that does land on the chin of Amir Khan.*

Woodhall was able to make a confident prediction at this stage. *'We've seen all this before. I can't see this going much longer'.* By now

Bunce had had enough. 'It's generally considered that I'll take the hardest line,' he said:

> *Here's the thing. He's expecting nothing, I say nothing, to come back and it's two years now and surely somebody's going to move out of the way and throw a counter and when that day comes I hope I'm ringside.*

In round three, as Woodhall had predicted, Bull went down and was counted out. Steve Bunce repeated his warning:

> *We've got a problem here Mike, no-one is standing, no-one is moving and when that French guy moved, Amir Khan struggled for ten rounds to get close to him. Steffy Bull came out of retirement, for a good pay day, live in America, live on TV, and he didn't connect with a single punch.*

Mike Costello added: *'I've seen enough of that to be honest.'* Costello knew there was some controversy surrounding the fight and made a point of listening to a recording of the commentary a few days later. He felt he could be satisfied with the line the commentary team had taken, because 'it's pretty much the tone in and around boxing'.

In the next fight, in July 2007, Steve Bunce's wish came true – someone 'threw a counter'. Willie Limond of Scotland posed a different challenge, both for Amir Khan and the commentary team.

Richie Woodhall spotted what was happening after the second round:

> *He took three right hands in that round, Amir Khan, that's probably the most he's took in a single round in his career... The problem is for Khan he's got a low left hand; it's coming back down to his chest and that's how Limond's connecting with that right hand over the top... They've studied Khan's style and Khan has got this low left hand and the Scot is coming across with the right hand over the top.*

In the sixth round Limond connected with three right hands in a row and put Khan down. Costello had to make rapid assessments about how badly Khan was hurt, how close he was to being counted out, and how effectively he responded. He finished the round with a graphic metaphor to leave the listener in no doubt as to what had happened:

We're only at the midway stage and Amir Khan is holding on in desperation. He takes another left hook, Limond goes for the overhang right, he misses this time, he takes a jab from Khan, Khan is in his own corner, he's still on unsteady legs. Willie Limond is virtually running after him. He opens up on the ropes to our right, Khan comes back at him with a right hand, worrying moments, desperate for Amir Khan. He lands a left hand to the body, Willie Limond two shots, left and right. Amir Khan pours scorn on the punches but they're hurting. Another jab from Willie Limond. Khan comes forward now, showing great bravery, but what has he got left in those legs with forty-five seconds to go in round six? Now maybe Willie Limond is beginning to feel the pace and Amir Khan with his mouth wide open, gasping for air here, over towards his own corner and Willie Limond is dancing after him, Amir Khan is virtually trying to run away. They're separated by the referee… Amir Khan's been taken into the trenches here and is trying to clamber out.

In the event Khan fought back to hold on for two more rounds, and won the fight when Limond was retired on medical grounds by his corner. This left the commentary team to reflect again on whether they had seen a well-matched fight. Mike Costello suggested it had been a good experience for Khan, and Woodhall thought him a deserved winner. Steve Bunce was still sceptical:

I tell you what, Mike, listen. I don't want to be the killjoy because it's always my job. You two never get to be the killjoy here. This guy Willie Limond is not a banger, he is not a puncher. We saw what happened to Amir Khan … He showed he was hurt for the first time … when Limond went looking for the knockout. I'll tell you what will happen tonight. Every single big super featherweight and every single lightweight in Europe will be on the phone now saying: 'Get me Frank Warren', saying 'I'll fight him and I'll take the small end of the purse'.

In his next two fights Khan disposed of Scott Lawton and Graham Earl, the latter a former European title-holder. The second fight was stopped after seventy-two seconds. David Croft was compèring the presentation for 5 Live and turned quickly to former champion Frank Bruno for a view. Bruno thought promoter Frank Warren was right to pace Khan's move to a world title fight slowly:

He's still a youngster. He doesn't need rushing... he needs plenty of rounds... When those Puerto Ricans come, when those Mexicans come, when some of those tough, hungry Americans come, it'll be a different cup of tea. And it won't be Brooke Bond.

1   Transcription courtesy of Cayton Sports Inc. (see website *Ringside Radio*)
2   Ludwig Stein, letter to *New York Times* July 3rd 1988
3   Interview with the author
4   BBC WAC R30/693/1 Earls Court File 1 1936-46
5   For this and later quotation from Andrews see *For ever and ever Eamonn* by Eamonn and Grainne Andrews (Grafton 1989). *Radio Times* advertised the Cockell commentary for 4 o'clock.
6   Andrews was to be the first subject of *This is your life* on British television and then its compère.
7   Email from Patrick Rossington
8   *Des Lynam – I should have been at work!* (Harper Collins 2005) p 44
9   Interview with the author
10 Minter won this fight with a knockout in round five and went on to win the world middleweight title
11 Interview with the author
12 *'Just a Word in Your ear'* by Raymond Glendenning (Stanley Paul 1953) p 110
13 *Come in Barry* by W Barrington Dalby (Cassell 1961) p 103
14–16 Interview with the author

SEVENTEEN

FOOTBALL – A GAME FOR SQUARES

Here go the players! For the moment Huddersfield are running off to the left – that is, the left-hand side of your plan – and Blackburn are running away to the right. As soon as they toss we will let you know the positions of the teams for the match. The captains of the teams by the way – Stephenson of Huddersfield and Healless of Blackburn Rovers – have just greeted each other in the customary way with a hearty handshake, and are now tossing the coin, carefully watched by Mr Bryan. Oh! Apparently Stephenson has won the toss, I imagine, because he has called his players away from the left-hand side of the goal from where we are sitting to the right to defend the goal on the right. And now on your left you have Blackburn Rovers – on the left-hand side of your plan – and the right Huddersfield Town, and they are just about to kick-off.

THIS IS GEORGE ALLISON in the commentary box at Wembley in 1928 for the FA Cup final. His listeners, he assumes, have on their laps the plan of the pitch (divided into eight squares) distributed by the BBC so they can follow the play more easily. Allison has beside him the 'number two' commentator, probably John Snagge or Derek McCulloch, whose job it was to call out from time to time the number of the square where the ball was. *The Times* was impressed with Allison's commentary:

> So efficient and vivid was the description given, that it is probable that the millions who listened to the match at home knew a good deal more about the subtleties of what was taking place than the thousands who were actually able to see the game.

Despite all the difficulties with the Football League over live coverage, described earlier, Saturday afternoon commentary was eventually to become almost as much as part of the ritual of sporting life as the matches themselves. Once the Football League agreed, the BBC would announce just after 3 o'clock the ground from which live commentary would come. By then, it was assumed, potential spectators to that and other games would already be through the turnstiles and not deterred from attendance by the prospect of listening to a match at home. The second-half commentary from 4 o'clock was the centrepiece of Saturday afternoon radio for several decades, and indeed the highlight of the football follower's week.

———————

THERE HAS NEVER BEEN MUCH DOUBT that football lends itself to radio commentary. The game meets one of the obvious requirements – it is popular, and there is widespread, not to say fanatical, interest in the results of matches, and people identify strongly with the individual teams. The normal length of a full game can be easily scheduled, the second half even more so. Matches offer the prospect of continuous action, of ebb and flow down the field, of moments of excitement regularly punctuating more routine play. There is much individual and team skill to identify and report on. Innovations in formations, and in the use of substitutes, have given the commentary team even more to discuss. Decisions by officials add incident and ready-made talking points. And not least is the passion of the spectators themselves, their cheers, their groans, their communal sighs of disbelief – all making a natural backdrop, and a vivid, additional dimension for the listener. So there is excellent raw material from which live commentary can be crafted.

However, there are considerable challenges. Fast, unpredictable play, with the initiative of the game swiftly changing, calls for a sharp eye and a very good connection between mind and mouth. Commentators not only have to say where the ball is, but what strategies are unfolding in front of them. There are twenty-two players (more if substitutes are used) to identify correctly, with many of them sometimes crowded into the goalmouth area for a set piece. The final moments before a goal may involve an indistinct flurry of arms and legs which leave the average spectator asking: 'Who scored?' There may also be periods of stalemate, when the play is far from entertaining. Contentious decisions or unruly behaviour (by players or spectators) put a premium on the ability of the commentary team to combine the flavour of the controversy with an element of judicious reflection. No wonder George Allison once said that the commentator must seem excited, but not *be* excited.

Allison dominated football commentary until the outbreak of war in 1939. He had what a contemporary in the BBC called 'a remarkable, deep-toned broadcasting voice'.[1] Allison also possessed an insider's experience of the game, becoming Arsenal's 'secretary-manager' during his time as a commentator. He claimed to know around five hundred contemporary footballers by sight – handy if it was true, as until 1933 players did not wear numbers on their backs. Allison believed that the way to make commentary work was simply to describe the play. He told one interviewer that commentary was 'fairly easy':

> You just repeat what you see happening … talk as the words come into your head. Something instinctive inside you does the rest. It's fatal to have any emotional interest in the match … the public are not interested in a set of superlatives. Listeners want to know what is happening and they also want to share in the game as it goes on. My great secret is to appear excited without really being so. In other words I have to act.[2]

On air, Allison was reliably 'BBC'. But Freddie Grisewood – one of the first BBC announcers – recalled that behind Allison's formal and courteous tones lay a natural comedian. He remembered Allison in the late 1920s doing a mock commentary on a closed wireless circuit audible only in Savoy Hill:

> *And then the ball comes to so and so. Does he kick it? Not on your life. He falls head over heels on his back, the silly ass. What a footballer. Come on, you bat-eyed blitherer, do something.*[3]

Allison often said that the secret of successful commentary was to forget that there were millions of people listening. He assumed that he was describing the game for one person only – 'a sweet old lady up in Redcar'. This was his mother. The other listeners, he said, were just eavesdroppers.[4] Allison talked in later life of the cramped conditions in which he worked and of the crowds milling round in front of his commentary box, obscuring his view at key moments. Spectators would sometimes help him out – 'It's a goalkick, guvnor' – so that he could keep listeners informed. No TV monitor in those days for instant replays.

Allison was given only limited guidance on how to do the job. Indeed the BBC more or less let him invent football commentary for himself and, since there were fewer complaints about him than anybody else, they were happy for him to get on with it.

In the later 1930s, de Lotbinière did begin to put down in words how it should be done. By now the use of a second commentator calling out the squares had become something of a music hall joke and been abandoned. De Lotbinière wrote to an assistant in Edinburgh in 1939 advising on how an international match should be covered.[5] One of his main concerns was with 'geography' – where the commentator was in relation to the pitch and where the ball was 'in relation to the field.' Similarly he asked that players be referred to as much by position as by name as 'a great many listeners will not be familiar with all twenty-two names'. At this stage an expert summariser was only used at half-time, and at the end of the game, and Lobby advised that the commentator's main concern should be to follow the play, and not to comment too much.

De Lotbinière had the advantage of not being a great football follower, and he could easily place himself in the seat of the casual listener. For this reason perhaps it was the emphasis on geography, and on locating the place of play, which was his main contribution to thinking about the technique of football commentary. He returned to the theme in the 1952 BBC Handbook (italics as in the original):

> Take the commentator who describes a football match between Newcastle and Portsmouth like this: 'Milburn out to Walker – he's beaten Ferrier – he's racing along the touch line – he's opposite the penalty area – he centres'. Some listeners may realize from all this the exact whereabouts of the ball, but many will not even know which goal is in jeopardy and so the commentary can mean little or nothing to them. Instead the commentator must do some cross referencing: '*Newcastle now on the attack* – Milburn out to Walker *on the right wing* – he's beaten Ferrier – he's racing up the *far* touch line – he's opposite the *Portsmouth* penalty area – he centres'.

Allison's simple account of how he described a football match – '*you just repeat what you see happening*' – could never be an adequate recipe for commentary. De Lotbinière had reminded commentators of a further dimension: the need to place the play clearly on the pitch so listeners could follow it in their mind's eye.

THE POST-WAR YEARS AT THE BBC were the period of Raymond Glendenning and Alan Clarke. Glendenning, as we have seen, was a versatile commentator, and football was one of his main sports. Glendenning occasionally had beside him Charlie Buchan, the former England footballer and founder of *Charles Buchan's Football Monthly* magazine, but this was really before the days of the summariser. More often Glendenning had to weave in his own background material. Here he is on the FA Cup semi-final between Birmingham City and Derby County in March 1946. This was a period of fast play, with Glendenning talking at almost three hundred words to the minute. Broadly Glendenning follows the Allison approach, describing every move, but he still manages to squeeze in a reference to his pre-match pitch inspection:

> *Duncan tries to kick it upfield, not very far. A very neat pass by Turner, out to Edwards on the Birmingham left wing. He's dribbling up now, he puts the ball right down into the Derby penalty area. Away goes Dougall, chasing it like blazes – will he stop it going over? And he forces Nicolas to play the ball, and he's got it right on the touchline there, and finally – Oh, no – Nicolas has come away with it, a very fine tackle there, and he recovered the ball and put it right up the wing to his own right wing, Harrison. Harrison now into the centre of the field. Birmingham coming back, the ball's halfway inside the Derby County half still, and Mulroney knocks it down with his hands, tries a terrific shot at goal, but he controlled that ball, a chest-high bouncing ball. The ground has dried out rather more than I expected since I was on it this morning. The players are finding it rather difficult to control the ball in a swirling wind. It's a very dry ball. The ground has lost that bit of tackiness that would have helped the ball player.*

But when Hungary played England in the historic game at Wembley in 1953 Glendenning, like the English players, was caught out by the skills of the Hungarians:

> *Hungary … playing too much of the ball at the moment … and there's Kocsis, the inside left, playing in the inside right position – it comes back to the right back – he lobs it across the goal and its neatly nodded right to Puskás's feet, he lets it lob across his chest, its straight into … a beautiful goal! Straight into his man who was running in there, and he had the English defence absolutely standing still.*

Alan Clarke had first come to the BBC's attention doing services' games at the end of the war. He became one of the most consistent performers until the mid-sixties, sharing the 1966 World Cup Final from Wembley with Brian Moore. Clarke did not attempt to name the players involved in every pass, but like Glendenning he followed almost every move on the pitch and told the listener where play was – *'the ball's gone into touch, in front of us here, on the Arsenal right wing.'* He knew his players well and could follow rapid play around the pitch without losing his clarity or syntax. Clarke was particularly skilled at taking his foot off the pedal during quieter periods of play while still communicating a sense of interest in the play, and he was always alert to how the game was unfolding. He brought light, unobtrusive touches of humour into his commentaries. This, together with his natural gift for finding the right word, made him one of the most elegant of commentators.

In those post-war years Clarke, Glendenning, Maurice Edelston, Simon Smith and others made a big impact, not only on listeners but on players too, as Tom Finney recalled in a programme broadcast in 2007.[6] Some of the younger listeners were to follow their radio heroes into the commentary box. Brian Moore had listened as a schoolboy to Glendenning covering racing and boxing, as well as football and thought Glendenning had the best commentating voice of them all. Moore in his turn was to become an inspiration for others. Alan Parry, who began on BBC Radio Merseyside before moving to London and has commentated for BBC TV, ITV and Sky as well as BBC and commercial radio, recalled how all the young lads in the street where he lived would listen to the radio commentaries and then rush out to play, pretending to be stars they had just been hearing about.[7]

Brian Moore moved to television in 1968 and this helped create openings for the two men who dominated football commentary for a long spell in the 1970s and 1980s – Bryon Butler, who replaced Moore as football correspondent, and Peter Jones. Butler's voice was rounded and comforting – Mike Ingham has described it as being 'like a warm overcoat in winter'[8]. He spoke with style, partly perhaps because – according to Alan Green – he 'tended to drop prepared paragraphs of prose' into his commentary.[9] Bob Burrows, his boss at BBC Radio, thought Butler happier with written journalism than with commentary.

Jones did match reports on local radio while working as a teacher and then joined the BBC on a full-time basis. He had a lilting, silky voice of great clarity, and became an outside broadcaster of great distinction. He could invest public and ceremonial occasions, such as the opening of the Olympic Games, with a balance of solemnity and good humour. Some felt he occasionally struck a self-important pose. But he used his skills to moving effect at the Heysel Stadium in 1985 and at Hillsborough in 1989 when great disasters overtook the game. On both these occasions, when emotion or the desire for speculation might have overcome him, he concentrated only on what he could see. For between two and three hours at Heysel he spoke with restraint and authority.

In the 1970s football commentary changed. Describing the actual play, almost uninterrupted, no longer seemed to be enough. There was more to comment on, things that would add variety and significance to the details of the match. Writing in the early 1980s Brian Johnston credited Peter Jones with moving football commentary on from the days of Glendenning and Clarke. For the commentary to work effectively, the commentator now had to do more than describe the passage of the ball. Johnston attributed the change of style to changes in football itself, from a game when star players often held onto the ball to a game of continual fluidity and almost non-stop passing:

> Peter has evolved what I call 'thinking aloud' commentary. When play is in midfield and there is little likelihood of a goal, he will speak his thoughts as opposed to describing the game. He may muse over what tactics the team is trying, what is going on in a certain player's mind, how the game will affect the teams' positions in the table, how the manager is feeling and so on. He will do this for a few moments and then pick up the play again as one of the goals is threatened. Other commentators now do the same, and soccer commentary is far less descriptive of actual play than it was.[10]

Peter Jones was one of the best-known voices on British radio when – attending the Boat Race in 1990 – he collapsed and died from a heart attack. Those who succeeded him as commentators on the very top games – Mike Ingham and Alan Green – both quote the key advice he gave them – 'use light and shade, always offer a contrast. Paint pictures. Use your voice to emphasise what's important and what isn't'. Both certainly went on to do that – and more.

FOOTBALL ON RADIO had a new lease of life after the BBC lost the television rights to live Premiership games. BBC Radio retained its contract with the Premier League (until 2007 it was the Premiership) and the other leagues for live radio coverage. When he was head of 5 Live, Bob Shennan stressed that it is its association with football as much as anything which distinguishes the station in the world of live sport:

> Football drives the audience for a radio station like us season in season out. There's a lot of very good football, we have access to all of it but the crucial thing is that there's so much of it and there's a rhythmical, regular commitment. Almost every day for most of the year there's something for us to be talking about or bringing commentary on. So the notion of 5 Live as 'the home of' is crucial and clearly the Premiership and the top clubs are the most attractive.[11]

In 2006 commercial station talkSPORT won the rights to broadcast live Saturday afternoon commentary on Premier League games from 2007 to 2010, although it has to select its match after the BBC has chosen the game it wants. Before it won this contract talkSPORT commentators had sometimes narrated games to listeners from televised coverage they were watching in the studio.

By 2008 BBC 5 Live broadcast commentary on several hundred matches a year and commentators faced the task of making each one individual. John Murray:

> You need to be interesting and entertaining. We do so many football matches a year and travel to so many grounds. We can describe European grounds and cities listeners may never visit but we also have to remember that most listeners haven't been to most of the home grounds. You have a chance to tell people about these places.[12]

Nick Barnes, of BBC Radio Newcastle, stressed the importance of this in local radio:

> I love to build up a picture for people sitting in their car or listening at the kitchen table. At local grounds in lower divisions I can talk about the environment – that old doomed scrapyard at Rotherham, the prison you can see from the gantry at Swansea and the washing in the back gardens.[13]

Mike Ingham went to the BBC via local radio (in Derby) and became the BBC football correspondent. He recalled his early induction into the world of commentary as a boy:

> You had to rely on radio for live coverage of the matches and I became addicted to the Saturday afternoon football service with uninterrupted second half commentary. The commentators were usually two from Alan Clarke, Brian Moore, Simon Smith and Maurice Edelston – these guys had great voices, oozed authority and always made you feel you were sitting in the stadium with them.[14]

Ingham, with a warm and graceful voice, became a fine descriptive narrator whose style exemplified accurate, straightforward commentary. He tempered his judgements about the game's controversies with a feel for the complexity of the issues at stake. Working alongside him as a summariser, Graham Taylor noticed how careful Ingham was to sum up a game before making a judgement:

> He has an overall view of what is happening on the pitch and he doesn't try to jump in straightaway at the start of his commentary and be critical. He will carefully make an assessment before he opens up. So if he's the one to start the game he will watch it unfold – you can almost hear his brain working. Then after about ten minutes he makes an observation.[15]

STYLE OF COURSE ALWAYS CHANGES and this is true of radio commentary. Just as Stewart MacPherson changed the BBC's conception of a commentator after the Second World War so Alan Green began to do the same fifty years later. Green sought to defy the conventions of commentary and invent his own. No commentator so polarised opinion, certainly not so deliberately, as Alan Green. He carved out for himself a special position on BBC radio, given licence to say things, as BBC managers admitted, that others were not allowed to say.

Two things were soon evident about Alan Green – that he grew up in Belfast and that he once worked as a news reporter. Even after living in England for many years his voice was still an Ulster voice – sharp, emphatic and vibrant, though it could be clothed quickly in scorn. And he always maintained his awareness of what might be worth telling, of *the story*.

Through both commentaries and phone-in programmes Green established himself as the King of football talk, the man with a direct line to the 'terraces' – 'a fan with a microphone'. In a BBC promotional video clip in 2007 Green presented himself as a brash know-all who just happened to have found an easy way to earn a living. 'What do I know about the game? Nothing.' He attracted many critics. Included among the lesser charges levelled against him were: 'A triumph of ego over information', 'A parody of himself', 'A verbal bully'.[16]

But he retained many supporters. A blind listener, Hazel Dudley, having often listened to Green while sitting at Anfield, wrote:

> My favourite commentator without doubt is Alan Green. He paints pictures. He can tell you what the weather is like, what the players are wearing, what the spectators are doing as well as giving a comprehensive account of what's going on in the game. He raises his voice to a crescendo when there's a goal about to be scored, and then if it's a miss you can easily tell just by listening. I know when I'm at Anfield I stand up for a scored goal at the same time as everyone else. No-one beats Alan Green.[17]

So what is Alan Green's place in the story of radio commentary? He soon revealed that he was very good at the fundamentals. To the World Service listener, joining in the heart of a match, he quickly announced the score, how much time had gone, his own viewpoint in the ground, where the play was, who had been substituted, who had scored the early goal. And from early on in his career he exemplified another prime requirement: he was a gifted narrator. In football there is much fast play, ebbing and flowing unpredictably across the field, involving several players, the momentum gathering pace, slackening and then bursting into action in another direction. In less than a minute this can involve 10 or 12 players but, when he wanted to, Green could keep abreast of it. Wonderfully fluent at the microphone he could enter intuitively into the rhythm of a game, taking the listener with him:

> *It's back at the halfway line with Campbell, Campbell lifts it towards Lauren. Scholes came in to challenge – fairly. Now it's Lauren again – oh, neat flick by Lauren, finding Flamini. Flamini on towards Henry in the penalty area, well headed clear by Silvestre, drops to Lauren, Lauren on his right foot, turns onto his left foot, there's the cross into the penalty area, headed away by Gary Neville. Scholes meets him on the edge*

of his own box, finds his captain Roy Keane and Keane spins away from Ljungberg – not once but twice – into Scholes, back it goes and Heinze whacks it right foot into safety up over the halfway line.

But what Green developed was more than just a description of the movement of the ball around the pitch. It was more the telegraphed summary of a crucial moment, which described the essentials of what was happening – a move done and dusted in barely a second: *'Great shot. Takes a deflection. Corner'.* Chelsea are leading Bolton 2-1 when they are awarded a free kick just outside the box: *'Here comes Lampard. Driven in. Three-one'.*

A simple aside captured perfectly the moment when a player was close to over-reacting: *'Careful, Wayne'.* Graham Taylor, who has worked alongside Green for many matches as a summariser, said: 'He's your goalscorer. In the penalty area his choice of words, his speed of delivery, his inflexion, is first class'.

Green's football commentary soon became laced with a series of fierce tackles – with players, officials, managers, even portions of the crowd. Always on the lookout for poor play or poor behaviour, his condemnation began to develop a moral overtone: *'Woefully inadequate'* (a poor pass), *'an awful ball, plays it in wretchedly deep'*, *'a wicked deception'* (a player feigning injury), *'Now he's back on his feet – what a disgrace'*, *'Fearful abuse'* (by players on a referee). Like many listeners he came to revel in the moment when a culprit was punished: *'Gattuso's going to be booked – what a shame'.*

Referees were soon established as a favourite target. *'The German referee has got it wrong again – unbelievable'*; *'That's soft from the ref, really soft'.* Managers never escaped, indeed they were held responsible for player misbehaviour: *'Where does it stem from? It stems from the managers'.*

There was a famous falling out between Green and Sir Alex Ferguson, who gets it in the neck here for pressurising a referee:

At least three minutes of stoppage time, depending on what influence Sir Alex has on the referee – it could be four minutes, it could be five... Fergie, left arm outstretched, pointing to his watch, shouting at Rob Styles. Never seen that before... From the Manchester United manager. Surprise, surprise, we've got four minutes of stoppage time. I could write this script.

'Corporate' spectators who failed to follow the game became another target. *'Take that sandwich out of your mouth'* (a reference to the 'prawn sandwich brigade' at Old Trafford). *'Sixty-three thousand watching and most of them couldn't care less'* (referring to UEFA's allocation of tickets at the Champions' League final). At Arsenal one Wednesday night the ball was played towards the executive boxes some ten minutes before the interval, and Green already has the occupants *'thinking of their cheese and prawn sandwiches'*.

His intuitive feel for the flow of a game meant that he almost always spotted the big moment, and was seldom behind the action when it mattered. But it was sometimes a close run thing. Here, busy promoting the evening phone-in programme, he misses an Arsenal build-up and just catches the final moves:

> *Ten minutes to half-time here on Sport on Five's huge match this Tuesday evening and there is a special 606 tonight coming live from Highbury. I'll be presenting it. The lines will be open around about nine o'clock, which is in about twenty minutes' time. 0500 909693 to ring if you want to give me a call. Vieira... good ball forward towards Henry just outside the penalty area. Bergkamp with a run... here's a chance for Arsenal... two-one Arsenal!*

Sometimes Green's passion, which made him desperate to voice his own opinions, came at the expense of the commentary itself. On a Sunday afternoon in August 2007 he took over for the final twenty-two minutes or so of the game between Liverpool and Chelsea shortly after the referee Rob Styles had mistakenly given Chelsea a penalty. A little later there was also some confusion over whether Styles had given Essien a second yellow card, but then neglected to send him off. The penalty decision was about as bad as refereeing decisions get, directly affecting the result of a major game. It was of such significance that the referees' association publicly apologised the next day and Styles was demoted to lower-level matches for a period.

Green's commentary period was punctuated every minute or so by exclamations of anger and frustration with the referee. Styles had given *'a pathetic display of refereeing'*. He was *'absolutely appalling'*. Styles *'has lost it'*. Styles had given *'a shocking display'*. Styles *'just doesn't know what he's doing'*. The referee's performance was *'breathtaking in its incompetence'*. Styles was *'making up the rules as he went along'*. Styles was *'totally incompetent'*. The penalty was *'an absolutely awful decision'*.

To add flavour Green took it all personally, or pretended to. *'I get criticised for criticising referees and then see a display like this'*. But *'I was right and the referee again was wrong'*. Criticism swiftly turned into scorn.

'*Everybody watching here. . . everybody watching on TV, everybody listening – we've all got it wrong. Only Rob Styles is right'*. And scorn turned into malice: '*The referee's five yards away and he can't see it'*.

It was an extraordinary rant, one in which 'the voice of the fans' was allowed to drown out the voice of the commentator.

Alan Green likes to tell how, at an early stage of his career he was warned by management at the BBC not to be so opinionated in his commentaries and to leave it to the summariser to play that role. 'Give me a summariser who has opinions, then,' he retorted. Graham Taylor comments:

> When nothing happens, he's dangerous, he's so full of opinions... By the time he's finished he's done everyone's job. He can sometimes express an opinion you disagree with, but leave you no time to disagree.

Those who have worked alongside Green adapted to the demands in different ways. David Pleat watched the game as a strategist and saw patterns and strategies emerging before they became apparent to others. He needed time on his own at the mike to get his comments about team formation and strategy across, and he was assiduous in his desire to be fair. What a pleasure to hear a broadcaster acknowledge, as Pleat did during a Premier League game: '*I can't give you a view of that* (a red card) *because I was just making a note on my pad.'*

Graham Taylor relaxed easily into the role of summariser and during a game gave regular updates to the listener on how each team was taking, or losing, the initiative. Green sometimes performed a kind of duet with Taylor, in which they shared common thoughts, though Green usually had the last word.

By contrast, Mark Lawrenson specialised in the pithy interjection, adding value to what the commentator had said, or putting another point of view. At their best, his exchanges with Green displayed the inter-play of quick-fire passing on the field. Once Lawrenson had worked with Green for a while, he knew when the commentator was passing him the ball, and – more important – how to take it off him when he needed to. He developed the facility to insert a succinct summary of the essentials of a move, while Green paused for breath: '*Good pass from Giggs, great move from Carrick, fine save by Hahnemann'*. As Green wonders aloud (this is August) when a player will be match fit, Lawrenson inserts just one word between Green's, skilfully catching the listener's ear: '*October.'* When Green railed at a referee 'taken in' by what he believed was a player feigning injury, Lawrenson calmed him down: *'Alan, if a player goes down the referee has no choice but to stop play.'* And Lawrenson always made sure that the realities of professional football were not overlooked. *'What kind of a challenge is that?'* asks Green scathingly after a fierce tackle. *'A good one if you're a centre back'*, comes back the instant reply, leaving Green silent. For a second.

Green made sure that if he said a game was good, it was indeed good, because he would tell us if it was not: *'Oh, ref, please blow the whistle. Let's not have any injury time. Thank God it's over'.* It follows that if Alan Green said *'It's an immense game of football we're witnessing here at Old Trafford'*, then it really was a thriller, with Manchester United playing well, even by their standards.

Alan Green brought to commentary the pulsating excitement of football at its best, more vividly perhaps than all those who preceded him. He and the quieter, more considered, Mike Ingham came over the years to complement each other well. Perhaps Alan Green should be allowed the final comment on himself, but in the form of his own assessment of José Mourinho given during commentary on a Chelsea game in 2006:

> *There are aspects to (him) I cannot stand – his obvious arrogance, his willingness to spout forth on any subject imaginable, frequently riling the opposition when he doesn't need to, but by goodness he's an excellent manager.*

1   Robert Wood *A World in Your Ear* (Macmillan 1979) p77
2   *Modern Wireless* December 1931.
3   Freddie Grisewood *One thing at a time* (Hutchinson 1968) p146
       Grisewood became the first presenter of the long-running programme
       Any Questions? in 1949
4   George Allison *Allison Calling* (Staples Press 1948) p41
5   BBC WAC R30/428/1 Commentators 1936-9
6   *Back to Square One* Radio 4 January 2007. On the same programme
       Alan Green commented: 'Tom Finney would get the bus to games and
       look up to the commentators. Wayne Rooney wouldn't know me from
       Adam.'
7   *Fifty Years of Sports Report* ed. Audrey Adams, Collins Willow (1997)
8   Email to the author
9   Alan Green *The Green Line* (Headline 2000) p 73
10   Brian Johnston *Chatterboxes* (W H Allen 1984) p106
11–15 Interviews with the author
16   Letters to the editor reprinted on *Sport.Telegraph* website
17   Interview with the author

EIGHTEEN

GOLF – 'SHHH'

We walk the course, inside the ropes, and as close as we can get to the golfers without disturbing them. You creep along each hole, looking for vantage points. You may be crouched behind a bunker or alongside a tree. It's best to be downwind. Even a gentle breeze carries a whispered commentary a very long way and it's my experience that there isn't a golfer alive who can't hear a pin drop from fifty yards. Heaven help the radio commentator who's heard by a golfer addressing a putt.[1]

IT'S THAT MAN AGAIN. Alan Green would not normally talk in a whisper but here he was helping out his golf colleagues during the Open Championship. He had met the problem that has beset those broadcasting on golf from the start.

In 1927, during the first flush of enthusiasm for commentary, the BBC had explored whether commentaries on golf might be possible. Some engineers thought they would be, but in May 1927, when the Open Championship was at St Andrews, the Dundee station of the BBC was informed by London: 'We shall not require any lines as we do not intend to carry a running commentary'. Management minutes suggest that the idea had been turned down because the final holes were played at an inconvenient time (the Championship finished on a Friday afternoon in those days) and 'an eye-witness narrative was considered the best means of handling matters.'[2] Three years later, in 1930, the BBC Handbook reported that commentary on golf was ruled out 'by reason of expense'.

It was Henry Longhurst who carried out what he later claimed to be the first 'live' outside broadcast on golf in Britain. Longhurst does not date the event but it seems likely to have been in the late 1930s. The BBC set up a commentary box on stilts on the Little Aston course at Birmingham in a position where the commentator could see two greens and three tees. Longhurst saw a fair amount of play from his vantage point. Indeed he remembered that a former Open Champion,

Arthur Havers, 'completely fluffed a short approach shot in front of our window.'[3]

Longhurst tried again at the English Amateur Championships at Hoylake but encountered the challenge which has confronted on-course commentators ever since:

> We soon came up against the elementary stumbling block that in order to describe the play you had to see it and in order to see it you had to be within range of the players and they could therefore hear everything you were saying, which was not only extremely embarrassing but led to persistent cries of 'Shhh' from the silent spectators.

To try and overcome this difficulty, Longhurst and his engineers placed themselves on a knoll beside the fifth fairway for the semi-final matches – they were well out of the way of the players but with some sort of view of the play. The broadcast was to be at an advertised time and the signal for the commentator to begin was to be given by an engineer on the roof of the clubhouse nearby. At the appointed moment a white handkerchief was lowered and Longhurst began his broadcast. By then unfortunately both semi-finals had been completed and the players had moved on.

The first attempt in Britain to describe live golf by someone moving around the course following the action was in 1939. The commentator was the writer and essayist Bernard Darwin, who went out onto the course at the Royal Liverpool Club with two engineers, one carrying a small transmitter and the other the batteries:

> Once, talking out of the side of my mouth into an odious little pocket microphone, I tried to follow and describe the playing of a hole from behind. Birkdale is a place of giant sandhills and with my lame leg I felt very like John Silver ploughing his way through the sand in the great scene at the block house. Later I was teed up immobile on the top of a mountain and described, shot for shot and filling up the intervals as best I could, the play at the fourth hole, which turned out entirely commonplace, with every stroke perfectly dull and respectable. The first attempt was said to have been inaudible, whereas the second was audible, but whether this was really an advantage must be doubted. It is possibly prejudice on my part but I am convinced that golf does not lend itself to this form of description.[4]

GOLF WAS TO TAKE even longer than cricket to become an established subject for radio commentary in the UK – de Lotbinière made no mention of it in his lengthy paper of 1942. It was many years before the resources and techniques were found to turn the apparent constraints presented by the sport to advantage. In 1951, radio listeners heard live commentary for the first time on the final holes of the British Open Championship – Max Faulkner winning at Portrush in Northern Ireland. The regional BBC station set up a makeshift studio on the roof of the clubhouse, and commentary facilities at three points round the course including the final green. But for some years afterwards coverage remained largely confined to reports from fixed vantage points around the course, at first by Henry Longhurst and then by Tom Scott.

Broadcasters faced a number of problems in covering a tournament. Much sport takes place in a stadium. By contrast a golf tournament is dispersed across a wide area, most of it not visible from one or even two fixed points. It is a slow game. It takes two golfers anything up to fifteen minutes to play a hole, and there may be only seven or eight moments of action during that time. Golfers play their shots in almost complete silence and any commentator near enough to a green to see a putt can only whisper into the microphone.

Slowly however the technology was developed which enabled the story of a major championship to be captured for listeners. Mobile transmitters which commentators could carry on their backs were a crucial breakthrough.

The drama of a big tournament owes much to the way that the changing fortunes of different golfers on adjacent holes impact on each player's prospects. Continuous fluctuations in the leader board provide the dynamic of a championship. Thus, once the technology and the resources had been found to cover several holes at once – by having mobile transmitters, supplemented by access to television coverage – live accounts from different holes could be woven together into a period of continuous action. The reports from each hole often impacted acutely on each other and the structure of the tournament thereby became an asset to the broadcaster rather than a challenge.

Ironically the potential to provide a dramatic climax on radio has been greater since the British Open championship was re-arranged in 1957 to suit the demands of television: since then the order of play on the last round has ensured that the tournament leaders are all playing the final holes at the end of the day. This gave tournaments a more compelling momentum and natural climax. Radio could now more easily capture the intricate tensions which lie beneath the game's placid surface, and share them with its audience.

IT WAS THE EMERGENCE of a group of world-famous players in the 1960s, followed soon afterwards by the success of Tony Jacklin and other European stars, that first prompted the BBC to extend its golf coverage. John Fenton had joined the BBC in 1943 straight from school as a 'Youth in Training', graduated through the ranks to the production team of *The Goon Show* and was made golf producer in 1965. He did much to establish golf in the radio sporting calendar, with more live coverage from out on the course.

In 1974, when Fenton was sent to cover the Masters for the first time, there was little expectation of live commentary. His initial task – since the BBC had made no detailed arrangements for him – was to find a telephone in a quiet place from where he could send his report to London. That first year, he made friends with the manager of the Augusta National, who allowed him to use the telephone in his office. Another year he covered the event – perhaps the biggest in golf – from a public phone at the back of the press tent.

At this stage, Fenton recalled, coverage of the first two days of the British Open was still restricted to news reports, but there was some live commentary on the Saturday and Sunday:

> I would go around with an engineer and a mobile transmitter – Renton Laidlaw would cue to me and I would cover a hole or half a hole. Choosing where to stand was difficult. You had to be somewhere where the player couldn't hear you, you had to be downwind, but where you could see what was going on. You developed a very hushed whisper; you could get very close. I remember once at Sunningdale I was literally sitting on the edge of the green, about two feet from Faldo, and they cued to me. I became known as 'whispering' John Fenton.[5]

The players themselves also played a role in promoting more live coverage. In the mid-1970s the Professional Golfers' Association approached Bob Burrows, then Head of Sport at the BBC, about giving the game a higher profile. Burrows recalled that the 1977 Open Championship at Turnberry was a turning point:

We took both *Sport on 4* and the whole of *Sport on 2* out from Broadcasting House and presented it from Turnberry.[6] We had a very good relationship with the sports engineering team, especially Ken Keen and Dick Elsdon. We were able to put people on the course with radio mikes. John Helm got an interview with Lee Trevino direct from the 17th fairway and Don Mosey did live commentary from the 18th green. It really transformed our coverage.[7]

It helps if the sport delivers too, and The Open certainly did that year, with a thrilling last round between Tom Watson and Jack Nicklaus, before Watson won on the last green by a single stroke.

Following that major innovation in 1977, golf coverage continued to grow. Renton Laidlaw, who did most of the reporting, worked for the *Evening Standard* newspaper in London and brought all the best skills of journalism to his golf coverage on radio. George Bayley worked initially as a schoolteacher in Newcastle. He nursed an interest in radio, undertook some newsreading for BBC Radio Newcastle and moved on to covering golf, a game at which he was himself a fine player. His smiling, friendly figure became a feature of the commentary team for seventeen years, developing new ideas for on-course coverage and increasingly given the role of following the potential winner. His soft and mellow voice came into its own on the greens as, in urgent whispers, he urged putts into the hole: *'Get in, get in, get in, get in...'*

Ryder Cup matches between the USA and Europe generated growing interest. Some of the memorable encounters of the 1990s were not covered on terrestrial television and were followed in greater numbers on radio than on TV.

In 1989 Tony Adamson was appointed the BBC's first golf correspondent. By the time of the 1995 Ryder Cup he had established himself as a voice of authority and he helped the BBC win a Sony Award for Best Sports Programme and Best Coverage of a Live Event. 'I watched the Ryder Cup on Radio 5,' said Kate Battersby in the *Daily Telegraph*:

> Driving along Marylebone Road I noticed several drivers around me leaning forward, their faces frozen, and as Faldo's putt dropped there was much clenching of fists and banging of steering wheels. Then as we all realised that we were among many listening to the same station we all laughed at each other.[8]

MODERN GOLF COMMENTARY has many ingredients that make it work. But if it has moments which bring it most to life they come when the game moves near to the flag. Coverage of the final putts on a green provides the centrepiece of the broadcast. And the putt that could win the hole offers the greatest scope, and the greatest dangers, for the commentator. It is preceded by tense moments of waiting, like those when sprinters wait for the gun. The challenge for the commentator lies not only in deciding what words to use, but how much can be left unsaid.

Here is Iain Carter, who succeeded Tony Adamson as BBC Radio golf correspondent in 2003, covering one putt by Tiger Woods at the 2005 British Open at St Andrews. He gives us the commentary team's take on the line, the consultation between golfer and caddy, the path of the ball, and the suggestion of contentment and assurance as Woods strides away:

> *We reckon it's dead straight. Tiger Woods is at a little committee meeting with the caddy, Stevie Williams. Williams is now standing there, leaning on the flag behind his boss, and Tiger Woods is coming downhill, downwind. He's just got to set this one rolling and it should drop in for his par three here at the eighth. (Pause) And it does. Right into the middle of the hole. And that was a very, very assured stroke from Tiger Woods. He's heading off to the ninth, the driveable par four, and he's got his par three at the eighth in his pocket.*

A successful live programme from one of the big tournaments has to string together one hole after another like this in rapid succession. That means having several teams out on the course and a temporary studio from which the coverage can be co-ordinated. For the co-ordination to work, the presenter and producer need access to the television coverage. And it inevitably follows that some commentary will be done from the TV screen.

At the US Masters, the BBC is allowed only two fixed positions on the course: at 'Amen Corner', close to the twelfth tee, and by the sixteenth tee. From each of these positions the commentator has a good view of another green. Iain Carter recalled that the first time BBC Radio combined commentating 'off tube' with live reports from the course he and his colleagues were presented with a new set of challenges. Carter described how one crucial putt by Tiger Woods was covered:

It was a technique that just evolved as the moment happened. Woods chipped the ball way, way left of the hole, at the back of a bank and then the ball reached the top of the bank, stopped, rolled back, took two borrows and then went onto the edge of the hole and dropped in. Andrew Cotter was the commentator out on the course. I could see the TV close-up back at base ... There was a moment when Andrew said *'Now it's trickling back'* and there was a break and I could see it was going in and I yelled *'It's going in'* and then Andrew came back with *'It's teetering on the edge, it's fallen in.'* And then the whole place erupted and we had the genuine sound from out there, and there was a marrying together of the two voices, one saying what he could see and the other saying what he could see and the whole uproar – and that was something that probably had never been done in radio before, where you had one person doing it from tube, one person seeing it in the raw. It's entirely instinctive. The moment comes and you have to capture it.[9]

CROWD NOISE FORMS an important part of the soundtrack of much commentary, sending signals to the listener about the unfolding of an event, and enabling the listener to share in the sense of anticipation which is at the heart of watching sport. But the essential counterpart of noise is silence, and one without which listening would be incomplete.

The stillness of several thousand people around a green is one of the great silences in sport. Here radio meets a particular challenge, as four or five seconds of silence can seem a very long time. But if the unfolding of play at a hole has created suspense, listeners may share in a moment of excitement even though nothing is said. At such moments the task of the commentator is to refrain from commentating.

At the ocean course at Kiawah Island, South Carolina, in 1991, Tony Adamson was at the 18th hole when Bernhard Langer had a five-foot putt on which hung the destination of the Ryder Cup. Adamson was in the commentary box above the hole, looking down on a green that was surrounded by four or five thousand people. The Atlantic Ocean, he recalled, was just behind him:

I was aware all afternoon that you could hear the ocean.

I said: *'There are five thousand people round this green. Bernhard Langer is in the loneliest spot any golfer can be in. All he can hear is the Atlantic Ocean.'* I stopped there, and just punctuated the silence by saying – *'five feet for Bernhard Langer. Looks pretty straight to me.'* And my co-commentator then could hardly speak and all he said was *'Tony, I can hardly speak'*. And I said *'I know how you feel'*. And then we let more silence happen. And then I said: *'He's over it now, he's decided on his line'*. More silence, *'It's on its way'* More silence. And then all you heard was the American cheer as he misses and I let the cheer go, for I was desperately disappointed for Langer. I had to go with the noise. *'Europe have lost the Ryder Cup, Bernhard Langer has missed on the right, and he is distraught. He can't believe it'*.[10]

THE ACTION ON THE GREENS is what gives much of the buzz to golf coverage but over eight to ten hours the commentary team have to provide other moments of inspiration. Sometimes these are opportunistic but deliberate as when Alan Green persuaded Seve Ballesteros to describe a difficult chip shot that his playing partner Philip Walton was facing on the Oak Hill course in New York State. Sometimes they are unplanned, as when Chris Rea was driven into a bunker by his engineer while commentating at Wentworth.

Much also depends on the inter-play between members of the commentary team, including the expert summarisers. The latter are there not just to provide analysis and comment but to help create an atmosphere of discussion and banter that the BBC believes makes the coverage entertaining.

The American Jay Townsend, himself a professional golfer, started working with the BBC at the 1999 Ryder Cup. The BBC chose him partly for his 'entertainment value'. Carter stressed the importance of Townsend's sense of humour, 'because that makes [him] the sort of person that people want on the radio'.

Carter used Townsend's analysis as the occasion allows:

> I'm always very conscious of the need to give summarisers the opportunity to explain and not tread on their toes … and when I work with someone like Jay Townsend he will often start to signal with his hands whether he

thinks a putt is right to left, left to right, uphill, downhill or whatever. Depending on the timing when the putt is going to be hit, if I think I've got enough time, I'll just say: *'What's the break here, Jay?'* and he can then explain it. Equally if it's going to happen very quickly I just say *'This one's going to break right to left'*, and just use his expertise that way.

Here are Carter and Townsend working together during the 2005 Masters. Tiger Woods and Chris DiMarco have been neck and neck and are on the 18th green. Woods needs this putt for the title. The sense of anticipation, always a key part of sport, is intense. Carter provides his characteristic scene setting – the geography of the green, the body language of the player, the watching family and spectators. For the final moments, the sentences are short and sharp, and spoken quietly:

Carter:
He's now standing midway between ball and hole, just to the left of the line of the direction that the putt will take. And now he's going around the clock face and he will be effectively the big hand at six o'clock as he hunches down onto his haunches and looks and surveys, eyes wide, concentration playing right across his face beneath that black cap, and he is staring, looking for inspiration. And now looking at it from the other side of the hole, coming round behind the hole. His wife and mother look on. The entire crowd holds its breath. What a moment. Eight feet for the Masters.
He takes the marker away, gets down on his haunches once again, left hand on his left knee, right hand holding his putter. Now he's standing up and he's strolling forward. A decision has been made. He knows the line he's taking. What would you advocate, Jay?
Townsend:
I'd say it's a right edge putt. You don't want to give the hole away. Fairly level putt – you can go ahead and put a nice, aggressive stroke on this one.
Carter:
This to win the Masters. Eight feet for Tiger Woods. The putter head is behind the ball, he widens his stance a fraction ... he's ready now. Woods for the Masters. Sets the putt on its way (crowd erupts) and misses – misses to the left.

Townsend:
He didn't play enough break...
Carter:
And Woods didn't take the break and he's gone through by three feet and Chris DiMarco – over to you son.[11]

ON JULY 22ND 2007 the last round of the Open Championship at Carnoustie provided a remarkable drama. Minute by minute it unfolded, each scene more unexpected than the last. It provided a testing opportunity for the commentary team to show how golf can work on radio.

When the leaders went out on the course that day Sergio García was two shots ahead of the field. By 4.50 p.m. Andrés Romero, by now on the fifteenth hole, had made his ninth birdie of the round and had taken the lead. He played another birdie at the sixteenth: two ahead. But Romero dropped three shots on the final holes just as Padraig Harrington and García, who were playing three and four holes behind respectively, picked up shots. So Romero left the stage. It was Harrington and García who played out the final scenes, at first on separate stages and then together during the play-off. Each had periods in front, and each faltered. No serious dramatist, scripting the play, would have dared put Harrington in the water – twice – at the eighteenth. Nor have García hitting the flag with a tee shot during the play-off.

The commentary was compèred from a temporary studio box near the 18th green where John Inverdale, helped by a scoring computer, had an overview of what was happening. Mobile teams of commentators and summarisers followed each of the leaders, and the producer wove in reports from each hole, as his colleagues raced down the fairways to keep up. Between them, presenter, commentators and summarisers had to ensure that they gave the listener the right arithmetic: 'If X putts this, Y will probably need a birdie on the next hole to stay in the race' and so on. Pauses between shots allowed for occasional news from other sports – *'Let's hear about a wicket at Lord's – here's Pat Murphy'*.

Unlike the commentators on the course, Inverdale also had access to television coverage and was able to draw on replays of key moments, and close-ups of the golfers, adding details about body language to the listener's picture. The soundtrack was no less important, not just the cheers and sighs of the crowd, but – when the commentator fell silent – the solitary swish of the golf club as a shot was played.

Out on the course the commentators had to capture each shot, and give it character. *'An assassin's drive,'* said Iain Carter of one shot by Sergio García from the tee. Although he sometimes pauses at the moment the ball is struck, Carter's technique is generally to give his commentary momentum by talking the listener through the preparation and performance of the shot. Describing García chipping up onto the green, Carter knew we had also heard the customary hoot from a Scotrail train going past the course:

> *So here he is with this chip. It came up just six inches short of the bunker, so he's got the face of the bunker staring him in his face and then he's got around about twenty paces, something like that, to the pin, which is cut right at the back of the green. Probably a bit more than that actually, thirty paces, so he's got to get the ball up sharply and then he'll let it release, I would have thought, down to the hole.*
> *So here he goes. Just bumps it forward, uses the banking, lets the ball now trundle towards the hole – and it's going in, it's going in, it's going in. All the time I'm talking to you it's getting close. It's a wonderful chip, he's put it to five feet and that was pretty nerveless stuff. And what timing from that train driver, right on the backswing.*

During those last few holes at Carnoustie, the summarisers added technical detail: rules for dealing with a water hazard, the options for reaching the green, the effect of wind on how long a hole plays, the 'yardage' from ball to hole – *'224 to the front edge – 216 over the burn'* said Jay Townsend. On the seventeenth hole Mark Roe explained that, putting for a birdie, Sergio García faced two small hills and a double break:

> *He has great fortune with his second shot there, flirting with the bunker, just a yard from the trap where it landed, but it kicked on down. This is such a hard putt to read. It's got three breaks in it. It's downhill, then it levels out, then it goes downhill again, it moves right to left, left to right, then right to left at the hole – it's very tricky.*

Iain Carter and fellow-commentator Mark Pougatch set the wider scene: the crowds, the buildings, the landscape and sky, the families waiting, Miguel Jimenez sitting on the grass, smoking a cigar and watching his compatriot Sergio García. Iain Carter invited listeners to join the spectators in the auditorium of the 18th green:

There's not a single seat to be had here on the vast grandstands on either side of the green, and one that's effectively a slip cordon to the flag, as well as all the windows and bedrooms of the Carnoustie Hotel, behind that white building there. There are people standing on verandas, the huge clock's showing nineteen minutes past six in the evening. What a moment this is. There's even a shaft of sunlight down to the south of the course, high grey cloud overhead...

The final resolution of such an event as The Open comes after four days of tension for both golfers and commentators. And at that moment it is sometimes the human dimension which is the most compelling. In describing this the line between observation and mawkishness is a fine one. As the eventual winner prepared himself at the last hole, John Inverdale reached for some way to 'call' the moment: *'Padraig Harrington, This is Your Life'*. A summariser reported that he had just bumped into Harrington's wife: *'I've been up to Caroline and given her a kiss'*. And, when Harrington completed the eighteenth hole, Mark Pougatch caught the moment shown next day in every newspaper: *'And on runs his son Patrick ... there's a great bear hug'*.

THUS GOLF COMMENTARY has come some distance since the 1930s, when Longhurst waited anxiously for the white flag to fall. Ways have been found, to use Bernard Darwin's phrase from 1939, of 'filling up the intervals'. Transported from hole to hole, the listener has access to continuous action. Golf – that apparently sedate game – has revealed itself as among the most riveting of radio sports.

1   Alan Green *The Green Line* (Headline 2000) p132
2   'Eye-witness narrative' was the term used by the BBC for a *report* – as opposed to a live commentary – on an event
3   This and later extract from Henry Longhurst *My Life and Soft Times* (Cassell 1971) p254
4   Bernard Darwin *Life is Sweet Brother* (Collins 1940) p210
5   Interview with the author
6   *Sport on 4* was a Saturday morning magazine programme looking at sport in depth; *Sport on 2* was the Saturday afternoon commentary programme
7   Interview with the author
8   Quoted by Tony Adamson *The Ryder Cup* in *50 Years of Sports Report* (Collins Willow 1997)
9–10   Interview with the author
11   DiMarco holed his putt and took the match to a sudden-death play-off which Woods won

NINETEEN

TENNIS – RADICAL CHANGES

Mrs Moody serves to the backhand
Miss Round chops back again but deeper
Mrs Moody drives rather softly
Miss Round a fast, furious drive to the far corner
Mrs Moody lobs it up
Miss Round drives again from the baseline
Mrs Moody across court
Miss Round across court and very fast
Mrs Moody down the backhand line
Miss Round there
Mrs Moody a drop shot
Miss Round races in and gets it and plays across court
Mrs Moody. Oh! Mrs Moody plays a cross-court drive back at her
Miss Round goes for it, falls, hits the ball but doesn't get it back
over the net.
Game to Mrs Moody

BBC BROADCASTS FROM WIMBLEDON began in 1927 and this is one of the first recordings available – Teddy Wakelam describing the women's singles final in 1933. The days of such sedate play, and such plain and largely unemotional accounts, are long gone. In those days spectators at Wimbledon responded to the play by clapping enthusiastically but not a shout or scream could be heard. The game became more and more athletic, the players more glamorous, the crowd more extrovert. The commentators too became more engaged, painting the play in sharper colours. Here is Jonathan Overend at Wimbledon in 2007, as Venus Williams serves to Marion Bartoli.

> *Composing herself. Second serve, break point down.*
> *Forehand return, Williams, down the line.*
> *Backhand from Bartoli cross court.*
> *Forehand down the line on the other side from Venus Williams,*
> *who's toying with the French woman right now.*

*Two-handed backhand from Venus, slightly shorter ball for
Bartoli to attack.*
She goes cross court, hits the line.
*Incredible defences from Williams, who now is into the centre
of the court once more with a backhand.*
*Bartoli sends her scampering into the forehand corner, and now
into a backhand corner. Bartoli just can't get rid of Venus Williams in this rally.*
*Here's a forehand from Bartoli down the line but Venus can
deal with it down the centre.*
Another backhand down the line from Bartoli, wonderful stuff
(roars of crowd intervene). *Bartoli's won the rally. Ball out
wide from Venus, just an incredible exchange between the two.*

The BBC's coverage of the Wimbledon tournament developed radi-
cally over the years, and with it changes in the way that broadcasters
tried to make tennis commentary work on radio.

AS EARLY AS 1930 the BBC announced in its handbook that tennis
provided 'excellent material for running commentary'. This was not
to remain a unanimous view but with ready co-operation from the
All-England Lawn Tennis Club Wimbledon coverage quickly became
a firm favourite in radio's sporting calendar.

The sport certainly offers a number of ready-made attractions to
the broadcaster. It has both female and male stars and a large following among both women and men. It offers head to head contests
between individuals. Periods of fast-flowing action are interspersed
with natural pauses. These are supplemented by Wimbledon's inbuilt
soundtrack – the contrasting passages of silence and applause that
signal to the listener the story of each point. Most of all, perhaps, the
game has a subtle scoring system which allows for gripping swings of
fortune, whereby each player can be on the brink of victory or defeat
in turn. It can make for dramatic listening.

Teddy Wakelam, assisted in the early years by a Wimbledon official, Colonel Brand, was the BBC's main commentator from Wimbledon between 1927 and 1939. Tennis also provided the subject of the
BBC's first live sports commentary from outside the UK when Wakelam covered the Davis Cup tournament from Paris in 1933.

It took a few years for the BBC to work out how best to incorporate
the Wimbledon tournament into the main broadcasting schedules,

especially as in the 1920s and 1930s there was only one BBC network. The length of most individual sporting events, for example football matches, could be predicted in advance. Not so a tennis match, which could last anything up to one, two, three or even four hours and might reach several potential finishing points en route.

In other sports the BBC knew weeks or months in advance who would be playing whom and on which day, whereas the broadcasting schedules were normally drawn up – and the *Radio Times* printed – long before it was known who would meet who in, say, a Wimbledon semi-final.

So the policy was developed of having commentators on stand-by and going over for matches deemed to be of particular interest, or at a crucial stage. However, where an important match was broadcast the demands of other programmes sometimes took precedence. Wakelam liked to tell the story of his commentary on a men's semi-final which, after more than two hours of mounting excitement, had reached 6-5 in the fifth set. A BBC official sat beside him to ensure that there was a smooth hand-over to the studio at the time advertised in *Radio Times*:

> When the score had reached 30-15, my companion touched me on the shoulder and held up his hand for silence. In his beautifully modulated and honey-toned voice he then gave out the announcement: *'We are leaving here now and going over to the Girls' Friendly Society Concert at the Albert Hall'*.[1]

But it was Wakelam who established the original strategy for tennis commentary on BBC radio – that of trying to describe every shot, with very few additional comments. He and Brand were both qualified tennis umpires and their focus was on an objective description of the play, saving any comments until the moment, after every two games, when players went to the chair:

> Our own view of doing things is to act very much as a kind of glorified umpire-scorer, occasionally interspersing our stroke-by-stroke commentaries and point-by-point scoring with short descriptions of the particular kind of court craft which this or that man is employing and enlarging on things in general as 'change-over' and 'between the sets' intervals allow.

In this one sport de Lotbinière was somewhat at odds with his audience. He was not convinced that it was possible to make tennis commentary work. In 1942 he wrote:

> The nature of the game does not lend itself to commentary and it is almost impossible to prescribe any treatment that is wholly satisfactory. The play is too fast to follow in detail and the sameness of the strokes makes for monotony[2]

Lobby perhaps had not fully reckoned with the hold Wimbledon was to have on the British public.

———————————

AFTER THE WAR, with Wakelam retired, it was Max Robertson who was the voice of Wimbledon on BBC radio and he became the BBC's longest-serving tennis commentator. Like many of his contemporaries at the BBC, Robertson was educated at public school and university, though he left Cambridge without completing his degree. Seeking work in Australia, he gained some commentary experience on the new radio stations there before joining the BBC in 1939. He began Wimbledon commentaries in 1946.

Robertson established himself largely through two qualities: the speed and clarity of his coverage, and a microphone manner reflecting the apparent decorum of the Wimbledon tournament. His light, pitter-patter delivery seemed especially well-matched to the passage of the ball to and fro across the net, and he could raise the tempo for faster games, rarely missing a shot. Robertson stressed that he was out there on court for the listener, and that this style of commentating was emotionally demanding:

> Doing a modern running commentary on a good singles match is like playing it yourself from both sides of the net. The constant effort of anticipating and giving as accurate a current description as possible, sustained over long periods of time at extremely fast speech speed, demands both mental and physical stamina. At the end of it the commentator feels the elation of the winner and very often the exhaustion of the loser.[3]

An extract from Robertson's commentary on the women's singles final between Maureen Connolly and Louise Brough in 1954 suggests how much, at that stage, he was following the Wakelam approach. This was a dramatic personal encounter between the diminutive young American woman, 'Little Mo', and her older compatriot whom she had displaced as champion – a contest which 'Little Mo' won. During the rally Robertson stays very close to the tennis. Maureen Connolly is serving at five-all in the second set:

> *She serves to the right-hand court. Backhand reply by Brough. Forehand by Connolly down to the backhand. Brough gets it back. Forehand by Connolly, cross-court this time, low and fast. Forehand by Brough, rather slower. Connolly that slightly sliced forehand down to the backhand this time. It comes back from Brough. Connolly a looped forehand down to Brough's forehand. Same from Brough. Now Connolly lower on the forehand cross-court. Brough cross-court on the forehand – just out over the side line.*

Only after the rally does Robertson allow himself a small personal touch: *'Brough turns round with a rueful little grimace to herself'.*

Robertson was skilful in adding one important element to his commentary. Drawing on the pauses in play between serves – and assisted by the fact that in those days spectators rarely gave voice – he would use moments of silence to capture the sense of anticipation in the arena. During the legendary game between Jaroslav Drobny and Budge Patty in 1953, with the score at 17-16 in the second set (this was before tiebreaks), Robertson mentioned quietly that Drobny had taken out a handkerchief and wiped his brow. The listener knew that meanwhile Patty was preparing to serve. There followed a full five seconds – a long time in radio commentary – in which Robertson did not say a word.

BUT THE ROBERTSON APPROACH to commentary was not to survive. Styles of broadcasting, and the expectations of listeners, changed and tennis came to be seen as a considerable challenge. Bob Shennan, for some years head of BBC 5 Live, called it 'an incredibly difficult radio sport to commentate on'.[4]

One problem came from changes in the game itself. The speed of rallies, and the range of modern players' skills, made continuous shot-by-shot description increasingly difficult. Listeners' expectations were also changing, in part as a result of changes in commentary styles in other sports, where broadcasters began to search out the flavour and personality of what they were seeing, and to talk to summarisers during the play.

In addition sports fans came to expect up-to-the-minute information on what was happening across a tournament like Wimbledon, not just a commentary on one particular game.

The original approach was slowly abandoned as commentators realised they could give listeners a better idea of what was happening by capturing the essentials of a rally, rather than mentioning every single shot. Radio producers, who now had to compete more for listeners' attention, needed to produce a varied and stimulating programme, rather than just a blow-by-blow account. Former tennis players were added to the commentary team. The language of commentary became more informal and more attention was given to the personalities of the players. The BBC began to place commentators at several courts, enabling them to switch quickly from match to match, and capture key moments around the tournament. Thus the problems presented by having several matches under way at once were turned to advantage.

A significant step in the transition from the old style of tennis coverage to the one used today came when Bob Burrows assumed the post of Head of Sport and Outside Broadcasts on BBC Radio in 1975. The merger of Outside Broadcasts and Sports News into a single department, leading to the creation of the post taken by Burrows, had significant effects on the nature of sports coverage, and Wimbledon was a prime example. Burrows wanted a more versatile and newsworthy programme. With the co-operation of the All England Club he brought in major changes. He recalled:

> The coverage was very staid. Television only covered two courts, and I knew there was a lot more happening around the tournament that wasn't getting attention. So we introduced extra commentary positions around the courts. Some of the old Outside Broadcast people were rather set in their ways and we brought in up and coming people, some of whom had been trained by Angus Mackay. Peter Jones was the first to present the programme from Wimbledon and we had a range of different voices during the day to ensure there was light and shade in the commentary – Max Robertson, Gerald Williams, John Motson and others.[5]

Previously the studio announcer in central London had linked up with commentators at Wimbledon, but now a new format was developed whereby the whole afternoon's programmes were presented from the tournament. The commentary team was augmented so that more matches could be covered, and more additional material – interviews with players, well-known visitors, and spectators – was introduced. The programme offered a wider coverage than BBC television, which in due course was forced to follow suit.

Max Robertson, who in the 1950s had been assisted at Wimbledon by Rex Alston, Freddie Grisewood and others 'on loan' to tennis when needed, remained as a senior commentator but new names were brought in. Gerald Williams joined the radio team from journalism and became BBC tennis correspondent in 1976; Des Lynam covered Wimbledon on radio before moving to television; David Mercer, formerly a solicitor in Wales, and a tennis umpire, began working for the BBC in the early 1980s and became tennis correspondent in 1990 when Williams also moved to television. Others included Richard Evans, an experienced tennis journalist familiar with the organization and politics of the game around the world, and Tony Adamson, BBC golf correspondent for many years, and still a member of the Wimbledon team even though he has retired from his full-time post at the BBC.

Some of Robertson's colleagues had begun to question whether it was possible, or indeed necessary, to describe every shot. The problem with Robertson's technique, said Des Lynam, was that 'one had absolutely no chance of knowing where the tennis ball might be until one heard the score announced at the end of the point'.[6]

Lynam recounted how he and Gerald Williams devised an alternative to the Robertson approach to commentary:

> (We) worked out a style in which we verbally followed the server. By describing what was happening to him or her, you could more or less tell the story of each point without gabbling too much ... By concentrating on what was happening to the server – 'She serves, but is passed down the line', for example – the listener was given a better chance of understanding what was going on.

Tony Adamson said that when he started commentating at Wimbledon in the early 1980s Gerald Williams passed on similar advice – 'Always start the rally with the server and follow the rally that way. You can almost cut out the other player, as long as you give the listener the geography of the court'.[7]

These changes impacted on Max Robertson. By the end of his career he was combining his traditional method of shot-by-shot description with more subjective and personalised comment. In the women's final at Wimbledon in 1983, Martina Navratilova out-played Andrea Jaeger in the first set and the commentary team was keen to see Jaeger enliven the occasion by getting back into the game. Robertson shared the broadcast with Gerald Williams. Robertson as always was fast, a little clipped, meticulous. He paused after every point for announcements of the score by the umpire to be heard, an important way of putting the listener onto the court. Personal comments about the players, and spectators' feelings towards them, had now become part of the commentary – *'(Jaeger's) sense of humour and fun has been absolutely infectious – everybody loves her.'* There was even a cautious mention of Navratilova's partner: *'Martina waves to her friend Nancy Lieberman and Nancy Lieberman stands and applauds.'*

Here is Robertson during a Navratilova service game. He moves onto first-name terms with the players:

She serves, fortunately for Jaeger it was into the side line, it would be an ace otherwise, she can't move at the moment, this is the most sorry sight. Next one is right, a two-handed reply down the line and Martina nets a forehand volley. Martina from the far end, the roller end, serves down the centre, a forehand return short, Martina goes back nicely with her knees and takes a backhand on the rise and now smashes – just out. Well, Andrea can do with any little bit of comfort Martina can give her, any mistake, a crumb. Martina serves wide to the forehand, gets a let. Andrea went for a big forehand, hit it miles out of court... both playing with large-headed racquets, Martina's has a square head to it at the top.

A two-handed reply – Martina's forehand half-volley across court, up comes Jaeger and gets a backhand – little dink across court – that more like the Jaeger against Billie Jean King – she actually moved, she actually ran, she's laughing all over her face as she comes back. I do like this girl. 'Unbelievable', she's saying, 'at last I've got a point.'

Martina serves towards us to the backhand and into the net – pit a pat, pit a pat of the ball boys so quick, so exact, so efficient.

A lot of break on that and Andrea's beaten her and Andrea's broken. A lot of break and lift from that service by Martina and Andrea welted her forehand with topspin down the line past her backhand. That should give her courage.

In 1933 Wakelam had allowed himself, during one rally of four-teen shots, only one fragmentary moment of emotion (*'Oh!'*). Fifty years on the ebb and flow of play is dramatised, the players are ad-dressed in personal and affectionate terms, and the commentator's own emotions are on display. The discourse of public and private life had changed and commentary had changed with it.

BY 2007 COVERAGE OF WIMBLEDON on BBC 5 Live Radio had tak-en the changes made in the 1970s a step further. 5 Live migrates to the tournament for two weeks each summer and builds its afternoon and early evening schedule round the tournament, transmitting some of its regular programmes from a studio at the ground. In 2007 the station had three studio bases at Wimbledon, broadcasting facilities from seven courts, and a roving microphone. The aim is to ensure that Wimbledon coverage draws in tennis listeners while retaining as many as possible of the station's regulars.

Bob Shennan stressed the importance he attached to maintaining a wide audience:

> During the last half dozen years or so our whole approach to the coverage of the event has changed. It is much more about the whole event, rather than the specific matches, except in the most obvious cases. We also know that our audience wants us to convey the big picture as much as to talk about the number two American woman playing at that moment. We're trying to get a balance between offering something to the aficionados and offering something to people who have a broad interest in the event as much as in the individual matches.

The commentary team contains reporters as well as commentators and summarisers and in 2007 around twenty-five different people were used at the microphone during the fortnight. The reporters were there to bring in news items and interviews from the tournament and to provide contact with spectators. These were designed to capture the breezier atmosphere of contemporary Wimbledon, for instance by talking to the Marcos Baghdatis fan club gathered at an outside court. 'It's about debate, opinion and involving the listener,' said the editor Jonathan Wall. 'Our main aim is to offer accessibility. If we hadn't changed the programme, people might have left us for other stations.'[8]

The technique for describing the play developed by Gerald Williams and others was taken further by Jonathan Overend, who became the main BBC tennis correspondent in 2003. His great fluency and clarity and his ability to change the tempo and pace of his commentary as the play demanded lent itself to tennis commentary. The technique he adopted was not to follow every journey the ball makes but to capture the underlying dynamic of the rally so the listener sensed which player had the initiative.

The familiar phrases describe the major strokes: the forehand pass, the forehand approach, the backhand slice, the stop volley, the smash. But the key to the narrative technique is the short phrases which tell the listener not only what shot is played but where the ball has gone: he serves long and wide, the backhand reply is long, the forehand's gone wide down the line, it's played deep into the backhand corner. Through these phrases the commentator – and the listener – keep up with play.

Overend also introduced a key phrase – *into the rally we go* – as a bridge between the fierce opening exchange after a serve and the possibly calmer and extended exchange of shots that follow. Where the play is repetitive enough a phrase like 'they're going face to face now diagonally across the court or backhand to backhand' can cover a string of shots across the net when the play is temporarily stalemated. This is a tiebreak between Mauresmo and Davenport. Overend takes us through the rally but as soon as it finishes, he is ready to pounce, bring the score up to date and swiftly weave in news from the neighbouring court:

> *Here's the second serve at four all and it's good but short. Forehand return from Davenport, blocked forehand from Mauresmo, cross-court goes Davenport and cross-court goes Mauresmo. And they're going forehand to forehand right now, diagonally across the court, then Mauresmo's across onto her backhand side and mishits. It goes long. And from 4-1 up in the tiebreak, Mauresmo has lost four points in a row and Davenport now leads 5-4. Venus Williams now 5-2 ahead on centre court against defending champion Maria Sharapova.*

The fast and complex action of tennis requires the commentator to be able to call up key phrases at an instant, while deftly anticipating the play. Overend had 10 or 11 seconds to describe this seven-shot rally played at speed. He began with a pause to allow us to hear the sound of a racquet hitting the ball, and Nadal's grunt:

Nadal serves, backhand slice return from Federer, the return was down the centre, backhand cross-court from Federer, a huge forehand from Nadal as he steps up the pace, Federer deals with it on the defence but then (he raises his voice as applause surges around him) *a forehand cross-court from Nadal is a clean winner, and a wonderful shot wins him the point.*

One key word – 'a *clean* winner' – conveys the decisiveness of Nadal's forehand.

The gradual process of change in the coverage of Wimbledon on BBC radio has incorporated another transition. It was once primarily a monologue, with the summariser making only occasional comments. It is now a conversation involving two, three or maybe four people and this has changed the listening experience.

The process of inviting former champions, the first of whom was Fred Perry, into the commentary box began in the 1950s. But for many years the ex-player was kept firmly in his or her place, speaking only between games, with the occasional exclamation between points. Even in 1983 Max Robertson's commentary on Navratilova's service game, transcribed above, was interrupted only by one brief aside from Christine Janes. Not only were the summarisers' comments usually brief, but there was limited technical analysis of what was happening, and not much input of inside knowledge from the tennis circuit. Some summarisers provided only routine musings on the fortunes of the players. (*'Oh, what a terrible match she's having.'*). 'It used to be 'British players' day out' at Wimbledon,' recalled Jonathan Overend.

That changed considerably – the ex-players began to talk a lot more and provide more analysis. Commentary is seen to work best when there is a mix of description, analysis and banter, with fast inter-cutting between each. Because the commentary process now embraces the distinctive style of its station, the contributions must be snappy and to the point. A degree of argument and of humour is expected, and a sense that something unexpected may be just round the corner – so stay tuned. Summarisers were expected to contribute to the cut and thrust in the commentary box, know their tennis and sound relaxed. Tony Adamson described working with Frew McMillan:

Frew McMillan is the best. He invariably says something he hasn't said before, something nobody else has hinted at, something he's seen, that adds enormously – he's down with them – he treats every game as important, he's very professional.

Michael Stich and Pat Cash – both former Wimbledon Champions – provided the main expert analysis during the 2007 men's final. Their comments often drew on a feel for what it was like to play against a particular player – *'A sliced backhand always troubles Nadal'*, *'He is making Federer move and Roger likes to be in the middle, in charge.'* Or they offered an insight for the non-tennis-playing listener – *'A faster serve can be easier to return.', 'The left-hander's serve swerves away from Federer.'* They supplemented Overend's own analysis with technical assessments – during the women's final in 2007 Stich explained how the Venus Williams serve puts Bartoli in difficulty:

> *Great serve to the body – very effective to serve there especially against a double handed player such as Bartoli, on both sides playing double-handed.*

During a big game like this there is a sense of tension in the commentary box. Overend acts both as compère and commentator. He puts description of play at the core, and he always holds the ring, but he facilitates regular inputs from summarisers. The team operates like a small group of friends in the stands, the interplay between them like the balls ricocheting around the court. It can be quite frenetic, and occasionally fatiguing, for any listener who wants to hear an uninterrupted passage of play. During the first set of the men's final in 2007 between Federer and Nadal, for instance, there were (in less than an hour) nearly fifty contributions by Pat Cash and more than thirty by Michael Stich, as well as a few by Andy Murray.

A degree of disagreement is accommodated, though within boundaries. When Annabel Croft suggests Venus Williams is *'in command'* Overend dissents, and as they discuss this we twice hear the swish of the racquet – a double fault. Overend brings us up to date: *'You'll have heard the sigh of the crowd. You'll have heard two shouts of 'Out!' That will probably tell you its thirty-forty.'* He might take the listener away from the shot being played to explore a point of analysis, or finish a joke, but he almost always got back to the game in time.

Away from Wimbledon, when 5 Live broke into its schedules for the final of the US Open between Federer and Djokovic for example, the commentary loosened even more. Overend speculated about Sharapova's presence in the players' box – *'should tongues be wagging?'* Occasionally he let one or even two serves go while the summarisers were chatting. He remembered that he may have some listeners quite new to tennis – *'You need three sets on the board to win a grand slam, remember.'* The members of the team were all pals together and now and again Overend, tongue half in cheek, had to call them to order – *'If you could just answer one of my questions that would be helpful.'*

So tennis commentary has changed considerably since the early days. Wakelam's approach reflected a more restrained style of play, and a more restrained style of broadcasting. Tennis and radio now operate in a more competitive and businesslike environment. The language of tennis commentary has become more informal, the tempo faster, the interjections often sharper.

But one thing has remained constant – the need for commentators to work within the confines of their stations. Jonathan Overend is clear that tennis coverage is primarily the responsibility of a network, not a sports department:

> What is important to remember is that we are now working for the radio station, not BBC sport. We're part of the 5 Live network, we're part of the station, and we need to keep in with the theme, the flow, the style. We need to give the listeners enjoyment in an informative and informal way. We can't do formal in the old way.

'Keeping in with the flow' is what Wakelam had to do too, when he handed over to the Girls' Friendly Society Concert. He had to respect the requirements of the pre-war BBC brand; in 2008 it is the 5 Live brand which calls the tune.

1	This and the later quotation are from *Half-time* by HBT Wakelam (Thomas Nelson 1938) p223 and 291
2	BBC WAC (R 30/428/2 OB Commentators 1940-47)
3	Max Robertson *Stop Talking and Give the Score* (The Kingswood Press 1987) p17
4–5	Interview with the author
6	This and later quote from Des Lynam *I should have been at work* (Harper Collins 2005) p 94
7–8	Interviews with the author

TWENTY

CRICKET AND THE RISE OF TMS

NEARLY EVERY OVER it seemed was a maiden, only a very occasional single occurring … we had to do something because the commentary, of course, had been advertised, so every hour or so we went over, to recite with dreary monotony: 'Durston is bowling from the Vauxhall end – there he goes running up to the wicket. Over goes his arm. Sandham has played the ball back to the bowler – Durston has fielded it, and is now walking back to his bowling mark – and there he goes again, running up to the wicket.' And so on, almost ad nauseam… That afternoon put paid to cricket for a long time as a real 'running commentary' sport.[1]

Cricket commentary began badly on BBC radio and was soon abandoned. It was eventually developed largely because two people recognised how those very qualities which had at first made it seem inappropriate for commentary could instead be turned to advantage. The wait while a fast bowler runs up, and the gap between overs, could provide windows for comment and reflection. Building on this, cricket commentary gradually acquired a distinct character, enriched by some historic radio voices. For more than fifty years its vehicle has been a unique programme – *Test Match Special (TMS)*.

The aim of *TMS* has been to provide not only an account of the game, but thoughtful and entertaining conversation around it. Its team of commentators and summarisers forms and re-forms in different groups throughout a season, moving from ground to ground like troubadours. While the cricketers play at cricket, they play at commentary, and we play at listening, moving in and out of the game as we get on with our lives. *Test Match Special* knows that its listeners like to come and go.

From the unpredictable events on the field of play, the *TMS* team construct their narrative of the day. Their lines are unscripted and their conversations largely uncontrived. Their story never really ends, since there is always another day, another match or indeed another series. Their style of discourse was not invented overnight, nor is it now settled for good. It has changed in temper with the society around it. Once formal, almost deferential, and occasionally poetic, it became conversational and opinionated, and occasionally more 'hard-edged.' Along with much else in life it has become determinedly 'interactive'; as a result some enjoy it more, some less. It often enriches the pleasure that cricket-lovers find in the sport and it has gained some listeners more attracted to the conversations around the game than the cricket itself. By its very nature it allows for a variety of voices and registers. Occasionally it irritates. Such is the nature of any conversation. Nonetheless, to provide, for a total of thirty hours spread over five days, a consistently good level both of information and cricket talk, is remarkable. There is nothing like it in sports commentary. Indeed, there is nothing like it on radio.

From the start, in May 1927, the BBC made clear its belief that this new thing it was trying out – live commentary – would not really work with cricket. 'Obviously … a running commentary on a cricket match by the method used for rugger internationals or the Grand National would be impossible,' said *Radio Times*. Sensing that cricket commentary could not be like that on football or rugby, where the action was short-lived and continuous, the BBC lighted on a different approach. They sent a commentator to a match, but only put him on air from time to time to give an account of the state of the game. Listeners were reassured: 'They will not have to sit through descriptions of maiden overs while the batsman sends to the pavilion for his cap.'

But the BBC was unsuccessful in its initial choice of commentators. Neither Canon Frank H Gillingham, who gave the very first BBC cricket commentary from Leyton in May 1927, nor the former England captain Pelham 'Plum' Warner, who did the first broadcast from Lord's, were effective. Gillingham had played cricket for Essex and apparently made considerable impact as a preacher on his day, but as a commentator he won no converts and was soon dropped. Warner undertook several commentaries during 1927, but his voice lacked vigour and enthusiasm. The BBC retained him from time to time for cricket talks but they swiftly dispensed with his services as a commentator.

The BBC then turned to Teddy Wakelam, who had done the first rugby commentary from Twickenham and was popular with listeners. Wakelam was sent to The Oval for a county game. But cricket did not lend itself to the style Wakelam had used for commentating on rugby and football. It led him to the conclusion – quoted above – that the 'dreary monotony' of cricket did not lend itself to commentary. His verdict helped convince the BBC, at least for several years, that the sport was not suitable for live radio coverage.

THERE WAS NO SINGLE REASON why the BBC changed its mind about cricket. The process took many years and in the immediate post-war period it was still regarded as an unsuitable sport for commentary. But during the 1930s one person did begin to demonstrate its possibilities. He was not a great cricket enthusiast. His first loves were rugby and boxing but he had a good radio voice, and he had the ability to capture the setting and atmosphere of sport in a novel way.

Howard Marshall trained and worked as a journalist before joining the BBC in 1927, where he soon became a news editor. BBC managers quickly noted that his voice was suitable for broadcasting and in 1930 he became a 'sports and special events commentator'. By the time he came to cricket he had had several years of experience at the microphone, relating to different audiences for different purposes. Brian Johnston, who heard Marshall as a young man, thought this was important: 'He was able to build up time at the microphone which is the best possible way of learning to broadcast.'[2]

Marshall began initially with 'eye-witness' reports at the end of a day's play. The first of his commentaries of which extracts remain was made from the England v Australia Test at Lord's in 1934. Here Marshall describes Bowes bowling to Wall – the gaps indicate pauses in his speech:

> *Here comes Bowes running up, he's going to bowl. He bowls, Wall playing him with considerable difficulty but still playing him. Ironical cheering from the crowd, I don't know whether you can hear it. Bowes walking very slowly, purposefully to his pile of sawdust, just about to bowl … Wall facing him, up comes Bowes, Wall shaping to play him, Bowes bowls. Walls staggers back onto his right foot, and plays a nondescript cut at a ball outside the off stump, misses it altogether and it goes thump into Ames' gloves … Here comes Bowes again, Wall facing him, Bowes bowls and once more Wall lurches across his wicket, misses it altogether and Ames takes it.*

So we picture the desperate Wall, whose Test batting average was 6, trying to save his team from defeat. And we can easily imagine listeners at home warming to the characterisation – *ironical cheering, nondescript cut, lurches across his wicket*. Here was a man who could use language.

Marshall made these commentaries on his own, without any 'summariser' to discuss play with, or to provide a short break in which he could gather his thoughts. This may explain why, although the voice is indeed pleasing – warm, rounded and full of anticipation – the listener in 2008 is acutely aware of the pauses between each moment of action, and the hesitation between each piece of description. For those who heard Marshall in the 1930s however this was part of the appeal. Arlott praised his 'deep, warm, unhurried voice', Brian Johnston his 'slow, deep, burbling voice.' By the late 1930s, and especially during the Australian tour of England in 1938, Marshall was attracting a wider audience. And crucially he was now supported by the new Director of Outside Broadcasts, Seymour de Lotbinière. Lobby knew that good commentary must follow some basic principles. But he also knew that different sports required different approaches: Marshall seemed to him as much the man for cricket as, say, Graham Walker was the man for motor cycling.

It is Marshall's close of play summaries, as much as his live commentaries, which convey what he contributed to cricket *talk* on the radio. These broadcasts were often given during the closing minutes of the day's play, sometimes incorporating a reference to the players leaving the field. They were made, it seems, from handwritten notes rather than a fully-prepared script and it may be this which gives them a conversational air. As he explained in *Radio Times* in 1934, the informal tone was something for which Marshall consciously strove:

> With the scorecard and your notes before you, the microphone is forgotten, and you chat as you would to a friend who is interested in cricket. If you do stumble and hesitate now and again – I know I shall and I hope you will forgive me – you do at least preserve spontaneity and a certain colloquial freshness of expression.[3]

It is in this sense of chatting to a friend (not *with* a friend) as much as Marshall's feel for the atmosphere of the game that lie the seeds of the later *Test Match Special* approach.

Marshall was particularly good at describing the setting of a match and his accounts were always humanised – both watcher and participants are given character and feelings. At the end of one day's play against the West Indies in 1933 he reported:

It is a lovely summer evening with the sun shining and the players casting long shadows on the turf, and a big and enthusiastic crowd sitting round the ground... I always like the Oval – it's a friendly, informal sort of place.

At the close of a relatively uneventful and poorly attended match at Lord's Marshall captures the sadness of those whose pleasure has come to an end:

Then the little gathering of faithful spectators sighed and gathered up their belongings and put on their hats – for the match was as good as over.

Marshall was also a lead broadcaster for the BBC on state occasions. Indeed he was perhaps more at home, and even more greatly respected, in this role than he was as a commentator. When he described Hutton's great innings at the Oval in 1938 he carried an authority gained in a hundred other broadcasts, including the coronation of 1937. His experience as a reporter on state occasions, and his standing as a commentator, also served to reinforce his later role as the BBC's senior war reporter. His reports from the North African campaign display the same clarity of observation and the same poetic touches as his reports from Lord's. Here he describes the battle for Longstop Hill in Tunisia:

To our right below us the Tabooba road and the sunlit plain stretches mistily away towards Tunis – very beautiful with wild flowers, golden marguerite and poppies, smokily blue gentians and in the middle of them flashes of gunfire from our twenty-five-pounders.

Some of those who heard Marshall on cricket thought he was sometimes a little behind the game, that you heard the applause for a boundary before he had described the shot. But Marshall was breaking new ground. He knew that the pace and excitement of the football or racing commentator did not belong to cricket. He was seeking something more conversational and more vivid, something which incorporated within the standard BBC registers of the day that 'certain colloquial freshness of expression'. It was to prove an important legacy.

In 1939 when the West Indies cricket team toured England came an important innovation: unbroken ball-by-ball commentary on each Test match on the Empire Service wavelength to listeners in the West

Indies. A subscription radio service – Radio Distribution – had been set up in Barbados in 1935 and it was this company which put some pressure on the BBC to supply full ball-by-ball coverage. This was almost certainly the first ever unbroken commentary on a whole Test.[4] But there was no such service for listeners at home. The Test match commentaries of 1938 were more extensive than in previous years but continuous coverage was never contemplated.

Indeed, in the post-war years the battle for cricket commentary on the BBC had to be won again. As late as 1947 the BBC Handbook announced that 'Cricket matches are long drawn out and do not lend themselves readily to commentary.' Yet All India Radio provided unbroken ball-by-ball commentary on home test matches in 1948 and in the summer of that year the BBC sent back continuous ball-by-ball commentaries to Australia on its overseas service. By 1948 the concept of a commentary team as we know it today was fully in place. There were four commentators, including one from the visiting country (Alan McGilvray) and a 'silent number five' (this was the scorer, Arthur Wrigley). A year later commentary on the matches against New Zealand was continuous, but only for New Zealand listeners.

It was to be a further nine years before home listeners heard unbroken coverage of a Test match. A major obstacle was the reluctance of the BBC to release domestic wavelength time for commentary for five whole days at a time. As cricket coverage grew in popularity during the 1950s however there was a growing awareness that if commentary continued to be tied to fixed periods, the most exciting periods of play might be missed. Robert Hudson played a key role in persuading producers at Broadcasting House – and most notably Charles Max-Muller – that the network known as the Third Programme could be freed up for part of the day.

In May 1957 *Radio Times* announced that 'something completely new happens on British radio on May 30th.' Anne Roberts, an eleven-year-old schoolgirl in Taunton, was one of those who noticed. 'I sat down with a scruffy little notebook and listened, making a note when wickets fell.'[5]

Unbroken ball-by-ball commentary, divided between two wavelengths during the day, had begun. *Test Match Special* was born.

———

UNKNOWINGLY HOWARD MARSHALL had prepared the ground for a man who was to become the best-known voice in cricket. John Arlott was sometimes critical of Marshall's technique but he admired his voice and he must surely have been the one commentator Arlott heard, if only on recordings, who dared to adopt so wistful and poetic a style.

But there were many influences on Arlott, some of them quite disparate: the mother and aunt who brought him up, and fostered his love of reading; the novels and poetry he discovered in his youth; his early visits to watch cricket; his disappointment at missing out on a university education ('I would have given my ears for it,' he told Michael Parkinson during a television interview); his training as a policeman; the time he spent talking with Hampshire players in the 1930s.[6]

When Arlott left school in Basingstoke he took a clerical job but then joined the police force, where he served for nearly ten years. He first came to the attention of the BBC during the war when he submitted poems which the producer Geoffrey Grigson invited him to read on radio. He joined the Corporation in 1945 and was working as a producer of literary programmes in the BBC Overseas Service when a chance opportunity arose to commentate on a game at Worcester, involving the touring team from India. Coverage of the tour matches was broadcast on the BBC's Far Eastern Service and was closely followed by cricket lovers in India who had access to radio.

Dicky Rutnagur, who grew up in Bombay and went on to become a commentator himself, remembered hearing as a boy Arlott's first broadcasts, and the pictures Arlott drew of the Worcester ground:

> Arlott personified England. You felt you were there in the ground, you felt the atmosphere. With Arlott's voice you felt you were in England and you saw the Cathedral before you.[7]

But managers and commentators at the BBC did not take immediately to Arlott's voice. De Lotbinière famously told Arlott that year, before sending him on an overseas tour: 'While I think you have a vulgar voice, you have a compensatingly interesting mind.'[8]

The main staff commentator who worked with Arlott, Rex Alston – a former public school teacher – was equally critical: 'At first his delivery was monotonous and his broad Hampshire accent did not make for easy listening.'[9]

Arlott considered elocution training but was dissuaded by a friend, the actor Valentine Dyall. Arlott's was certainly not the traditional BBC voice, with its clipped, received pronunciation. It was softened and enriched by an attractive west-country burr, faintly suggestive of cricket's supposedly rural origins. Its impact was sharpened by the contrast with his colleague in the box, Rex Alston, meticulous in getting the details of the cricket right but a man whose clear, thin, schoolmasterly voice had none of the warmth and variety of Arlott's. But they found a way of working together and by 1948 were presenting themselves to readers of *Radio Times* as a contrasting double act:

> Rex Alston is the one who always gives the score, and keeps the entire story up to date while the game is in progress. John Arlott is the one who rambles with poetic licence about things and people.

There was however more to Arlott than a voice. His command of language – the range of vocabulary, the cadences of his sentences, the imagery – put his commentary on a different level to those around him. And Arlott also had, and this is sometimes overlooked, the great fluency and clarity of diction which all commentators need. To hear him was to hear a man who found pleasure in the sound of good language and good speech. In full flow Arlott's speech rhythms came close to a polished prose style, particularly when drawing on his proud sense of cricket history. Here he is at Trent Bridge in 1954 as Denis Compton equals Jack Hobbs in number of Test centuries scored:

> *This means to say that these two come together in the same world, and, great worshipper of Jack Hobbs as I am, it must be said that in his time Compton has had a different but comparable greatness, playing often against the tide, over the years when we were losing and I think it is a bracket that Jack Hobbs would not resent and of which Compton, with his usual modesty, would be happily proud.*

Arlott also brought to the art of commentary a measured restraint. He never raised his voice in an attempt to excite the listener. He left that task to the event itself. In 1948, when Don Bradman came to the wicket for his last innings in Test cricket at the Oval, Arlott had just taken his turn at the microphone. No observer could conceive what would happen next, that to the second ball he received Bradman would be out.

Arlott's response is to hand over the microphone, as it were, to the crowd and we hear their prolonged applause as Bradman leaves the field. Arlott has time to realise that Bradman may have been moved to tears by the welcome he had received at the wicket:

And what do you say under these circumstances? I wonder if you see a ball very clearly in your last Test in England, a ground where you've played some of the biggest cricket of your life, where the opposing team have just stood round you and given you three cheers, and the crowd have clapped you all the way to the wicket. I wonder if you really see the ball at all.

But even this might not have been enough if Arlott had not also had an ability to bring the cricket itself to life. The foundation here was a careful observation and accuracy, skills he attributed to his training in the police. Equally important was his feel for the setting of cricket, for the individuals who played the game, and a sense of the drama implicit in even the most routine of encounters on the pitch.

Arlott recognised at an early stage what the key ingredients of good commentary were. He had listened to Howard Marshall and he had also registered that the wartime broadcasts made by Ed Morrow and others had created 'a new formula' for outside broadcasts. He called it 'the second phase of broadcasting.' He said the wartime reporters had replaced 'the politeness of the mannered broadcast.' They gave broadcasting 'urgency, on-the-moment drama and yet also the common touch.'[10]

In 1948 Arlott wrote a short book *How to Watch Cricket*. Cricket, he observed, is like a play: 'Its end cannot be foreseen... its dramatic unities fuse and create the suspense of high drama.' He questioned whether there really was a problem, as some of his colleagues suggested, in describing superficially dull play:

How shall the commentator put into words this apparent inaction, this sultry heaviness of the air, the steadiness of the bowling, the grim relentlessness of the batting? Shall he do it by bald blunt statement, which must prepare his listener for minute after minute of numerically dull play? Or can he show the true nature of this tug-of-war – the tightness of the bowling and fielding, the grim, experienced, technically perfect batting of Hutton and Washbrook? How can he show that the work of these two batsmen has the quality of deep knowledge and experience to be found in the oldest of the crafts of the country?[11]

Arlott had something to say, in those moments between each ball, because he had a great feel for players, and what is suggested by their technique and appearance:

Baig, a small, neatly made, rather boyish looking player, a very correct player, his head nicely over the line of the ball, his strokes unhurried, a nice free flow of the bat, his right hand very low on the bat.

During periods of high action Arlott raised the level of his imagery. Here he is again at Trent Bridge watching Compton bat against Pakistan:

Now in comes Khan, bowls to Compton and he cracks that back down to mid-off, but mid-off is... I was going to say respectfully deep. Mid-off's position is a 'women and children first' position. They're obviously about to take to the boats and there are several players who if they went back three yards further wouldn't be on the field of play at all. The Pakistan side is as scattered as I've seen anyone since England didn't like Bradman... well now Kardar seems at the moment to have about five fieldsmen and seven missionaries, you know as they used to say in Victorian days, sent into distant parts. They're still in Trent Bridge but only just...

Seemingly at will and without preparation, Arlott could invest an apparently routine moment with original character, whether a bowler:

And Snow, shirt pulling out at the waist, polishing rhythmically, almost absent-mindedly, with the ball on his flannels, turns, furls his right sleeve, walks inwards, straightens up, comes in, body thrown well forward...

Or a batsman:

O'Neill goes out and disapprovingly prods the spot rather like a lady with an umbrella, and returns to his place.

Words are plucked from other contexts to characterise vividly a moment of action: of Everton Weekes in full flow: *'an impudent stroke'*; or inaction: *'past the somnolent Toshack at mid-off.'*

Arlott took broadcasting seriously. Like other commentators, he was called in to help augment the BBC team for the 1953 Coronation. (Howard Marshall, who had left the BBC in 1945, was also persuaded to return for this occasion). Arlott was placed at Piccadilly Circus, where many thousands had waited for almost twenty-four hours to see the procession emerge from Regent Street. Here he seems to bring together comfortably some scripted prose with more spontaneous observation:

> *They slept last night side by side, and cheek by jowl, on the pavements, on the newspapers long since trampled underfoot. They were wet together last night, dried in the breeze this morning, wet again later today, dried again with sun and wind, and now warm with happiness. A friendly wave for everybody, everybody's a personal friend, whether they recognize them or not. And hands are waved out of little shop windows, out of the clock up there among the illuminated signs that however dark the sky have flung their bright colours out across the circus today – gold, green, blue and yellow.*
>
> *And all round they're not stands, but people thronging, packed closely together, with children up on their shoulders, little flags waving... Slowly this procession makes its stately way round the great sweep of the circus with a quality that somehow twists the heart in the chest and you can feel this coming up down there from people who've waited so anxiously and who are, you know by their faces, more than satisfied. The RAF, drawn up there below, during the day have become their friends, and this band down there, the band of the Number Five region, RAF, they're sung with them, rallied them, applauded them, as they've marched up and down.*

It is not surprising that the heroes and heroines of this scene are the people watching, and that Arlott celebrates their solidarity. This unusual broadcaster was made more unusual still by his dissenting political voice. His mother was active in Liberal politics, and Arlott stood twice as a Liberal candidate for Parliament. He was a moralist for whom the great political challenge in sport in the 1960s and 1970s was South Africa. This placed him in an unusual position in the commentary box, where most of his colleagues favoured continuing links or professed neutrality. 'His clubby *TMS* colleagues,' remembered one Indian listener, 'spent their time finding excuses for the apartheid state.'[12]

Arlott made it clear that he was not only against a tour by a whites-only South African team, but that he would not commentate on it. The argument some put was that a boycott risked mixing politics and sport. Arlott put that argument away in a Cambridge Union debate:

> *Anyone who supports this motion will not exclude politics from sport, but will in fact attempt to exclude sport from life* [13]

IF THERE WAS A WEAKNESS in Arlott's commentary it lay in his sometimes inadequate understanding of the technicalities of the game. 'How good he was as a player I was never quite sure', wrote Brian Johnston cautiously.[14] It was probably not Arlott's fault that one BBC official told his superior in 1946 that Arlott had been a county player. It seems that the closest he got to county cricket was playing for the Hampshire Club and Ground side.

Alan McGilvray, the senior Australian commentator of his day, respected Arlott and admired his ability 'to make a rainy day sound interesting'. But he was critical of what he called the 'lyrical' style of English broadcasters. 'Their commentaries were rich with colour and atmosphere, but it didn't seem to matter if they missed a ball or two,' he wrote.

McGilvray described Arlott as 'not the most knowledgeable of cricket broadcasters, technically':

> His limited background in cricket occasionally came through, particularly early on. I remember Ray Lindwall taking him to task one day in 1948 because he described Lindwall's deliveries as 'turning from the leg'. Lindwall was moved to explain to Arlott that he didn't turn the ball. He swung it in the air, perhaps cut it off the pitch, but he didn't turn it.[15]

Trevor Bailey made a similar comment:

> He was essentially professional, not always good on cricket but a very professional performer. He did make mistakes occasionally, once he got onto technique.[16]

And indeed there are moments listening to Arlott again today when you sense he is at the edge of his expertise, and Bailey is helping him out. *'That one moved back at him,'* says Arlott, *'Chappell LBW bowled Snow.'* There is a slight pause while Bailey searches for the right register, then: *'I think it was caught at the wicket.'*

Such weaknesses were not significant in the context of Arlott's wider contribution to commentary. His way of describing and talking about cricket established what must almost count as a new form of radio, a distinct and compelling form of oral narrative. That lived-in, resonant voice, the vivid sketches of the players, the wider canvases on which he described the great Test match grounds, all commanded the listener's attention. Above all the dramas of the game were fed to listeners' imaginations through the prism of a thoughtful, reflective mind. 'It's a contemplative game, you see,' Arlott said. 'It's a game which produces art, painting, writing, poetry ... and I suppose commentary is just a step down from that.'[17]

In later life there was a growing air of world-weariness in Arlott, especially after the death of a son in a motoring accident. Although he found pleasures in the world, not least in food and drink and art, and could be immensely sociable, alongside his geniality came an increasing sense of disenchantment, and even melancholy.[18] Moments of what he saw as bureaucratic stupidity in the game – such as the failure to get a match re-started after rain – now became the object of his wrath.

Arlott drew on the start made by Marshall, especially in the degree to which he communicated so strongly to listeners his own presence at the ground. He was helped by having with him in the commentary box others, notably Rex Alston and Brian Johnston, whose styles threw his into even greater relief, and who allowed him the space to be himself. But he was instrumental in winning a devoted audience for cricket on the radio.

His was a cultured and entrancing take on an unusual sport. Many found that his ruminative and loving commentaries enriched their own feelings for the game. Because of the breadth of his knowledge and his curiosity, commentary remained interesting even during periods of slow play. And most of all he was, in the words he himself used about a fellow-journalist, 'careful with speech; he valued it too much to allow it to become dross.'[19]

The poet Dylan Thomas described him as:

> ... not only the best cricket commentator – far and away that – but the best sports commentator I've heard, ever: exact, enthusiastic, prejudiced, amazingly visual, authoritative and friendly.[20]

Almost on his own Arlott destroyed any lingering doubts there were in the BBC about cricket commentary. More than that, he won a following, not only in Britain but overseas, for day-long narrative on cricket. He helped to make *Test Match Special* not only possible but inevitable.

THE PROGRAMME SOON BECAME an annual feature in the broadcasting calendar. By 1957, when continuous ball-by-ball commentary began, expert summarisers, usually former Test captains, had been added to the commentary team. Cricket followers, many of whom still did not have television, quickly came to depend on having access to continuous coverage of home Test matches. Few listened all day but the important thing was that the programme was there whenever they wanted it.

In its early years *TMS* was, despite Arlott's presence, distinctly prosaic. His ruminations were deviations from the dominant style, a style which owed much to Rex Alston, a lead commentator until 1964. Alston could hardly have been more different from Arlott, not only in voice but in manner. Alston, said *The Times* in its obituary in 1994, 'had a pleasant, courteous laid-back microphone style, with characteristic public school inflexion.' Today's listeners would find the *TMS* of the 1960s relatively formal, and marked by the very distinct roles of commentator and summariser. Freddie Brown and Norman Yardley for instance normally came in at the end of overs with technical comments, as did their successors Fred Trueman and Trevor Bailey. The over itself belonged to the commentator.

During the 1970s the style and tone of the programme began to change. There were perhaps two reasons, one cultural, one personal. The wider society had become more open since *TMS* began. There was some erosion in traditional patterns of deference and people in authority were not taken quite so seriously. People talked to each other more as equals, and in less formal registers. Disagreements, even conflicts, became part of the discourse of broadcasting. It was hardly enough any more for a programme to be respected; to gain listeners it had to be entertaining.

The individual catalyst of change was, ironically, both a veteran broadcaster and an old Etonian. At his preparatory school in the 1920s Brian Johnston had something of a reputation as a mimic and was nicknamed 'The Voice'. Bored by his first job – working for the family coffee firm in Brazil – he produced and acted in theatrical reviews. In the Guards Armoured Division at the end of the war he was active again in drama productions. On being demobbed the family hoped he would rejoin the coffee business but Johnston revealed to them that he had decided instead to seek an opening in the world of the theatre.

In 1945 he heard of an opportunity at the BBC. As part of the selection process he was required to conduct interviews with people in the street and, unusually, he experimented with a tape recorder and sent in the results. He got the job. He had a variety of assignments over the next twenty years, mostly involving outside broadcasts, but he made his reputation with the 'Let's Go Somewhere' feature in which he subjected himself to bizarre experiences, such as lying on a railway track as a train went overhead, and spending an hour inside a post box. So by the time he joined *TMS* (he was a regular from 1970 onwards) he was already an experienced radio entertainer.

Johnston had also established himself as a cricket commentator on television but had been removed from the television cricket team, in part at least, for being too flippant. With his arrival in the radio commentary box *TMS* began, as Robert Hudson later put it, 'to move slightly downmarket, from the respected to the popular.'[21]

This change in style, largely influenced by Johnston, did not happen overnight. It was a natural transition, reflecting a change in personnel and the general loosening of the BBC's conventions at the time. The main change was that description and analysis of cricket was now supplemented by more conversation between members of the commentary team – the kind of talk in which spectators indulge when they are at the game. Marshall had talked of chatting to a friend, but by this he meant something quite different: commentator to listener. With Johnston a new maxim emerged: listening to the programme should be like eavesdropping on a group of friends.

This particular group of friends talked a lot about cricket, and the conversation was often entertaining. But it also grew increasingly cosy, with a strong emphasis on jokes between and about members of the commentary team – novel and refreshing when they started, but tiresome when they became repetitious. Johnston's partners in the commentary box collaborated in these ventures, though with varying degrees of willingness.

The style did attract a new group of listeners, some of whom had previously not followed cricket much at all. It was this group who chose the programme for the conversation as much as the cricket. Judging by the letters the BBC received, it included a higher proportion of women listeners than before. Some came across the programme almost by chance and liked the sound of it. Johnston's voice had a light and undemanding tone, and it was welcoming.

Johnston responded with warmth to gifts and messages from listeners. He served up leg-pulls much as he would in 'real life' and brought his distinct brand of verbal humour to the commentary box. It was perhaps above all his fascination with dreadful puns that revealed him to be the inveterate schoolboy. When Venkat and Reddy were batting for India against England he asked:

> *I wonder what would happen if Venkat were facing and the umpire said: 'Are you ready?' He would have to say: 'No, I'm Venkat.'*

It would not have occurred to any other member of the *TMS* team to say this, and, had it occurred to them, they would not have said it. For Arlott, by contrast, a pun had to have rather more to it, and was generally delivered as a dry aside. In 1948 when the English batsman FG Mann was dismissed by the South African bowler 'Tufty' Mann, Arlott sighed: *'Another example of man's inhumanity to man'.*

Johnston's influence on the style of *TMS* was decisive. Where commentary was concerned he was a consummate professional, and rarely missed a ball. But he also added a new ingredient: his own sense of fun and enjoyment. Many people found this infectious. West Indian Tony Cozier worked beside him for nearly twenty years:

> Brian stamped his personality on the box. With his *joie de vivre*, his sense of humour, everybody relaxed. *TMS* was The Johnston Special really. Within the box itself BJ was captain.[22]

However, as the atmosphere of light-heartedness grew, some thought *TMS* spun out of control, especially after John Arlott's retirement in 1980. End of the pier humour, great fun at the end of a pier, became distinctly intrusive during a commentary. The playfulness became almost relentless at times. 'It often descended into triviality and ego-centricity,' said Mike Brearley in his obituary of Arlott.[23]

In 1982 the magazine *Wisden Cricket Monthly* published a strongly critical article by a reader which described the programme as 'an exercise in self-indulgence' and 'lacking in gravitas'.[24] It identified Johnston as the main culprit. Correspondence about the article showed a diversity of opinion but the article had struck a chord with many – one letter referred to the 'sniggering, wine-bibbing, self-backslapping rump'. The reference to wine was directed not at Johnston but at the influence of Arlott, who made no secret of the fact that good commentating could be accompanied by good drinking.

Curiously one of the commentators, Don Mosey, and the only member of the commentary team then on the BBC staff, joined the fray and in an article associated himself with some of the criticisms.

He argued that there was a lack of balance in the team and wrote of its 'sloppiness and indiscipline'. In truth Mosey had never been a happy member of the crew. He had been disappointed not to get the job of cricket correspondent but claimed credit for urging the BBC to bring Trueman into the team and for being 'partly responsible ... for steering *TMS* from its clinically competent but faintly antiseptic course to the distinctive character it achieved in the 1970s when listening figures rocketed.' Subsequently in his autobiography Mosey said the programme had at one point become 'a shambles of personal indiscipline'.[25]

One other factor alienated some listeners. Mike Selvey, the former Middlesex and England pace bowler who joined the programme as a summariser in 1994, was astonished to find how reactionary the views of some of his colleagues were, and that one wore the tie of a whites-only cricket club in Johannesburg:

> I remember a phone-in about when South Africa should be re-admitted to international cricket ... and there was a lot of sanctimonious twaddle. There was Johnston who made it very clear where his sympathies lay. He would wear his Wanderers tie. They shouldn't have been out in the first place, as far as I could make out. And I remember saying very clearly that when Nelson Mandela cast his democratic vote ... that was my answer.[26]

Looking back there is something of a consensus among those involved with *TMS* that for a period of time the programme itself had an excess of frivolity. Jonathan Agnew acknowledged that 'it went through a phase when it was silly.'[27] Mike Lewis, a senior editor with BBC Radio Sport, said, choosing his words carefully, that *TMS* 'didn't quite know where it was going'.[28]

There is no doubt that Johnston was a much-loved broadcaster and entertainer. His touring show, *An Evening with Johnners,* drew large audiences and the accompanying CD and audio cassette was a best-seller. His breezy and conversational style at the microphone, rooted in a mix of music-hall and early television entertainment, anticipates the antics of much talk radio in the modern era.

Johnston knew cricket and played it regularly. His comments on the cricket itself were noticeable for their instinctive friendliness towards players and officials. His success in winning new listeners for *TMS* helped to secure the programme at a time when competition for air time might have threatened its future. Through his bright, easy manner Brian Johnston provided, as much as Arlott did, a legacy for *Test Match Special*, and one that the programme has never entirely lost. It became more approachable.

THE ROOTS OF *Test Match Special* are in Howard Marshall's warm evocation of the game, in Arlott's lyricism and sense of cricketing heritage and in the frolics of Brian Johnston. It has expanded over the years, from summer Test matches to winter ones, only surrendering its position when the commercial station talkSPORT won the contract for some of England's overseas tours between 2000 and 2005. The considerable stability of its staffing from the end of the 1980s until the retirement of Peter Baxter as producer in 2007 (including producer, commentators, summarisers and statistician) brought with it, at times, a certain cosiness. But when a new season begins the familiar voices which signal that cricket is back again provide listeners with a sense of reassurance.

It is the BBC cricket correspondent Jonathan Agnew who set the tone for the latter-day *TMS* on a day-to-day basis. Unusually for a modern-day commentator, Agnew had played sport at the highest level. He played cricket for England but was working as a journalist when, in an inspired move, Peter Baxter invited him to try his hand on radio. Unusually, Agnew began as a summariser before moving to the commentary role.

Agnew is always focused on the game but for him contact with the listener is also a key feature:

> *TMS* is just a chatty sort of a programme. We're working on your behalf in a way, so we are explaining things to you, there's that kind of personal touch to it... We're not actually shoving it down your throat... And so I think that's why it's been successful – we are company, first and foremost, and then for people who like cricket. I do get thousands of emails now – and that's the message that comes through, that people like chat, they like company.... the same old familiar voices chattering away...

Agnew has combined this informality, assisted by an youthful, almost boyish, voice, with an underlying seriousness about the role of the programme and about his own job as a reporter. One example lies in changes that have taken place with respect to drink. Christopher Martin-Jenkins commented:

Maybe there was a time when we were a bit too inclined to have a glass. Jonathan Agnew has more or less decided that we shouldn't be touching alcohol during the day's play.[29]

Agnew became very sensitive as to how much entertainment a period of play is providing. He was able to switch from the serious to the less serious and back again comfortably. A dull period of play at Durham was enlivened by reference to a haunted castle nearby: more than one hundred emails from listeners resulted. But he did move the programme on from the Johnston days, a fact welcomed by most members of the commentary team. While *TMS* still retained its capacity to be frivolous, Agnew gave it a more hard-edged tone at times. He earned his spurs during the incident when England cricket captain Michael Atherton was alleged to be using dirt in his pocket to rough up the ball. Agnew decided that his job required him to speak out:

That was a watershed as far as I was concerned... workwise it was the toughest month of my life. Pictures kept coming up, new pictures, plus the fact that I could see what he was doing. I was amazed that for so many people around the place their eyes seemed to fail them. And it still splits the press box now...

Agnew was keen to assert the independence of *TMS* from the English Cricket Board, which owns the broadcasting rights:

The ECB would very much like to have us on side ... all broadcasting partners together etc. but actually that would compromise the people running the game that we are commenting on. There has never been any question of there being any editorial control or compromise through rights issues.

He was forthright in his doubts about the ECB decision to give Cardiff an Ashes test in 2009 and about the place of day–night international cricket, even when he is commentating on it:

Night-time cricket in England is nonsense – players can't perform at their best. We only play because of the TV contract.

Agnew became so much the soul of *TMS* that it became difficult to imagine the programme without him. He combined the natural good humour of an entertainer, a commitment to good journalism, and an enthusiasm about the possibilities of digital broadcasting. He had always been an advocate of a programme with humour, entertaining enough to entice people to an interest in cricket. But he also wanted the programme to be intelligent. In 2007 he invoked the words of the original BBC Charter, saying the programme must try to 'inform, entertain and possibly educate'.[30]

Over the years producer Peter Baxter assembled with care a group of commentators and summarisers. In addition to Agnew, the core of the programme over many years read: Christopher Martin-Jenkins, Henry Blofeld, Vic Marks, Mike Selvey, and, after retiring as a player in 2002, Angus Fraser. This group gradually evolved a variety of on-air relationships, and the bonds between them varied intriguingly like those between members of a family. On the outside, sometimes flirting, sometimes sparring, with its members, was the elusive figure of Geoffrey Boycott. The programme was enriched by the mix of voices and attitudes that these, and others, provide.

Christopher Martin-Jenkins (CMJ) once called his colleagues to order after some self-indulgent jokes about autobiographies, announcing: *'That's enough in-house stuff, we've got a serious contest here'*. His extensive cricket knowledge and astute assessments became central to the programme's credibility. His calm, soft voice, notably free of the aggression of much modern sports talk, gave the programme an underlying tone of courtesy.

CMJ's contacts with first-class cricket were reinforced when his son Robin began playing for Sussex in 1995. CMJ helped to ensure that the programme remained rooted in cricket. A diligent and observant commentator, curious about the way a game was unfolding and appreciative of good play, he liked his summariser to make a proper assessment. When Collingwood was out, and CMJ asked former England and Middlesex captain Mike Gatting whether the batsman had played an injudicious shot, Gatting at first was cautious and attributed the dismissal to the quality of the bowling. CMJ pressed him: 'Was it an *unwise* shot?' Gatting saw there was no escape:

> *It's a shot he plays well, but you've got to be slightly more careful when you get onto the fourth or fifth day. It was a brave shot to be playing… possibly a silly shot early on in his innings. So for any youngsters: always try and get in and get the pace of the wicket before you try and do something difficult.*

Martin-Jenkins was satisfied.

Henry Blofeld can be heard on recordings from the 1970s commentating in his familiar precise voice, with the characteristic drawn vowels, but with little elaboration or decoration. Encouraged by the producer to develop a more personal style he invented a fascination with pigeons, buses, helicopters and the like which, while irritating to many, brought him devoted followers. He worked deliberately to sustain this eccentricity, suddenly announcing that he had seen a 'succulent crane' with the feeling that he had done his bit for an over or two. Blofeld's extensive knowledge of cricket and his choice phrases added to the listener's picture of the game – Warne's 'predatory walk up to the wicket', the Lord's pavilion 'looking like a squat Victorian matron'. His position as the programme's tame eccentric was confirmed in due course when he followed Brian Johnston into the halls. In the autumn of 2007 he announced a series of 'Evenings with Blowers' around England, presenting himself as a 'quintessentially English' raconteur.

Vic Marks and Mike Selvey were recruited to the programme as summarisers in 1984. One a spinner, one a seamer, and of contrasting dispositions, they were designed to add further variety to the commentary team. Marks brought good connections with west-country cricket and a slightly whimsical, gentle voice to the proceedings. He established a close rapport with Agnew, who sometimes shared his somewhat wry perspective on life. Marks' reflections on the death of Arthur Milton in 2007, offered presumably at very short notice, showed how *TMS* can be enriched, during a passage of quiet play, by access to a rich and humane vein of memory.

Mike Selvey emerged in the 1990s as the least establishment in voice and opinions of the *TMS* team and also the least willing to join its remaining flirtations with public-school playfulness. He quickly displayed an astuteness about cricket, and struck an open and measured air about innovations in the game. Selvey welcomed the conversational element to the programme but thought it made it more challenging for the summariser:

> It's conversation. I don't like to think of it as two separate people working apart from each other... I like to think of it as two blokes sitting on a bar stool if you like. I'd like to think it's no more and no less than if two blokes were asking: what happened there? It's a little less formal and it's a lot harder than it used to be... It's my responsibility to explain, to try and stimulate the conversation, to find talking points.

Angus Fraser was recruited to the ranks of summarisers during an England winter tour of 2001/02 when he was not selected for the Test team. He added a slightly lugubrious note, as if still recovering from a long bowling stint, but he brought many assets, not least his involvement in the work of the International Cricket Council. When moved to do so he was the most trenchant of summarisers, not least during the ball-tampering saga in August 2006. Fraser soon revealed a good feel for the weaknesses of his colleagues. 'Some are more humorous than others and you have to pick your time to have a bit of fun.'[31]

When that time arrived, Fraser might pounce. CMJ, who is usually reticent about his own cricketing prowess, made the mistake of mentioning an innings he had played at Lord's as a student, when two of his partners were run out while he was on 99. Fraser realised that this gave him an opening to get his own back not on one colleague but two:

> Fraser: *Did you run two people out?*
> CMJ: *Well, that's just about the truth of the matter, yes.*
> Fraser: *laughter* (which echoes round the commentary box).
> CMJ: *Had there been no scoreboard showing my score, I don't think they would have been run out that way.*
> Fraser: (incredulous) *Are you blaming the scoreboard?*
> CMJ: *No. I said that had I not been aware of what my score was, in other words...*
> Fraser: *Are you blaming the scoreboard?*
> CMJ: *I'm blaming my disgraceful immaturity.*
> Fraser: *Boycott modelled himself on you, didn't he?*

When he first began to work on *TMS* in 1995 Geoff Boycott swiftly established a special style of contribution. In 1998, after he was convicted in France of assaulting his former girlfriend, he was dropped by the BBC and did not return until 2005. In that time the only British radio station to stand by him was talkSPORT. In addition to sharp technical assessment, especially of batsmen, he brought another ingredient to the mix, revelling in challenging the programme's remaining conventions of restraint. He appeared to live in fear, not of giving offence, but of being another mealy-mouthed southerner.

Boycott's periods on air were punctuated by his incisive put-downs, and the programme was sharper for them. Of a fielder who missed an easy catch: *'If he'd stood still, he could have caught it in his mouth.'* On Mohammad Yousuf: *'He's a poor fielder, he stands out in the field.'* Then for a terrible moment it occurred to Boycott that he might not have made himself clear, and he added: *'He's useless.'* At the end of the Test in Multan in November 2005 when Pakistan, rather unexpectedly, bowled out England for 175 to win the game: *'This was a pretty good fifth-day pitch and they've bottled it quite frankly.'* And, as so often, he was spot on.

It became a part of the fascination of *TMS* that a chance remark might excite Geoffrey Boycott to an outburst. Or was it always a chance remark? CMJ asked him during that Multan test whether he had ever been asked to be an international Test match referee. *'They only want sycophants'* was the reply. During the Oval Test of 2007, Agnew casually mentioned, while reading out the county scores, that Yorkshire were playing a championship game – and a Roses match at that – the morning after a floodlit limited-overs match. Geoffrey was soon in full vein:

> *How brainless is that? Tiger Woods would love that – another tournament the night before the British Open. It's crackers. It's stupid.*

Boycott has spoken about how well he and Agnew worked together on air:

> I love it with Jonathan. He and I have a lot of empathy, a bit of fun, you can take the mickey, you can have interaction. I much prefer someone with whom I have some empathy.[32]

If there is one situation where Boycott's assertiveness rankled it was when he turned on a young commentator to test his mettle. In 2005, when not all the experienced members of the *TMS* team were available, Arlo White joined the programme in Pakistan. Boycott soon moved onto the attack: *'Have you played much cricket, Arlo?'* Peter Baxter acknowledged that in this first encounter between the two 'Boycott trampled all over him.' Baxter said that when he confronted Boycott about this Boycott replied: 'Oh, he's a young lad and he can take it'.[33]

Harsha Bhogle, the Indian commentator who worked on *TMS*, got similar treatment, and confronted his tormentor successfully:

> Geoffrey once turned round on air and effectively asked me how much cricket I'd played. When the session was over I said to him: 'Geoffrey, I've worked very hard to come to where I am, and if someone asks for my credentials I couldn't throw *Wisden* back at them and say here is my record, so if someone questions my record I have less to stand on than you. As a result you're making life very difficult for me.' I was staying at my parents' house in

Bangalore and he called me – he'd taken the trouble to get the number from someone – and he called me and said: 'You know I've thought over what you said, and I think you're right and I shouldn't have said that.' We work very well together and there's mutual respect now.[34]

But Boycott's trenchant views endeared him to a growing number of listeners. The ultimate tribute to his standing was always that in any controversy it was his views above all that listeners sought. They valued his love of cricket and his deep knowledge of the game. Boycott's philosophy is clear:

I decided early on I wasn't going to be a clone. I wanted to be my own person. When you start you don't know how people will react. I batted like that – I did it my way – and that's how I do radio. Above all, you must be honest and say what you think. If you gloss over something you'll look stupid. Above all I want respect. I want the listener to say – from him I'll get it straight.

Peter Baxter, who retired as producer in 2007, began to add further variety to the programme during his final years in charge. Among them was Simon Mann, who displayed intuitive understanding of cricket and added a warm, resonant voice to the team. Summarisers included Graeme Fowler and Graham Gooch. Fowler, a highly experienced coach, communicated great pleasure in being at a game. Gooch perhaps set the standard in terms of technical analysis. Just occasionally Alec Stewart evaded the clutches of 5 Live coverage to venture onto *TMS*, and relished the opportunity to send up Geoff Boycott. But Stewart himself never escaped the ragging. It was Angus Fraser who, in a discussion about 'walking' slipped in a reference to *the one occasion when Alec walked – his leg stump was knocked out.*

THE FLAVOUR OF *Test Match Special* is perhaps best captured by a 'visit' to the programme for a whole session of play. It is 2006, and in reply to England's 528, Pakistan are 409-7 overnight. The programme comes on air at 10.45.

Henry Blofeld opens the day's programme with Angus Fraser and Mike Gatting, both former England players and veterans of the county scene at Middlesex. Under Blofeld's benign eye they discuss the selection of the England team and then do a little comic turn, disputing their own performances as players. *'Ah'*, says Bill Frindall, the statistician, from the wings, *'another Middlesex domestic.'*

Play begins. Blofeld describes every ball, identifies the fielders and frequently updates the score. There is no great urgency to the play and his attention begins to wander. He turns first to the size of Gatting's breakfast, a compulsory subject, and then begins a jolly tour of the ground, suggesting that in the hospitality boxes they're having *'their first glass of the morning'*. With particular relish he recalls the stampede of MCC members rushing to get the best seats when the gates opened at nine.

Jonathan Agnew replaces Blofeld. He and Fraser talk freely together during the overs, in a much more conversational style. They discuss Afridi's batting and the impact he could have: *'An hour of this man and Pakistan will be in the lead.'* Agnew adds pleasantly to the routine of ball-by-ball narration, bringing the players to life. *'Harmison kicks up his heels and comes in'*; *'Afridi brushes the ball away'*. Bowlers themselves, Agnew and Fraser are convinced that Harmison *'just isn't bowling enough'*.

It is time to have a go at a colleague. There is a pause after Afridi is out so Agnew and Fraser chortle over the news that Christopher Martin-Jenkins has been on a cricket talk programme on SKY TV that morning. This is done with a mixture of affection and disbelief, since CMJ is of a generation that rather pre-dates satellite TV and all its works. Did he wear a tie? And any make-up? Martin-Jenkins of course is next on the rota, and undoubtedly standing just behind them.

By the time Martin-Jenkins is at the microphone nine wickets are down and Mohammad Yousuf is just short of 200. There's talk of Graeme Smith's two double hundreds in England a couple of years earlier, and of what George Cox (a Sussex player from the 1930s) told CMJ in his youth about 'purple patches.' Listeners who have switched to another wavelength to hear *The Archers* are welcomed back. It's clear that leaving *TMS* for *The Archers* is like a certain kind of extra-marital liaison: it is regretted but seen as inevitable. There's confusion over the score. CMJ is meticulous about this aspect of his role, and with some help from Bill Frindall and the TV monitor, they realise the umpire has signalled 'one short.' A discussion ensues of what the signal for 'two short' might be. It is absurd but strangely compelling.

While they watch to see if Mohammad Yousuf reaches his double century CMJ is censorious about the length Harmison is bowling. He and Gatting discuss Yousuf's change of faith (he was previously a Christian but converted to Islam). Then when he reaches 200, they give him due praise, mentioning that Hoggard pats him on the back. CMJ expresses concern: he was commentating when the score reached 111, 222 and 333 and it is now 444. These numbers are significant to superstitious cricketers. He refers to a cricket poem by Siegfried Sassoon (you are allowed to mention literature on *TMS*).

CMJ runs through a list, provided by Frindall, of all the double centuries that have been scored at Lord's. Martin-Jenkins places everyone on the list, from whatever era, in their context. He does cricket history with affection. As he finishes – and it is Gatting rather than the commentator who announces the news – the final wicket falls. Perhaps, says CMJ reprovingly, Harmison will take note that it was a length ball. He pauses so the microphone can pick up the ovation for Mohammad Yousuf.

Between innings Blofeld reads from Bill Frindall's score-card and, reverting to an earlier era, compares it in perfection to a cake the team have been sent. Soon after the England innings begins he *'feels a shipping forecast coming on'*.

Radio 4 long wave listeners now go back briefly to Broadcasting House while the commentary continues on digital radio and the internet. Andy Rushton has been sitting alone in a studio awaiting the shipping forecast sent to him by email from Aberdeen. As the time moves towards twelve o'clock, he puts on the headphones that enable him to listen to the *TMS* broadcast. On the corner of his desk is a small monitor on which he gets the SKY TV coverage. Andy is a cricket follower and is skilful enough to glance at the TV screen occasionally while he is reading the forecast. He can therefore mention – as he hands back – that there has been no addition to the score or that *'England have added two more runs.'* He has to remember however that digital TV coverage is a second or two behind *TMS*.

About this time a new summariser, Geoffrey Boycott, joins Blofeld at the microphone. Boycott's mission is to bring a no-nonsense tone to the proceedings and he warms up on Afridi: *'He's a great talent but he's got no brains'*. Blofeld seems satisfied with that as a starter, knowing he can get more from Boycott later on. He turns his attention to the size of the crowd and decides its time for a Blofeldism. The ground is not yet full – *'not chockers, or brimmers indeed, if you so wish'*. In other words: *'The ground is not chock full or brim full; I'm putting this into Blofeld speak for my fans who I know have been waiting patiently.'*

Boycott is good value during his thirty-minute slot. The Pakistan seamers aren't much good. Harmison's action needs sorting and since the England set-up *'includes coaches, physios, computer analysts, Uncle*

Tom Cobley and all' they should be able to do something about it. Briefly satisfied, Blofeld turns again to the ground and announces that *'The pavilion is in very good form this morning.'* Meanwhile Strauss and Trescothick are moving along nicely for England. Blofeld makes sure he describes every ball.

He then strikes a rich vein with Boycott about his feelings for Lord's and his first innings at the ground. It leads to a cameo from Boycott about his early days in the Yorkshire team. It was 1963 and he had scored 90 out of 140 on a wet wicket, but could not remember his dismissal. He does recall the inadequate wicket covers and the sandbags used. An unsuccessful LBW decision (this in the game they are commentating on) leads to a look at the TV replay to check on the umpire's decision. Here is another opening to ask Boycott about his career, and his feelings about bad umpiring decisions. *'You don't mind the 50:50 ones... but those you know are mistakes, they hurt.'*

Agnew is back. Frindall has come up with information about Boycott's dismissal in 1963: bowled by Alan Moss. Agnew announces the lunchtime phone-in and encourages listeners to put their questions. Talking over the first four balls of an over, Agnew and Boycott discuss Fred Trueman and his fondness for reminiscing – *'half of it was true'* is Boycott's rather sour verdict. Then Boycott turns his attention to the Pakistan seam attack and Sami in particular: *'I'd be thinking – he's not going to bowl me out'*. But he counsels England to bat normally for a while: *'They can get a bucket of runs after tea'*.

As Strauss and Trescothick continue with their partnership, Agnew is joined by the visiting summariser, Rameez Raja. They discuss temperatures in Lahore, whether the wicketkeeper was right to go for a catch and whether Sami's haircut has diminished his strength as a bowler. He and Agnew chat merrily, and only just catch Trescothick's dismissal.

When CMJ returns he wants to know from Ramiz if the game of Fives is played in the north of Pakistan – *'Fives players get good at using their left and right arms'*. They discuss good cover point fielders from Pakistan. Rameez lets slip he has spoken to Inzamam, the Pakistan captain, about where he should place himself in the field. Kaneria is brought on to bowl and CMJ recollects Kardar, a leg spinner who played for India and Pakistan. It is lunchtime.

In the afternoon England played steadily on, losing wickets but finishing some 340 or so ahead. The play was interesting but not dramatic. More than five hundred times the mantra was repeated – *'Gul*

bowls, and Strauss plays it out quietly onto the off side. There is no run.'
Wakelam was surely right – this alone could never make for riveting
listening. But around this there is both cricket talk and conversational
play, sometimes absorbing, sometimes trivial. The challenge is to get
the balance right.

1   HBT Wakelam *Half-Time* (Nelson 1938) p226
2   Brian Johnston *Chatterboxes* (W H Allen 1984) p19
3   *Radio Times* June 15th 1934
4   The broadcasting schedule published by newspapers in Barbados
indicates unbroken commentary. Similar broadcasting schedules for
Test matches in Australia in the late 1930s, published in Australian
papers, suggest that coverage, though extensive, was never continuous
during the day.
5   Interview with the author
6   For much about Arlott's early life see the biography *Arlott* by David
Rayvern Allen (Harper Collins 1994); Arlott's autobiography
Basingstoke Boy (Willow 1990); and especially Tim Arlott *John Arlott – a
memoir* (Andre Deutsch 1994)
7   Interview with the author
8   *John Arlott – a memoir* p63
9   Rex Alston *Taking the Air* (Stanley Paul 1951) p92
10   *A New Way* by John Arlott in *Sports Report – Forty Years of the Best*
(Queen Anne Press 1987) p20
11   John Arlott *How to Watch Cricket* (Sporting Handbooks 1948) p50
12   Mukul Kesavan *Men in White* (Penguin Viking 2007) pxiii
13   *John Arlott – a memoir* p163
14   *Chatterboxes* p166
15   *The game is not the same* p79
16   Interview with the author
17   *John Arlott – the voice of cricket* (BBC Enterprises tape 1990)
18   I am grateful to Paul Clark for his memories of listening to Arlott as a boy
19   Arlott on the writer Ian Mackay quoted by Tim Arlott in *John Arlott – A
Memoir* (Andre Deutsch 1994)
20   *Ibid* p55-56
21   Robert Hudson in *Summers will never be the same* (Partridge 1994) p29
22   Interview with the author
23   *Sunday Times* December 21st 1991
24   *Wisden Cricket Monthly* September 1982 (original article by E J Brack)
25   Don Mosey *The Alderman's Tale* (Weidenfeld and Nicholson 1991) p177
26–28   Interviews with the author
29   A book about *TMS* published in 1981 included a paragraph by John
Arlott in which he described how the pleasures of wine-drinking were
part of the *TMS* commentator's lifestyle. The paragraph was omitted
from the second edition of the book.
30   Interview with Nagraj Gollapudi *Cricinfo* September 2007
31–34   Interviews with the author

TWENTY-ONE

IT'S NOT OVER YET

WHAT MAKES A GOOD COMMENTATOR?

In the course of research for this book some forty commentators were asked this question.

About a quarter put the quality of the voice first, or rather the quality of the voice and of the speech – naming such aspects as fluency, clarity and distinctiveness. Gavin Eaves, who learned his trade doing live reports on BT Supercall in the late 1980s, offered a striking phrase – the need to 'be in charge of your own words'.[1]

A further twenty-five per cent thought that knowledge and understanding of a sport was the priority. They spoke of the need to be 'steeped in knowledge of the sport', 'devotion', being 'a very good reader of the game', having an 'eagerness' to learn about the game or 'a knowledge, love and feeling' for the game. Christopher Martin-Jenkins highlighted 'cricketing intuition' as a key requirement, a term that could fruitfully be applied to many sports.[2]

Almost half of those questioned put neither 'voice' nor 'knowledge of the sport' first. They chose some aspect of the skill and technique involved in the commentary process. They used terms such as: 'making it come alive', 'conveying the moment', 'observation skills', 'accuracy', 'anticipation'. One suggested these had to be underpinned by what he called 'broadcasting sense' – a feel for the possibilities of radio. Several referred to the need to manage excitement effectively.

None of those interviewed suggested that any one of the qualities on their own – voice, knowledge, skills – was enough, and almost all who opted for one criterion, quickly added the other two. Some commentators used a single word to bring together all these facets – one called it 'presence', another 'authority'.

RADIO CERTAINLY PLACES A PREMIUM on the importance of the voice, powerful enough to suggest a personality to the listener. Since the speaker has no physical presence, the voice assumes additional tasks, compensating for the eye and body signals that can no longer be used. So the voice of the commentator must not only be distinct and clear, and the speech fluent and easy to follow, it must suggest a person we want to spend time with, someone whose account of events we can trust. Some commentators have all these qualities: a distinctive timbre, a personal resonance and warmth that is instantly attractive.

But even then, voice alone can never be enough. It is essential but not sufficient. Listeners also need to feel confidence in the commentator's ability to 'read' the game or event, be aware of its history and be able to place events in context. This helps to provide that important sense of authority. Like a good voice, this is essential. An attractive voice, allied to good knowledge of a sport, will go a long way in making a commentator. But there are other, even more important, ingredients.

Commentators stand between us and the event. Their talk must follow quickly from what they see, and even at moments anticipate it. We need them, as one listener put it, 'to bring the play quickly and succinctly to the listener just as they're hearing the noise of the crowd.'[3] And they do more than describe what they see, they have no choice but to select what is significant, or what will most entertain the listener. They reveal the inner story. To do this effectively they need to be good story-tellers.

Story-telling is an ancient art that has played a part in all cultures.[4] However, in radio commentary story-tellers have a unique task, one they rarely had before: describing events with urgency, as they happen. This is the unique challenge for the commentator. And increasingly they do this, not in isolation, but as members of a team. Thus a new requirement has been added: the ability to handle live on air a range of conversations with the growing band of summarisers who have been brought into the commentary box. Voice, knowledge, broadcasting technique, small-group facilitator: the commentator needs it all.

These skills do not reside solely in one part of the population, yet, in the early years of British broadcasting it was considered unthinkable for a woman to read the news, or give the sports results, and for anyone with a regional accent to be an announcer or presenter. Change was slow to come but in the later decades of the twentieth century, the greater diversity of voices and personalities at the microphone, both men and women, added to the pleasure of listening to the radio. In sports coverage, although there was an increase in the number of women presenters and summarisers, the field of commentary remained a male preserve. However, towards the turn of the century, and just after, some notable exceptions emerged, for eample Donna Symmonds, Alison Mitchell and Jacqui Oatley.

THE SKILLS COMMENTATORS NEED are tested when they, and their summarisers, have to cope with disasters unfolding in front of them, sometimes involving loss of life. In 1977 the Brazilian commentator Edson Mauro was covering a Formula One race in South Africa. He described witnessing a death during his period at the microphone and the impossibility of responding adequately:

> Dealing with death during a transmission is very complicated... In the South African Grand Prix I saw Tom Pryce die. This had an impact in my life because he died in front of my eyes and I became wordless at that moment. He was driving at three hundred kilometres an hour, the fire truck was in the middle of the track, the driver did not see it and was beheaded by it.[5]

Tony Delahunty was reporting for Pennine Radio from Valley Parade, the Bradford City ground, on May 11th 1985 when the home team played Lincoln City in the last match of the season. The club had just secured promotion to the second division for the first time in fifty years and thousands of people, some of them coming from abroad, had travelled to the city to celebrate. Bradford, Delahunty remembered, was in carnival mood, the weather was beautiful, the brass bands were playing and 'it was a day of total celebration'.[6]

Delahunty was in a commentary position in the press box some thirty rows back in the stand when, a couple of minutes before half-time, his summariser, Mickey Bullock, said: 'Tony, it looks like smoke over there'. When he realised that there was a fire in the very enclosure where he was standing Delahunty spoke directly to people who were listening to his broadcast:

> *Let's get all those people out of there, let's get those people, just take your time, don't rush, take your time going down there, don't pull on the wires, keep the electrics over there, take your time, don't rush, don't push … wait for the kiddies … we're going to have to disconnect very shortly … we're taking a break, we're getting out of here...*[7]

Fifty-six people died in the fire at Valley Parade that day.

THERE IS NO SINGLE WAY to respond to unexpected and dramatic events, on or off the field. Different commentators respond in different ways – as they did at the Olympic Stadium in Berlin, on July 9th 2006.

France were playing Italy in the World Cup final. The score was one-all and there were ten minutes of extra time remaining. An incident between the French captain Zinedine Zidane and the Italian player Marco Materazzi took place off the ball, leaving Materazzi on the ground. Neither the referee nor the commentators could see what had happened and all had to wait for a television replay.

Mike Ingham and Graham Taylor were commentating on BBC 5 Live:

> Ingham: *And we're going to get an action replay now.*
> Taylor: *Oh! Zidane has to go!*
> Ingham: *Oh! Zidane! Zidane has just...*
> Taylor: *Zidane has to go...*
> Ingham: *... put his head into the chest of the opponent...*
> Taylor: *Well, Zidane must be sent off, he's got to be sent off.*
> Ingham: *Zidane must be sent off...*
> Taylor: *He's got to be sent off...*
> Ingham: *And that's the fourth official surely who maybe saw that. Zidane on his farewell appearance for France now has to be sent off in disgrace here in the World Cup final.*

On talkSPORT Jim Proudfoot, commentating with Alvin Martin, initially thought that a red card might not be given:

> Proudfoot: *We're seeing a replay now and... Zidane has headbutted Marco Materazzi in the chest off the ball... and a man who's had such a brilliant career ... what a sad end to it! I don't think he's going to get sent off because I don't think any of the officials have seen it but, in a World Cup that's been blighted by moments of idiocy, moments of feigning injury, the final has been blighted by Zinedine Zidane, one of the greatest players of my lifetime, putting the head on Marco Materazzi and it is for that that I hope he is remembered for this day. That is a scurrilous, treacherous, cowardly act from a great man, who should not have done that and I now hope that he does not lift the World Cup.*
> Martin: *I've never seen anything like it. I've never seen anything like it. That was pure thuggery...*

The French radio station RTL had a three-person commentary team, Cyril, Jean-Charles and Guy. Surprise was their dominant emotion, but the commentators were divided in their response. Guy thought that the nature of any provocation needed to be taken into account in judging Zidane's behaviour. Cyril suggested that Zidane had overlooked the fact that actions off the ball were being filmed. Jean-Charles was simply incredulous:

> Cyril: *Oh! La! La! La! What has Zidane done?*
> Jean-Charles: *Ah… but it's not poss…*
> Cyril: *Oh! La! La! La!*
> Jean-Charles: *But it's incredible! It must…*
> Cyril: *So if the linesman saw him, Zidane is out then. Even though it's Zidane. Right Guy?*
> Jean-Charles: *…Oh … Zidane gave him a headbutt! A headbutt!*
> Guy: *We need to see what happened before.*
> Cyril: *He certainly didn't mess about. Yeah, but we can't argue with this here Guy. It is unacceptable; it's a red card…*
> Cyril: *If it is a reaction Guy…*
> Guy: *…yes it's a reaction to something… something happened… er … as far as I'm concerned we need to see what happened.*
> Cyril: *Yes but it's the World Cup final Guy.*
> Guy: *So does he deserve to be taken out? But if he does, the other one probably does too.*
> Cyril: *There are one hundred and twenty cameras within the stadium – he mustn't do things like this.*

Riccardo Cucchi, working for Radio Giornarle in Italy, condemned Zidane's action, suggested that he committed similar fouls previously, but his commentary conveys a hint of regret:

> *It's a headbutt by Zidane! There has been a totally unjustified headbutt from Zidane who hit Materazzi right in the chest who then fell to the ground. Maybe the referee did not see it. Actually we did not see what happened because we were watching what was happening on the field where the free kick was taken, actually Del Piero's foul. Maybe the referee did not see it. Maybe one of the linesmen saw it, anyway it is a headbutt from Zidane against Materazzi. I don't think that there was anger between them. Sadly I have to say that Zidane is a great player, but this is not the first time that he has used the headbutt during his career.*

When the referee gave Zidane a red card, Mike Ingham on BBC placed Zidane's exit in the context of his position in world football:

> *We talked about Zidane winning the World Cup for France to-night and becoming perhaps one of the top three players of all time – along with Pele and Maradona – but that was disgraceful by Zinedine Zidane ... he just felled him with a horrendous headbutt.*

Jim Proudfoot sent the player on his way:

> *Leave the field, leave your career, you have let yourself down in the most vicious, horrible, imaginable way possible...*
> *... (Zidane's) whole career has been besmirched by one moment of idiocy, of lunacy, of thuggery. And I have lost untold respect for him and I would imagine hundreds of millions of footballers around the world have as well.*

On RTL, Cyril acknowledged that the decision was inevitable. 'We have to put ourselves in the referee's shoes'. His colleagues were concerned about the impact that the sending-off would have on the result. 'We are also losing a penalty shooter... We won't be able to keep three at the front.'

On Radio Giornarle, Riccardo Cucchi searched for some explanation for Zidane's behaviour. Before he picks up commentary as the game resumes, he strikes a clear, and generous, note of regret:

> *Maybe they exchanged words, maybe something big, and at a certain point Zidane walked back and headbutted Materazzi who probably, let's say it, probably could have provoked him with some words in Italian which Zidane certainly can understand.*
> *... It's a shame for Zidane because this was the last game with the French shirt. Zidane is a great player, a champion, thirty-four years old, and he was fighting with his mates, he nearly got the winning goal, the winning goal Buffon saved so well. It really is a shame.*

Despite many pronouncements of its demise, radio has survived and indeed flourished. Among its great strengths are its portability and flexibility. It fits easily into the routines of daily life.

Radio has one other special quality. Unlike television, it tolerates and indeed nurtures the imagination. However well commentators paint the scene, they also allow us to add our own pictures to the words that come down the line. In a strange way, radio is a *visual* medium.

Even in a world full of electronic devices, radio commentary has the power to summon our attention. In May 2007 5 Live covered a semi-final of the Champions League between AC Milan and Manchester United at the San Siro stadium: a match involving two of the best-known teams in world football, representing two great industrial cities of modern Europe, and parading some of the finest players in the world.

It was a night of fierce weather in northern Italy. Simon Brotherton set the scene for listeners:

> *We can hardly see the other side of the stadium here, the rain is falling so hard now... sixty-seven and a half thousand fans packed into this arena as the teams come now in pouring rain onto this beautiful green carpet of a pitch.*
>
> *AC Milan line up in front of their club badge to the left of the halfway line in their traditional red and black striped shirts, white shorts and black socks. Manchester United in their changed kit tonight – white shorts, black shorts and white socks. They line up to the right of the halfway line... flash bulbs are popping all around the stadium, lightning flashing around outside. It's a stormy, wet and wild night in Milan and we haven't even started yet.*
>
> *... Again another crack of lightning illuminates the sky here against this monstrously large cavernous stadium and away to our right they're all holding up coloured placards displaying the words 'WIN FOR US' written in English. AC Milan will be a handful tonight. The rain falls. The players are ready.*

1–2 Interviews with the author

3 John Millar, interview with the author

4 The other great story-telling invention of the twentieth century, film, sometimes incorporates the radio commentator as a device to advance its plot. In *Cinderella Man* (2005), the story of James Braddock's return to boxing in 1930s America, the radio commentator, played by Philip Craig, provides the key narrative of the fights to the viewer. In one scene the fighter's wife and family are shown listening to commentary in a darkened room. Through them the viewer is taken into the ring where the fight is taking place, and invited to wince with every blow. In a number of other films, for instance *Raging Bull* (1980), *The Black Stallion* (1980), *My Life as a Dog* (1985), *Bull Durham* (1988) and *Seabiscuit* (2003), the introduction of radio commentators into the plot helps to establish historical authenticity.

5–6 Interviews with the author

7 Audio clip. BBC *onthisday* website for May 11th.

Index

Index